A TASTE OF ENGLISH WINE

A Taste of English Wine

Hugh Barty-King

PELHAM BOOKS

STEPHEN GREENE PRESS

To Jenny

PELHAM BOOKS/STEPHEN GREENE PRESS

Published by the Penguin Group
27 Wrights Lane, London W8 5TZ, England
Viking Penguin Inc., 40 West 23rd Street, New York, New York 10010, USA
The Stephen Greene Press Inc., 15 Muzzey Street, Lexington, Massachusetts 02173, USA
Penguin Books Australia Ltd, Ringwood, Victoria, Australia
Penguin Books Canada Ltd, 2801 John Street, Markham, Ontario, Canada L3R 1B4
Penguin Books (NZ) Ltd, 182–190 Wairau Road, Auckland 10, New Zealand

Penguin Books Ltd, Registered Offices: Harmondsworth, Middlesex, England

First published 1989

Typeset in Linotron 11/13pt Fournier by Goodfellow & Egan Ltd, Cambridge
Printed and bound in Great Britain by Butler & Tanner Ltd, Frome, Somerset

A CIP catalogue record for this book is available from the British Library

ISBN 0 7207 1839 2

The photograph on the half-title page is of St Nicholas Vineyard at Ash in Kent.

Contents

A HISTORY OF ENGLISH WINE

TASTE THE WINE TODAY

APPENDICES

Picture Credits

The author and publishers gratefully acknowledge permission to reproduce the following illustrations:

Half-title page Geoffrey Bond; *p.1* Ann Ronan Picture Library; *pp. 4, 5* the Hulton-Deutsch Collection; *p. 7* Miller, Craig and Cocking; *p. 8* reproduced by gracious permission of Her Majesty the Queen; *p. 9* the president and fellows of Corpus Christi College, Oxford; *p. 15* Mary Evans Picture Library; *p. 19* University of Toronto Library; *pp. 20, 23* The British Library; *p. 25* a Private Collection; *p. 30 (above)* A.C. Tait; *p. 30 (below)* the Painshill Park Trust; *pp. 35, 37, 39, 41, 43* National Museum of Wales (Welsh Folk Museum); *pp. 51, 194* the *Daily Telegraph; pp. 80 (centre), 83* the Martin Lumby Partnership; *pp. 80 (below), 113* Janet Price; *pp. 105, 164* Patrick Eagar; *p. 135* Leeds Castle; *p. 143* Tim Page; *p. 158* John Rigby; *p. 189* Viewpoint.

The other illustrations were kindly provided by the vineyard owners, wine makers, wine merchants and other people associated with the industry.

Acknowledgements

I will not list the many people who talked to me, wrote to me and posted me leaflets, labels and photographs – a large number, but of course only part of the very much larger number now involved. Their names are given in the text in the relevant place. But I would like to thank them here for taking the time and trouble to respond so fully and promptly to my questioning, to my letters – not only vineyard keepers and wine makers but wine merchants, supermarket wine buyers, hoteliers, festival organisers and the rest. They gave me *the flavour* which I hope I have been able to convey to readers who have neither the time nor the inclination to digest a heavy dish of facts and figures in reference book style which few would find readable.

It has happened that some of those who gave me much appreciated help have not been mentioned in the text and I would like to thank them here. These include Miss Jane Watts, Assistant to the Chief Executive of the English Vineyards Association; Mr Stan Phelps of the Wine Standards Board; Mr R. Charles Walmsley CB, FRICS; Mr David Harbourne, Alcoholic Drinks Division, Ministry of Agriculture, Fisheries and Food; Miss Coral Hill, Press Officer, M.A.F.F.; Mrs Mavis Collier and Mrs Janie Burford, Painshill Trust; Mr George Bell. I would also like to acknowledge Ian Paget and Geoffrey Bond, editors of the E.V.A. newsletter *The Grape Press*, which is the source of much of my information.

The late Jack Ward, to whom I am forever indebted, ended his gracious Foreword to my previous book – *A Tradition of English Wine* (1977) – with the words 'Time alone however can show to what extent the United Kingdom will be able to gain a legitimate place among the wine-producing countries of the world.' The 12 years that have passed since the publication of that book have shown, I believe, that England's place is not only legitimate but jealously admired.

Hugh Barty-King
Ticehurst
1989

Foreword

by Lord Forte of Ripley
Chairman, Trusthouse Forte

I cannot understand why some people are surprised when English Wine is served at a meal. After all, its history goes back to Roman times and the vineyards are not much further north than some of the best wine-growing areas of France and Germany. Perhaps we do not have the established traditions of our continental neighbours, but since the war an industry has grown here from almost nothing despite the vagaries of the climate.

The result has been the commercial production of a range of extremely palatable wines for consumption at home or in a restaurant. I have been most impressed by what I have seen when I have visited English vineyards and have been pleased to note how popular their products have become since we placed a number of vintages on regular wine lists in our hotels some time ago.

Hugh Barty-King is to be congratulated for writing this much-needed guide to English Wine and I am sure it will be an encouragement to both those who enjoy the pleasures of drinking it and those who have dedicated their lives to growing it. As these producers become even more expert in their art, I hope their houses earn a fine reputation not only at home but in the competitive markets overseas. May the sun shine on their vines for many years to come!

Charles Forte
December 1988

A Guide to Measurements

1 Hogshead = 52½ Gallons   1 Pipe = 105 Gallons
1 Litre = 1¾ Pints   1 Hectolitre = 100 Litres
1 Rod = 5½ Yards
2 Hectares = 4.9 Acres   2 Acres = 0.8 Hectares
3 Hectares = 7½ Acres   4 Acres = 1.6 Hectares
14 Hectares = 35 Acres   8 Acres = 3.2 Hectares

Introduction

HIS BOOK IS ABOUT a particular kind of wine – wine, that is, as in 'wine merchant' and 'wine cellar'. Provision merchants refer to butters and hams, the people who eat that kind of food to butter and ham. So here – since this book is addressed as much to people who drink it as to those who make or sell it – it is wine not 'wines'.

English Wine is the alcoholic beverage made commercially from the fermented juice of wine-grapes. These are grown on vines set in rows in open-air vineyards either in England or Wales, as opposed to eating grapes (known as dessert grapes) which are cultivated under glass. English Wine is not the same as 'British Wine', the alcoholic drink made commercially in Britain from grape juice concentrate imported from Spain, Italy, Algeria and elsewhere and retailed in wine shops, grocers, village stores and supermarkets as 'sherry-type' or under nondescript fancy names such as 'Rougemont Castle'. Neither is English Wine akin to 'Fruit Wine', alcoholic drinks made commercially and by amateurs from elderberries, plums or sloes, from potatoes, tea or parsnips, from nettles, dandelions or cowslips, known in the trade as 'Made-wines'.

English Wine is beyond compare. It is as intrinsically English as English tailoring, English madrigals, English shoes, the English sense of humour. It is not a type of continental wine; it is as old and original as all of them. Its distinctiveness comes from what many imagine to be what restricts it, England's lack of sun and the resulting slow ripening of wine-grapes grown in open-air vineyards. This, on the other hand, as oenologist Christopher Lindlar has pointed out, gives it a character dissimilar from any other wine:

> *The freshness of flavour given to English Wine by the verdant character of the fruit derives from the fact that we are growing grapes on the margins of the vine-growing zone of the northern hemisphere. The same as the difference in flavour of an English Cox's Orange Pippin apple and a French Cox, which is sweeter but has damn-all flavour, whereas ours has great flavour though is less sweet.*

Veteran English Wine maker Richard Barnes also believes that the distinctive fruitiness and crispness of English Wine is due in part to the fact that vines growing in the open air in such a climate have to struggle that bit harder than vines on the Continent.

INTRODUCTION

The wine's quintessential Englishness is acquired from growing first-class grapes and good wine-making based on scientific principles, moving away from empirical methods of years gone by and providing continuity and reliability of quality. Lindlar explains:

> *This cannot be done elsewhere in the world, and is a justification for English Wine. There would be no justification for English Wine if it was merely a luke-warm ersatz German wine or ersatz Chablis. We are not making pretend Mosel or Niersteiner; we are making something that is essentially English and has something about it which ought to enable the knowledgeable taster to identify it in a blind tasting among six other wines as being positively English, not by a process of elimination – 'this isn't German', 'this isn't French' – but by saying 'Aha! there is something in this glass which is England!'*

Karl-Heinz Johner from Baden, who has been making English Wine in Kent for the last 15 years, believes that he and other makers of English Wine have found a new flavour that did not exist before. It would be senseless to categorise it as either 'German' or 'French'. It is similar to neither.

> *Because of this northern climate, we have this slower maturation period, this slower ripening period, so we get more fruit from grape varieties that are growing on the Continent. We have higher acidity, and we have to adjust our wine-making process a little to improve body. There is no denying the acidity – sometimes green, sometimes even grassy – but it is light, fruity and very flavoursome, the hell of an attractive drink and in no way comparable with German wine.*

Ask Colin Gillespie to what extent English Wine has improved since he started making it in Somerset in the nineteen-seventies, and he will explain how in April 1988, delivering an order for his wine to a well-known London wholesale wine merchant, one of his bottles 'blew up on me'.

> *I don't know why. A small part of a batch had gone off. I told him I would take the case back and replace it. If that had happened ten years ago he would have thrown up his hands in disgust – 'Ugh! Never want to see any of that again!' But no. It is significant of the standing of English Wine today that the incident, which thoroughly embarrassed me, was no reason for him to cancel the order. On the contrary he confirmed it, and later asked for another 25 cases.*

No one is more convinced than Bernard Theobald, Berkshire viticulturist extraordinary, of the viability of vineyards in England, bearing in mind however that what is right for one site might not be right for another. Making a minimum of £1,000 net profit an acre over ten years after the first five years, for him compares very favourably with other farm crops. Only in a good year could early strawberry growers do a bit better in terms of profitability. 'I get ten times as much revenue from English Wine as from anything else,' he told Colin Parnell of *Decanter* in September 1982, 'and off one-tenth of the acreage'.

> *As the vines grow older and our skills increase, a vineyard is a capital asset appreciating in value. In twenty years I shall be disappointed if my vineyard is not worth £1 million. The right site, the right grape varieties, grown by the right man in the right way, that's the key.*

INTRODUCTION

So long as there are the 'right' men in England, with that sort of faith in the product, it would seem that never again will commercial viticulture be abandoned in England as it appears to have been for a quarter of a century between 1920 and 1945. That, however, was but a hiccup in a steady activity which dates back to the Roman Occupation and provides a fascinating story.

English Wine *is* the real thing – and has been for 2,000 years.

Could *English Wine* be just as good
 As *Vin de Table* and *Tafelwein*?
Could vineyards by the Rother yield
 As ripe a grape as by the Rhine?

Who ponders thus in muddled thought excels –
 As well range Stilton Cheese with Camembert!
What benefit from drawing parallels
 When English Table Wine's beyond compare?

We choose the vines our clime and weather suit;
 They pick varieties that favour theirs.
An English vineyard grows the English fruit
 With which no Continental growth compares.

Our island ambience creates a wine
 That is its own, is (dare I say?) unique,
Has all the quality implied by 'fine',
 Grape-fruity, flinty, crispy, sleek.

Could English Wine be just as good
 As Traminer, Mosel?
Don't ponder, *taste* – by that alone
 Can any doubter tell.

A History of English Wine

1

FROM THE ROMAN OCCUPATION TO
THE GREAT WAR

NGLISH WINE IS AS OLD as the English hills – well, not quite. *Vitis vinifera* did not grow on them as a native plant as it did in North America and Russia. The first vines to grow in England were brought over from Gaul by the soldiers and administrators who for 300 years occupied the most northerly province of the Roman Empire which they called Britannia. They were of the wine-grape variety and were grown in the open air in the gardens of villas and farmhouses to produce grapes from which a few Romans made wine for drinking at home to supplement the large quantities they shipped from Aquitania (the modern Bordeaux region) as the natives of the island had done before them, and from northern France and Germany. Such viticultural activities were not on any large scale and were in no sense 'commercial'. Some doubt they took place at all. But there were signs that perhaps there had been a vineyard at the Roman villa at Wingham in Kent when excavations were carried out there in 1882. There is a tradition that there was a Roman vineyard at Bungay in Suffolk and another on the Sussex Downs near Chichester at East Dean (Charlton); locals insist there was a Roman vineyard at Ightham in Kent.

In AD90 the Emperor Domitian issued an edict forbidding the *natives* living in Roman provinces, though not Roman citizens, from planting *new* vineyards on land which was their property – but there was nothing to stop them continuing to cultivate vineyards they had already planted. The ban remained in force for almost 200 years. When Marcus Aurelius became emperor in 276 he had the greatest difficulty in holding the empire together. He needed all the support he could muster from his provincial subjects in suppressing the claims of rival emperors. One of the ways he used to gain this support was to lift all former restrictions on the planting of vines and the making of wine. In the year 280 he announced that Domitian's ban was at an end. He allowed the natives of Gaul, Spain and Britain (though some hold that he was referring to Britanny) to have vines and make wine. For a hundred years before the Roman legions, who were believed to have planted a vineyard at Lincoln, withdrew from Britain in 397, the planting of vines by the natives of Britannia as well as Roman citizens was fully permissible.

It was then probably a matter of local farm workers being brought together in some form of co-operative wine making process. A likely location for such an exercise is North Leigh near Witney in Oxfordshire. On the hillside to the north-east of the villa which has been excavated there, the terracing can still be seen in the morning sun. The people who lived in the villa were probably Romanized Britons whose livelihood depended on farming. 'The siting of the vineyard in this area would make sense,' says John Lovegrove, custodian of North Leigh, 'by virtue of the fact that there were at least two other villas within a mile of the North Leigh site. The vineyard, if such it is, – and the general appearance of the site would tend to confirm that it is – would not in all probability have been planted before the middle of the third century.'

This is in line with the view of Timothy Loughton, who made a study of the subject in 1983, that viticulture in Britain did not really emerge until the departure of the Romans and three new factors coming into play: the growth of Christianity and the need for wine in its ceremonial; Britain being cut off from continental trading markets in the chaos that accompanied the Dark Ages; and the creation of monastic communities who had the patience and agricultural expertise to produce wine-grapes.

The civilisation built up so painstakingly by the wine-loving Romans was brutally dismantled by the hordes of barbarous Jutes, Angles and Saxons who poured in between 449 and 590. Those Christian Britons who managed to escape being slaughtered retreated to Wales and to the far west of the country, which was fast becoming 'England', taking with them their wine-drinking and vine-growing traditions. After Augustine's conversion of the English from Celtic to Roman rites, the monastic ideal took new root in England. Self-supporting religious orders were formed in large numbers, each growing their own fruit and vegetables, breeding fish and making their own wine for use at the Mass, for their refreshment after it and for entertaining distinguished visitors and itinerant preachers. This gave a new fillip to English viticulture which, after its Roman birth and prolonged infancy, acquired a distinctive pedigree and separate tradition which enabled it to take its part in the

The people of Anglo-Saxon and Norman England made wine from grapes grown on south-facing hillsides, and wine was drunk by everyone in the kingdom except the very poor.

everyday life of the kingdom. In the twelfth century William of Malmesbury looked back on the Anglo-Saxon scene in his Latin *Chronicle of the Kings of England*. 'The Vale of Gloucester,' he wrote, 'yields plenty of corn and fruit . . . No county in England has so many or so good vineyards as this, either for fertility or for sweetness of the grape. The wine has in it no unpleasant tartness or eagerness, and is little inferior to the French for its sweetness.'

The Normans, unlike the previous conquerors of England, were Christians and their conquest did not involve the destruction of monastery vineyards and castle wineries. When they came to the area around Ely they found so many vines they called it L'Isle des Vignes, and left them to grow and ripen as they had already done for so long. The arrival of the Frenchmen signalled the planting of vines by nobles, farmers and monks more intensely than ever. During the reign of William the Conqueror churches, monasteries and convents were built all over England, each with a corner of land set apart for the culture of vines and wine-grapes from which to make sacramental wine. The Normans who became the ruling class of England introduced French viticultural traditions.

Among the many laws made by King Alfred was one concerning the keeping of vines. This illustration is from a tenth-century manuscript.

A good, though probably not a full picture of the extent of the vineyards being cultivated in England at the end of the eleventh century was given in the Domesday Survey which King William ordered to be made in 1080 and 1086. Forty-two entries recorded vineyards comprising 46 place names in 14 counties:

1: Somerset
  1: Glastonbury
  2: Meare
  3: Panborough
  4: North Curry
  5: Muchelney
  6: Midelney
  7: Thorney

2: Gloucestershire
  8: Stonehouse

3: Wiltshire
  9: Lacock
  10: Wilcot
  11: Tollard Royal
  12: Bradford-on-
      Avon

4: Dorset
  13: Wootton
  14: Durweston

5: Worcestershire
  15: Hampton-by-
      Evesham

6: Bedfordshire
  16: Eaton Socon

7: Cambridgeshire
  17: Ely

8: Suffolk
  18: Clare
  19: Ixworth
  20: Barking
  21: Lavenham

9: Essex
  22: Rayleigh
  23: Hedingham
  24: Belchamp
  25: Waltham
  26: Mundon
  27: Ashdon
  28: Stambourne
  29: Toppesfield
  30: Stebbing
  31: Debden

10: Buckinghamshire
  32: Iver

11: Berkshire
  33: Bisham

12: Kent
  34: Chart Sutton
  35: Chislet
  36: Leeds

13: Hertfordshire
  37: Standon
  38: Ware
  39: Berkhamsted

14: Middlesex (Greater
      London)
  40: Colham
  41: Harmondsworth
  42: Kempton
  43: Kensington
  44: Staines
  45: Westminster
      (Chenetone)
  (46: Holborn)

The leading authority on the survey, Sir Henry Ellis, wrote in *A General Introduction to Domesday Book* in 1833:

> From the entries in the Survey and from other authorities we gather that in the Norman times few of the great monasteries were without their vineyards ... Other proofs besides those which Domesday affords might readily be brought that wine of native growth was formerly used in England. The quantity, however, produced never could have been sufficient for consumption by the inhabitants; and its inferiority is probably a better reason for having been supplanted by foreign produce than any stipulated destruction of the vines by treaty [he was refuting the suggestion that England had made a treaty with France agreeing to do this]. The encouragement of the vine as a fruit has continued in England at all periods.

It is unlikely that the only vineyards in existence at the time of the Domesday Book were those which rated a mention. It is reckoned for instance that there was a small vineyard

Map showing the positions of vineyards in 46 places recorded in the Domesday Survey, 1086.

within the precincts of the Tower of London; and it is odd that only one, at Stonehouse, was recorded in the famous vine-growing county of Gloucestershire, or in Staffordshire or Hampshire. Essex had the largest number of vineyards in the survey, a fifth of the total. Once planted they were cultivated by generation after generation.

The picture of vineyard ownership revealed by the Domesday Survey of 1080 and 1086 was very much more aristocratic than monastic. The pace was being set by the new nobility rather than the clergy, though of course the priors and abbots in areas like Glastonbury and Canterbury continued to cultivate the vine and make wine for the Mass and the convivialities which followed.

There was also a royal tradition of viticulture. Wine fit for a king was made at Windsor Castle from vines grown in the Little Park from at least 1155. The Abbot of Waltham, who was parson both of the old and new Windsor, received his tithe in wine pressed from the grapes which grew in Little Park. The wine-making at Windsor Castle was a commercial operation. It was primarily for the royal household to drink, but what was left over was sold 'to the king's profit'. The fame of it was still a talking point in the sixteenth century when William Lambarde said he had read that even if a tenth of the Windsor vines yielded, there was 'great plenty' of wine, which made him think 'that wine had been made long since within the realm, although in our memory it is accounted a great dainty to hear of.'

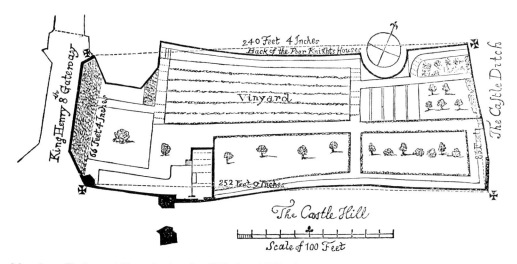

Map from Tighe and Davis's *Annals of Windsor*, 1858, showing the position of the mediaeval royal vineyard under the walls of Windsor Castle.

The vines were grown on a small plot 250 feet by 85 feet in what was the Castle Ditch east of Henry VIII's Gateway and under the high wall of the Military Knight's Lodgings. The site marked 'vineyard' on the plan in Tighe and Davis's *Annals of Windsor* (1858) has never been built on. Today it is a grassy stretch on the left of Castle Hill in the part of the grounds open to the public. Apart from the plot at Windsor, Henry II had royal vineyards at Purley, Stoke, Cistelet, and in Herefordshire and Huntingdonshire.

Down in the west country and in Wales, the great religious houses had managed to retain a comparatively calm existence while other parts of the island were engulfed in political and military intrigue. Giraldus Cambrensis, Gerald the Welshman, writing some 100 years after the Norman invasion, remembered tranquil days spent as a boy in the vineyard at Maenor Byr (Manorbier Castle), his birthplace in what was Pembrokeshire and is now Dyfed. He also told of vineyards in Glamorgan and Gwent.

'Occupations of the Month' were popular subjects for illustrations in mediaeval calendars: a Canterbury calendar of 1280 showed pruning vines for March (top left), treading grapes for September (top right) and drinking wine for January (left).

HENRY II, THE FIRST PLANTAGENET king of England, inherited from his father the demesnes of Normandy, Maine and Anjou. Eleanor, the divorced Queen of France, whom he married before he became king in 1154, brought with her as her dowry Poictou and Guienne, the great vine-growing area famous for its wine since the days of the Roman Empire as Aquitania and known in the twelfth century as Aquitaine or Guienne, today as Bordeaux.

Writers who have felt obliged to account for a 'decline' in English viticulture, have seized on the addition of Aquitaine to the realm of the King of England as the cause of it. But wine had been coming to England from Aquitaine and drunk by the English for a thousand years or more. It was no great novelty. The inclusion of Aquitaine in Henry II's kingdom would not have changed drinking habits overnight, though doubtless the 'wines of Gascony' (yet another name for the district) would have become very much cheaper. The quantity of English Wine was never great, and its character altogether different. French and English wine had never competed, and were never to do so. The scale of English viticulture, compared with the activity in France, was small, but that was beside the point. As Rev Samuel Pegge MA of Whittington pointed out in 1763, 'it is not to be supposed that *at any time* since the first introduction of the vine here, the inhabitants of the island produced wine enough for their own consumption, but rather that in all seasons they imported a great deal from abroad.' Wine was a universal drink in twelfth century England when, at a penny a gallon, it was drunk by all but the poorest.

There is no reason to think that those who kept the English vineyards at this time were ever discouraged by the large scale drinking of imported wine. They continued to make their modest contribution to the total amount consumed, unwilling to abandon a tradition which had been part of English life for more than a millenium – for certainly as long as it had been of *la vie Bordelaise*.

The arrival of large quantities of red French wine on the quays of London did not deter those with property in the capital from planting open-air vines in the thirteenth century. The year 1292 is the date on a grant of a house and vineyard in the parish of All Saints, Fenchurch; in 1295 the Earl of Lincoln had a vineyard in Holborn, where too John de Hotham Bishop of Ely had a vineyard in the London residence ('hostell') Ely House, the site of which was marked by the eighteenth-century mapmaker John Rocque with 'Vine Street', now called Vine Hill and approached by Vine Street Bridge.

Though there was little of it, or perhaps *because* there was so little of it, English Wine, to those who made it, was something rare and worth taking trouble over. The amount of attention required varied from site to site. The thirteenth-century writer Bartholme was amazed at the conditions in the west country. 'A good deal of Somerset must be land too fat and moist, in which the vine outrageth and beareth too many, too great and long leaves, bows and branches, and little fruit.' In spite of this he said, 'the abbots of Glastonbury who doubtless believed in the passing nobility of wine, than which nothing is more profitable if it be taken in due measure and manner, had vineyards on the sunny slopes of Pilton.'

No one attempted to create in England a 'wine industry' as there was in France and England. That had never been the case; and there is little reason to think that there were fewer vineyards and wineries in England and Wales because Aquitaine was ruled by the King of England. Making wine for sale was never the major concern. As André Simon, doyen of wine historians has written (*English Wines and Cordials, 1946*),

> *Having a staff of skilled vine-dressers and many vines to which much labour and money had been devoted for some years, Churchmen were loth to give up this culture; at the same time being able to obtain much better wines from the Continent at lower cost, they did not feel bound to drink the produce of their own vineyards and they attempted to sell at any rate some of it.*

Though not consciously an industry, the satisfaction of being able to make an English wine and one which people liked, made sure that the activity persisted. How many of the Domesday vineyards were still being cultivated 100 years after the survey was completed is not known for certain, but probably most of them. Certainly those at Meare and Panborough in Somerset were still there in the twelfth century, and there were now many more than the 42 noted by the commissioners.

In the thirteenth century the Archbishop of Canterbury owned 30 estates (manors). One of the biggest English wine-making operations of the Middle Ages, and the nearest to being 'commercial', was that undertaken to supply wine for His Grace's cellars. Vineyards for this purpose were planted at two of these manors, a big one at Teynham and a smaller one at Northfleet. Some of the Teynham wine was sold to the King. The earliest reference to the Northfleet vineyard is in a rent roll of archiepiscopal manors for 1235.

There was a vineyard in the city of Hereford in 1229, and there were many on the estates belonging to the Bishop of Hereford. In 1289 Bishop Cantilupe made seven casks of white wine at Ledbury and sent it to the bishop's estate at Bosbury where it was drunk the following summer. There were no glass bottles and no corks so the wine was usually drunk within 12 months. Any kept for more than a year was known as 'old wine'.

From an early time Winchester was famous for its wine, though not everyone would agree with John Twyne that the city acquired its name in that way. 'It was called the City of Wine,' he wrote (in Latin), 'and wine-growing stronghold and fortress where the best wine in Britain grew.' The poet Robert of Gloucester wrote (also in Latin): 'London is known for its shipping, Winchester for its wine.' A church at the north end, and on the east side, of Kingsgate Street was once known as All Saints in the Vineyards.

It seems that the Westminster vineyard mentioned in Domesday was not the one within the 12½ acres over which Edward the Confessor's Palace of Westminster spread itself. Its location is a mystery though its existence is undoubted. Writing in 1882 Dr Arthur Stanley insisted that 'in the adjacent fields were the Orchard, the Vineyard and the Bowling Alley which have left their traces in Orchard Street, Vine Street and Bowling Street'. Vine Street was re-named Romney Street in 1869. The vineyard whose site it marks will have been the 'Vine-garden within the Mill-ditch of Westminster' mentioned in a privy seal granted by Charles II to Edward Billing.

The mediaeval City of London abounded in vineyards. 'The street now denominated *the Vineyard* within the walls of the city of London', stated Samuel Pegge (1763), 'might have produced formerly, we think, very passable grapes; since in London, as it seems, they had vines very commonly in their gardens in the reign of Edward III (1327–77).' He was probably referring to the sheltered spot along the old city wall once tended by the Minoresses of St Clare which today goes by the name of Vine Street off the Minories. And the bridgemaster's accounts for 1382 show that vines were being grown in the open air in the Bridge House Garden at the south end of London Bridge at Southwark. It was likely to have been where, until 1955, there was a street called Vine Yard off Sanctuary Street, Southwark. But the motive for giving streets their names is rarely as significant as it appears. What of the Vineyard Walk off Farringdon Road, Finsbury? William Pinks, who wrote a history of Clerkenwell in 1881, thought there had been a vineyard there 'in monastic times' belonging to the Priory of St John of Jerusalem; but Gilliam Bebbington writing in 1972 considered it was part of the precinct of Clerkenwell Nunnery. The proprietor of The Old Vineyard public house which stood on the site displayed a sign in 1859 which read 'After the City Clerks partook of the water of the Clerks' Well from which the parish derives its name, they repaired hither to partake of the fruit of the finest English grapery'. Pinks denounced this as erroneous and absurd.

H.M. Tod FRHS writing on *Vine-Growing in England* in 1911 was in no doubt however that in the Middle Ages 'Kent vineyards extended from Thame to London and southward by Tonbridge and Sevenoaks to Tenterden and district and the marshes, not much less thickly than the hop grounds do now.' The Vinesfield in Rochester marks the site of the large plantation of vines in the enclosure of the Benedictine Priory of St Andrew – possibly the 'Monks Vineyard' which Charles Dickens referred to in *Edwin Drood*. There is still a pub called The Vineyard in East Row, and a Vines Lane. Fourteenth-century Sevenoaks had an estate known as The Farm on the Vine, later called Bethelham Farm and then Bligh's Farm. This was the home farm of the Archbishop of Canterbury's holding at Sevenoaks, and the area marked 'Sevenoke Vine' to the north of the farm on old maps commemorated the small vineyard cultivated for the Archbishop's table by his bailiff in Sevenoaks. The tradition has been kept alive by the famous Vine Cricket Club formed in 1734 – or maybe earlier. The abbots of the St Augustines at Canterbury had vineyards, at Northolme, Fishpoole near Littlebourne and at Coningbrook in Sellinge. The Kent Wine which was the end product, according to William Thorn, Abbot of Northolme, was '*ad commodum et magnum honorem*'.

Though in Edward III's day Gilbert Earl of Gloucester had his vineyard in Tewkesbury, he saw fit to plant another in the grounds of Tonbridge Castle which he owned. How long the vineyard survived is not known, but certainly the site's potential for vine-growing lasted into the eighteenth century. For when Horace Walpole visited it on 5 August 1752 he wrote to his friend Richard Bentley:

> *We lay that night at Tunbridge town and were surprised with the ruins of the old castle. The gateway is perfect, and the inclosure formed into a vineyard by a Mr Hooker to whom it belongs, and the walls spread with fruit, and the mount on which the keep stood, planted in the same way.*

ENGLISH WINE MADE FROM grapes grown in the vineyards bordering the Rother, the Medway and the Itchen never acquired the degree of potency or equalled the fullness of the red wine from the banks of the rivers which emptied into the Bay of Biscay, but it continued to be a rare and distinctive drink for men of taste, and in a class of its own – *magnum honorem*. This status was unaffected by the sequence of events which led to the Land of Claret being recovered by its former owners. In 1449 Charles VII, King of France, invaded Normandy and within 12 months expelled the English. Encouraged by this success he turned his attention to Guienne, and after three centuries of English rule the whole province, including the towns of Bayonne and Bordeaux, were 'finally swallowed up in the French monarchy'. Throughout the eighteenth century Gascon Wine had constituted some 80 per cent of England's total wine imports (3,000,000 gallons) at an average price of 3½d a gallon, compared with German Wine from the Rhine at 1s 2d a gallon, Italian Wine at 2s and Cretan Wine at 4s.

English viticulture and wine-making were as little affected by the loss of Aquitaine/ Guienne/Gascony as they were by its acquisition 300 years before. If anything the rise in the price of Gascon Wine which followed the restoration of the province to French rule boosted consumption of the fine, flinty English Wine whose delicate flavour had for so long, from the King downwards, suited the palates of the Establishment. Only two years before his defeat at Bosworth Field Richard III appointed John Piers 'master of our vyneyarde nigh unto our Castell of Wyndesore' for the term of his life. That England had a classic vineyard in its back garden for three centuries beside the Gironde and Garonne may have discouraged the island population from exerting themselves to the fullest extent in the cultivation of their own vines and the making of English Wine, but it is unwise to assume that by bringing Henry II the lands of Bordeaux as her dowry, Eleanor of Aquitaine delivered a wounding blow from which English vineyards and English Wine never recovered. In fact English viticulture, healthy before 1154 and even healthier throughout the remainder of the Middle Ages, was as much a mediaeval commonplace as fishing for eels and minstrelsy.

Those Middle Ages are always regarded as ending with the succession to the English throne of Henry VII in 1485, and with them a way of life overawed by religion and dominated by the Church. Society began to turn its attention to more worldy matters, to commerce, to manufacture, navigation, industry and the arts. If so far viticulture had been undisciplined and unscientific, in the new age it flourished as never before. When Henry VIII succeeded in 1509 there were 139 sizeable vineyards in England and Wales of which 11 were owned by the Crown, 67 by noble families and 52 by the Church. William Harrison who wrote at the end of the sixteenth century believed the country to be producing between two and three thousand tuns of wine a year, or 630,000 gallons. The best English Wine, he said, was called 'Theologicum' because 'it was from the clergy and religious men unto whose houses many of the laity would often send for bottles to be filled with the same.'

There seems to have been a certain slackening off in viticulture and wine-making in England at the end of the Middle Ages. Stories of a dramatic change in the English climate which affected open-air vine growing are exaggerated however. In *The Earlier Mediaeval Warm Epoch and Its Sequel* (1965) Professor Hubert Lamb gave the prevailing temperature in central England in July and August for 1500 to 1550 as 15.9 degrees Centigrade, the same as it had been from 1350 to 1400. Between 1400 and 1450 it had been 15.8 degrees and from 1450 to 1500 15.6 degrees. Lamb's statistics showed that it was no sensational change but 'cool springs, May frosts and to a less degree lack of summer warmth that in the end told against the vine in England.' But that is something English viticulture has always had to contend with, and still has to today. William Camden saw such decline as there might have been at this time as caused by something else. In his *Britannia*, published in Latin in 1586, he recalled William of Malmesbury's eulogy of Gloucestershire's fine vintage, and declared that any falling off from that high was due to any inexorable cause dictated by Nature from which Man had no escape.

> *Neither do I believe with the ideal and discontented husbandmen whom Columella* [the ancient Roman writer on agriculture] *reprehends, that the soil worn out by successive fruitfulness in former ages, is now become barren. But from hence (to pass to other Arguments) we are not to wonder that so many places in this country from their vines are called Vineyards because they formerly afforded plenty of wine; and that they yield none now is rather to be imputed to the sloth of the inhabitants than the indisposition of the climate.*

In hotter climates average results will come with minimum effort; in more temperate borderline climates closer attention, more hours of work and a greater degree of technical knowledge both in vine-growing and wine-making, are needed. Nature does not work so hard for vine-growers in the north as she does for those farther south. In England those who venture into viticulture have to take it slowly, giving thought to the choice of the most suitable variety of vine and to the most suitable site in which to plant them. If they get that equation right, English viticulture works, and its wine can be as good as any made in any other country.

The abbots and monks who lived in close regimented communities, growing their own food and making their own drink, certainly got it right. For them it was an industry, and as such – but in no other respect – it disappeared from English life when between 1536 and 1539 Henry VIII dissolved first 200 monasteries and 100 nunneries each of whose annual revenues amounted to less than £200, and then bribed or browbeat the rest into submission and had all the monastic houses vested in the Crown. After that the knowledge, enthusiasm and energy of the monks who worked the vineyards and wine presses were never to be replaced in quite the same way. However, although all religious orders were abolished, many expelled monks were appointed to benefices. An abbot who had been used to drinking wine made from his own grapes was unlikely, on becoming a bishop, to drop the habit. In the fervour of the Reformation the King issued many royal injunctions on such matters as the removal of superstitious images and the deportment of the clergy, but there was no dread ban on the clergy keeping a vineyard or on drinking the wine made from its grapes. Those who had mismanaged the more disreputable monasteries and abbeys which were scrubbed entirely off the map may have been the worst and laziest vineyard keepers, and good riddance to them. But it was equally possible that many were unacceptable to the commissioners for the very reason that they spent too much time tending their vines and too little caring for souls.

When properties such as Pershore Abbey and Battle Abbey became noblemen's estates the new, lay owners would have prized the bonus acquisition of a well maintained vineyard and wine press, and ensured that standards were kept up and, where they had slipped, raised. Vine-growing and wine-making in no way disappeared from England after the Dissolution of the Monasteries in the middle of the sixteenth century. The vineyard of Darley Abbey in Derbyshire, for instance, which must have been one of the most northerly in the kingdom, was still functioning in 1557 according to Samuel Pegge (1763). In Kent, vineyards were still being worked at Wardens and Fyll in Egerton, Boughton Malherbe and Hool Mill in Harrietsham in 1580. The noblemen of Elizabethan England were proud to fill their cellars not only with Rhenish and Gascon wine but with the fresh wine of the country as distinctively English as Colchester oysters, Stilton Cheese, downland honey, Cox's orange pippins, and the intoxicating poetry of William Shakespeare.

In spite of the Dissolution of the Monasteries in 1536 the pruning of vines and the treading of grapes continued to be everyday chores featured in sixteenth-century prayer book calendars.

When Will was writing *Henry VIII* he referred to what would have been common knowledge in England at the end of the sixteenth century – he was writing between 1590 and 1610. He gave these lines to Archbishop Cranmer who had known the vines of Westwell Priory in Kent given to him by Henry VIII:

> In her days every man shall eat in safety
> Under his own vine what he plants, and sing
> The merry songs of peace to all his neighbours.

In writing the speech of the Duke of Richmond on the Plain of Tamworth before the Battle of Bosworth in the second scene of the fifth act of *Richard III*, he drew on what he himself had seen all over England and knew was familiar to his audience.

> The wretched, bloody and usurping boar
> That spoil'd your summer fields and fruitful vines
> Swills your warm blood like wash and makes his trough.

James I (1603–25) had a vineyard on his estate at Oatlands Park in Surrey. Moreover he commissioned a Frenchman called Bonavil to write a treatise on Vines and Silkworms, though that was for the instruction of planters in Virginia not the royal vineyards in England. He also had a Physic and Vine Garden near St James's Palace. At a later date, close to Rosamund's Pond, not far from the site of this garden, stood The Vineyard Tavern, sometimes called The Royal Vineyard. Another Surrey vineyard at Charte Park near Dorking belonged to the Sondes family. It was bought by Beresford Hope who added it to the grounds of Deepdene which was built in 1652.

On the whole there were more optimists than pessimists. One of the former was Captain Nicholas Toke who planted a vineyard at Godinton in the Weald of Kent. According to H. M. Tod (1910) he 'so industriously and elegantly cultivated and improved our English vines that the wine pressed and extracted from their grapes seems not only to parallel but almost to outrival that of France.' After all, added Tod, 'the Commune of Beaune grows at least three classes of wine, and there is nothing to prevent Sussex growing wine equal to the second of these as well as the ordinary.' Edward Hasted, writing in 1797, agreed with him. 'There was a vineyard at Godinton in Captain Nicholas Toke's time from which was made wine of an extraordinary fine sort and flavour,' he said. Toke had five wives and died aged 93 in 1680. In the Weald of Kent at Great Charte in the sixteen-twenties Sir Peter Ricard had a vineyard and a wine press on which he produced six or eight hogsheads of English Wine every year – a hogshead was 63 old wine gallons or 52½ imperial gallons. In *The Compleat Husband-man* which he wrote in 1659 Samuel Hartlib instanced Ricard as one of the Ingenious Gentlemen who usually made wine 'very good, long lasting, without extraordinary labour and costs'. Sir Peter's wine, he said, was 'very much commended by divers who have tasted it, and it hath been very good'. And that in spite of the Wilde of Kent, as he called it, being very moist and cold. The Great Charte Vineyard was the one listed in Domesday Book at Certh which today is Ashford.

The key to successful viticulture in England, said Hartlib, was choosing the grape varieties which were 'most proper to this Isle'. He recommended four of them: the Rhenish-grape; the Paris-grape; the Parsley Vine or Canada-grape; and the Small Muskadell. The advantage of England, he said, was that the island was not subject to nipping frosts that could occur during May in France; the island air was 'more grosse' than on the Continent, not so piercing and sharp. England was not so subject to hail storms in the summer.

> *We make an abundance of wine here with profit, the charges of an acre of vineyard not being so great as of the hops . . . 2,000 vines an acre at 50s a year is the ordinary rate for the three diggings with their crooked instrument called Sventage, and the yield was usually four tuns an acre.*

He recommended getting a vigneron from France where there were plenty of them and they worked for lower wages than ordinary servants in England.

> *If we here in England plant vines as we do hops, it will do very well; but let them not be packt together too thick as they do in France in many places, lest they too much shade the ground and one another.*

His recipe for a good compost was brimstone, pigeon dung, lees of wine, blood and lime 'with moderation'.

AN INGENIOUS NOBLEMAN WHO anticipated Samuel Hartlib's ideas was Robert Cecil first Earl of Salisbury, the builder of the magnificent Jacobean mansion, Hatfield House, which still stands today – in the grounds of a very much older building which in 1109 had become a residence of the Bishops of Ely who had that vineyard in their London residence in Holborn. In 1610 Lord Salisbury decided to plant part of the garden at Hatfield House as a vineyard and sent the botanist John Tradescant to Flanders on a vine hunt. Antoine de la Boderie, the French Ambassador to the Court of St James's, or rather his wife, arranged for 20,000 vines (at eight crowns a thousand) to be delivered to Hatfield. They were planted in the four-acre walled area still known as The Vineyard on both sides of the steep banks of the Broadwater, a stretch of the river Lee. When his lordship's gardener Thomas Wilson heard that Madame de la Boderie was sending a further 20,000, raising the total cost to more than £50 besides the carriage, and that they would arrive in 15 days, he wrote to Lord Salisbury to protest. Those which he already had from the ambassador's Maitre d'hostell or from 'Mr Bell' were

> *more than the ground prepared will receive. We will make a nursery of them, sett thick together, on some small piece of ground adjoining, to supply those still which we shall find defective or dying. I have talked with Wryght of the Temple that made my lord Cook's pypes of erth, who tells me that ther is never a yard but my lord Cook must pay 12d for, besydes the cariage, digging the trenches and making up the ground again.*

In 1620 there is first mention in Middle Temple records of the Vine Court off Inner Temple Lane, and maybe Wilson's friend Mr Wryght had been involved in a vine planting exercise of some sort where lawyers had their chambers in the Fleet Street area of London. Wherever he got his advice from, Thomas Wilson made a success of his planting, for Hatfield House accounts show payments being made over the next two decades to gardeners for dressing the vines. John Evelyn paid Hatfield House a visit in 1643 and noted in his diary 'the most considerable rarity besides the house were the garden and vineyard, rarely watered and planted.' It was still being carefully maintained when Charles I was a prisoner there in 1647, though by the end of the Civil War it had become more of a pleasure garden than a wine-producing vineyard. There are no records among the many early references to the vineyard in the archives at Hatfield of grapes actually being harvested. 'One presumes that some wine was produced' said R.H. Harcourt Williams, Lord Salisbury's librarian and archivist in 1976, 'but no accounts of it were kept and we have no idea what it was like.'

Samuel Pepys found himself in Hatfield on 22 July 1661 and strolled over to see the house and its renowned garden.

> *After dinner, though weary, I walked all alone to the Vineyard which is now a very beautiful place again.*

He paid it a second visit in 1667. But four years after his first visit he had forgotten he had ever made it. In May 1665 he met a party of friends going to have dinner with Colonel Blunt, at Writtlemarsh near Blackheath, and they stopped and took him with them.

> *Landed at Tower Wharf and thence by water to Greenwich; and there coaches met us; and to his house, a very stately sight for situation and brave plantations; and among others a vineyard, the first that ever I did see.*

John Evelyn had been a guest of Colonel Blunt's before Pepys. An entry in his diary for 1655 told how he went 'to see Colonel Blunt's subterranean warren and drunk of the wine of his vineyard which was good for little'. He had previously visited (in 1643) a vineyard at Much Hadham in Hertfordshire – possibly the Vineyard Croft which became Vineyard Springs.

On 17 July 1667, Samuel Pepys had another taste of English Wine. He found the wine made by Admiral Sir William Batten excellent. It was from the grapes grown in the garden of his house in Walthamstow. Referring to the taking of some prizes by a ship in which he and Sir William had an interest, Pepys wrote:

> *I at Sir W. Batten's [where I] did hear the particulars of it; and there, for joy, he did give the company that there were there a bottle or two of his own last year's wine, growing at Walthamstow; than which the whole company said they never drank better foreign wine in their lives.*

When John Evelyn helped his friend and neighbour Henry Howard design an 'Italian Garden' at Albury Park near Guildford in Surrey in 1666, he incorporated a vineyard. Henry Howard, later Earl of Arundel and sixth Duke of Norfolk had bought the Albury estate from his elder brother Thomas Howard, in 1653. He enlarged the house and landscaped the garden in the Italian fashion with a 'canal' a quarter of a mile long and 60 feet wide. 'Above that' wrote John Aubrey, 'a vineyard of twelve acres of the same length with the canal upon the ascent of the hill which faceth the south. A good part of the hill is digg'd down to make the elevations easie.' The vines were planted below two parallel terraces each 400 yards long on a south facing slope above the level of the Tilling Bourne which had been widened to form the 'canals'. Today Albury Park is an old people's home and owned by the Duke of Northumberland.

Henry Howard's 12-acre vineyard beside a 'canal' at Albury near Guildford in Surrey – a drawing by Wenceslas Hollar of 1645.

John Evelyn was more than the designer of a one-off vineyard in an Italian garden in Surrey; he was a known champion of English viticulture and English Wine. He had no hesitation in acceding to the request of John Rose to write a preface to his book *The English Vineyard Vindicated* published in 1666. 'Being one day refreshing myself in the Garden at Essex-house' he wrote,

> *and amongst other things falling into discourse with Mr Rose . . . about vines, and particularly the cause of the neglect of vineyards of late in England, he reasoned so pertinently on the subject . . . I was persuaded to gratifie his modest and charitable inclinations to have them communicated to the world.*

John Rose was Gardener to His Majesty King William III at his Royal Garden in St James's, and was formerly gardener to the Duchess of Somerset. In his dedication 'to the prince of plants, to the Prince of Planters', Rose said he knew His Majesty could have no great opinion of our English wines as they had been made up to then. He had persuaded himself that the reason for their being less good than they could be, was not altogether the defect of the climate, at least not in all places alike, nor the industry of His Majesty's subjects. The cause lay in 'some what else' which he would endeavour to encounter.

> *So if, by your Majesties' gracious Acceptance of the Essay, Gentlemen shall be encourag'd to plant these sorts of Vines which I here recommend, and to cultivate them by my directions, that precious liquor may haply once againe recover its just estimation, be the product of Your Majesties Dominions and answer the ambitions of . . . John Rose.*

The 'some what else' was 'our own neglect and the common vicissitude of things'. People should not think that just because others neglected to plant vineyards there was no purpose now to begin.

> *Since the discouragement has only proceeded from their misinformation on this material article of the choyce of soil and situation, whilst giving ear to our forraign Gardners coming here into England, then took up those rules which they saw to be most practical in Countries of so little affinity with ours.*

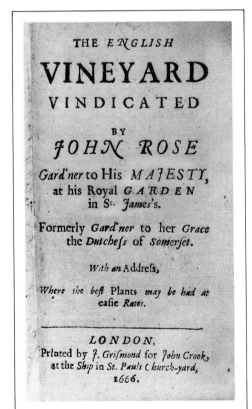

The title page of John Rose's book.

He was one of the first to see that to compare our achievements in the circumstances dictated by English soil, English weather, English topography and England's island locale, with those resulting from the very different conditions of the land mass across the Channel, was meaningless; and to proclaim that English wine-grapes and English Wine had a character and a tradition of their own.

One who like John Rose also had confidence in the future of a purely English viticulture was William Hughes who, in *The Compleat Vineyard* of 1670, pointed proudly to 'such vineyards and wall vines as produce a great store of excellent good wine'. We were, after all, he said, 'no nearer the pole than well-known German wines'.

Today's drinkers can only take it from people such as William Hughes that it was excellent good wine. They can never know how it tasted. Words cannot convey taste. But when an Oxford don like Dr Ralph Bathurst, president of Trinity College, was said by country historian Dr Robert Plot to have 'made as good claret here at Oxon AD 1685, which was a very mean year for that purpose, as one could wish to drink', it must have had a certain sophistication. In his *Natural History of Staffordshire* (1686) Dr Plot was even more enthusiastic about the viticultural skill of the right worshipful Sir Henry Lyttelton at Over-Arley 'which is situate low and warm, being surrounded with hills'.

> He has made wine so good there that it has been altogether undistinguishable from the best French wines by the most judicious palates; but this, I suppose, was done only in some favourable over-hot summer though, if Vines were placed advantageously, 'tis possible it might be done in an indifferent year.

Only slightly further south George Skipp was making red and white wine at this time from the grapes he grew in his vineyard at Upper Hall, Ledbury.

THE PRACTICE OF MAKING WINE FROM English wine-grapes grown in open-air vineyards had not been brought to a full stop by a change in the climate or by the transfer of monastic property to lay hands in the middle of the sixteenth century. The extent of the decline has been exaggerated. But there is no escaping the fact that viticulture, a difficult and demanding craft with rewards that varied from year to year, had become less attractive in the years that followed the Dissolution. For Samuel Hartlib the English had only themselves to blame 'that so little is attempted to revive them again' – vineyards, that was to say.

The conditions which made English Wine production possible had not changed, only the attitude as to how worthwhile it was to take advantage of them. Lack of adequate means of communication in seventeenth-century England meant that though the tradition of English Wine was still very much alive, few knew of it. More Ingenious Gentlemen were needed with the time and inclination to uncover for themselves what the years had obscured, and to be inspired to experience, as others had done, the unique satisfaction of growing their own grapes and making at reasonable cost drinkable wine of reasonable quality.

Samuel Hartlib's call was taken up in the following century by the anonymous author of *The Vineyard, Observations made by a Gentleman on his Travels*, published in 1727, who chose to call himself S.J.

It had long been the prevailing opinion, he told the Courteous Reader in his introduction, that the raising of vines to any tolerable perfection in England was altogether impracticable, and that all attempts of that nature would prove fruitless. Their opinions, however, were founded upon no better reason than want of experience. It was a common argument with many people that certain things were impossible because, had they been practicable, they would have been tried before. But the absurdity of such reasoning was too trifling to need any confutation unless the objectors could show that all attempts had proved ineffectual.

There had been several instances, he said, of people drawing wine from grapes of their own growth in England 'which they have found to excel many foreign wines in their pleasant, brisk and palatable flavour'. The current lack of English Wine 'was not owing to the unkindness of our soil or the want of a benign climate, but to the inexperience of our natives or a want of curiosity in such as are capable of convincing themselves by an easy experiment of the practicableness thereof.' The ancient Roman author Pliny, he pointed out, had commended English Wine for its goodness and an agreeable taste and relish. The very fact that the English climate was not over-warm was an advantage for English viticulture. Grapes brought to the markets of London from abroad were over-ripe and not fit for wine-making. The objection of the want of sun was easily confuted when the temperateness of England's soil was considered in opposition to the intemperature of France etc.

> *The wine of the Mosel, which lies so northerly that the grapes never come to the maturity which they do in the southern part of England, were yet, by the industry of the inhabitants, rendered fine, potable, pleasant and preferable to those of many more southern parts.*

Others joined his plea for men of quality to discard their prejudices. 'This we can say with certainty' declared Dr Hales of Teddington in his *Compleat Treatise on Practical Husbandry*, 'that very good wine may be made in England.' He had drunk with the distinguished Dr Shaw the wine which he had made from a little vineyard behind his garden in Kensington 'which equalled many of the lighter wines of France'. In his *Complete Body of Gardening* William Hanbury wrote, 'I have known good wine made of grapes in England and have drunk Burgundy no way inferior, as my taste could find out, to that noted wine which we have constantly imported from that country.' Philip Miller could not pretend to determine the cause of the current neglect of cultivating vines in England,

> *but such was the prejudice that most people conceived to any attempts of producing wine in England that for some ages past every trial of that kind has been ridiculed by the Generality of People, and at this day very few persons will believe it possible to be affected.* (The Gardeners Dictionary, 1747)

To Samuel Pegge the prejudice against even attempting to make English Wine was altogether too much, especially when, as in the case of Hon. Daines Barrington, it was based on a belief that wine-grapes had *never* been grown in England and that all accounts of their having been cultivated was a myth deriving from a misunderstanding of Latin. He stoutly contested the theory that the climate of England prevented open-air vine-growing. Did not some of the more austere wines grow in the Rhine valley and beside the Maine in latitudes as high as 49 degrees 'which may equal perhaps in coldness ours of 51½?'

Illustration from *A treatise on the Culture of the Vine* by William Speechley, gardener of the Duke of Portland at Welbeck, published in 1790.

The mood was changing. English viticulture must not be written off out of hand because of the unsuitability of the weather, but the means found to accommodate it to the vagaries and peculiarities of the English ambience. Symbolic of the change was the title of the talk given by Francis Xavier Vispré to the Society of Arts in 1784, 'A Plan for Cultivating Vineyards Adapted to this Climate'. Two years later he produced a comprehensive book entitled *A Dissertation on the Growth of Wine in England*. Two years after that William Speechley, the Duke of Portland's gardener, published *A Treatise on the Culture of the Vine*.

So MUCH FOR THE TALKERS and writers. Who took their advice and acted on their theories? Two exercises of the eighteenth century stood out from all others on account of their size, success and duration: Westbrook and Painshill.

James Oglethorpe was born around 1688, the son of a leading Jacobite, Theophilus Oglethorpe who had nine children of whom James was the last. In 1688 Theophilus bought the fine mansion near Godalming called Westbrook Place which had been built some eight years earlier for Sir John Platt. It stood in a park of some 80 acres at the foot of a humped hill. In 1718 it was inherited by James Oglethorpe who shortly afterwards built a massive wall up the humped hill and planted in front of it what some authorities are quoted as saying was probably the largest vineyard of its kind that England had ever seen. Oglethorpe planted his wine-grape vines on two straight terraces stretching the whole 400 yards in front of the wall. From them he made wine, though where the winery was is a mystery. Vineyard and winery were in full operation between 1720 and 1732 when Westbrook was in its heyday as a social-political centre. The young Member of Parliament for Haslemere and ardent social reformer held soirées and political gatherings almost every weekend at which the local English Wine flowed freely, accompanying the delicacy for which Westbrook also became renowned, the French snails which fed on the vine leaves.

He conceived the idea of founding a colony in America as a refuge for people stricken by poverty and for persecuted German Protestants. In November 1732 he sailed across the Atlantic with 120 settlers and founded what became Georgia. He stayed for two years, while his sisters occupied Westbrook and made it a hotbed of Jacobite intrigue – though James himself was no supporter of the Stuarts' claim to the throne. The young women saw that the vineyard was maintained, and the annual quota of Westbrook Wine. The story goes that for a time Prince Charles Edward himself stayed hidden at Westbrook during the Forty-Five Rebellion. If so, he probably drank to the downfall of the House of Hanover in a beaker of Westbrook Wine, while Brave General Oglethorpe, who had returned from Georgia in 1743, was re-taking Preston for King George.

The vineyard remained intact and the wine-making continued at least until 1754 when Westbrook was visited by Dr Richard Pococke who in his *Travels Through England* published in that year, said that Godalming in Surrey was 'where was General Oglethorpe's, where there is a vineyard out of which they make a wine like Rhenish'. After the general died in 1785 aged 89, the estate was put up for sale, and the sale particulars included the line: 'Also, Gardens and a Vineyard of considerable Extent divided and subdivided with lofty Stone Walls'. When it came up for sale 35 years later, the land was divided into five sections. One was 'Vine Yards and Gardens, 6 acres 2 rods 20 perches'.

So it seems that the Westbrook Vineyard had a life of almost a century. The purchaser in 1823 was Nathaniel Godbold who made a fortune out of patent medicines. In 1892 Westbrook Place was acquired by the Countess of Meath and was opened in August of that year by the Countess of Albany as the Meath Home of Comfort for epileptic women and girls. By then the vineyard was overgrown with fir and bramble, and only the walls – and the house – remained to testify to this great English Wine exercise of the eighteenth century, as they still do today.

The second of the 'modern essays near London' to which Philip Miller referred in *The Gardeners Dictionary* was the even more famous Surrey vineyard at Painshill near Cobham, some 18 miles south of the capital. It lay on the slopes of the high ground about St George's Hill above the Mole Valley. The same itinerant bishop Dr Richard Pococke who noted Westbrook came here in 1750.

> *We came to Painshill near Cobham, Mr Hamilton's, which is a most beautiful farm improvement . . . There are ten acres of vineyard here in two places; the grape gently press'd makes an excellent champaign, and pressed out and left on the husk produces a very good Burgundy; five or six hogsheads have been made in a year, and it sells at the inns here at 7s 6d a bottle. Cobham is a very small town full of inns.*

Mr Hamilton was the Honourable Charles Hamilton, ninth and youngest son of James sixth Earl of Abercorn. In 1738, when he was 34, Charles Hamilton took a long lease of Painshill, a smallish house with a large, wild park of some 300 acres which he set about transforming into a magnificent garden complete with the usual follies and temples. Part of the transformation was planting vines on the south slope of what was known as Wood Hill at the bottom of the garden beside the River Mole. The vineyard dropped down to a meadow which in 1773 was flooded to form the eastern extension of the artificial lake first dug in the seventeen forties which was filled by a huge water wheel from the river. In 1772 in the southwest corner of the vineyard, on the site of what had been a brick works, was built the 'Ruined Abbey' which still stands.

Hon Charles Hamilton, son of the Duke of Abercorn, whose vineyard at Painshill, Cobham in Surrey, produced much admired 'still champagne' between 1740 and 1774 – the 1732 portrait by Antonio David in the National Portrait Gallery.

The precise year in which Hamilton planted the vineyard is not known, but the vines were certainly bearing grapes by 1748 when he engaged a French vigneron to tend them.

David Geneste came from a French Protestant ('Huguenot') family who for generations had owned a vineyard at Beziat in Clairac in Guienne. He was born in Clairac in 1692, some seven years after Louis XIV had withdrawn his protection from French Protestants by revoking the Edict of Nantes. Geneste's sister Marie stayed in France, inherited Beziat vineyard and married André Borderie of Bourgade in 1723. Geneste decided to flee France, and at the end of the seventeen thirties, when he was about 40, landed in England. In 1739 he sent the first of a series of letters to his sister, now Madame Borderie. He married an English girl called Anne Bateman by whom he had two sons and a daughter. The first Mrs Geneste died in 1748, and in that year he was taken on as vigneron at Painshill Park by Charles Hamilton who paid him a guinea a week (a *louis d'or*). In a letter to his sister that first year he told her the vineyard was about 15 *cartonnats* in size – five acres. The grapes were very fine, and they planned to plant another ten acres next year. He had already managed to put aside a nest egg of £50 out of the tips given him by visitors. If he made a go of things he could make a good living, as no one understood vine-keeping in England. The Painshill vineyard was in a very bad state.

Hamilton planted two varieties of 'burgundy' grape vine, the Auvernat and 'the Miller Grape commonly called the *black cluster*' which was hardier than the delicate but tender Auvernat, and was in fact Pinot Meunier. The first year Geneste tried making some red wine from them but found it harsh and austere. 'But through the harshness,' he told sister Marie, 'I perceived a flavour, something like that of some small French white wine, which made me hope I should succeed better with white wine.' His white English wine surpassed all his expectations.

> In two or three years more, as the vines grew stronger, to my great amazement my wine had a finer flavour than the best champaign I ever tasted; the first running was as clear as spirits; the second running was oeil de Perdrix, and both of them sparkled and creamed in the glass like Champaign.

Many good judges of wine, he said, were deceived and thought it superior to any champagne they had ever drunk.

> But such is the prejudice of most people against anything of English growth, I generally found it more prudent not to declare where it grew till after they had passed their verdict on it.

He sold Painshill's English Wine to wine merchants for 50 guineas a hogshead. He sold £500 worth to one merchant who retailed it at 7s 6d to 10s 6d a bottle.

His success told him that much good English Wine might be made in many parts of southern England.

> Main parts are south of Painshill; many soils may yet be fitter to it, and many situations must be so. For mine was much exposed to the south-west wind (the worst of all for vines), and the

declivity was rather too steep; yet with these disadvantages it succeeded many years. Indeed the uncertainty of our climate is against it, and many fine crops have been spoiled by May frosts and wet summers. But one good year balances many disappointments.

In 1750 the vine varieties growing at Painshill included what David Geneste called Pied Rouge, Muscat Blanc, Muscat Rouge, Guillan Blanc and Sauvoit. The following year he was expecting to make eight to ten barrels of wine, but in fact he only made two, half of which was *verjus*. The same had happened to vine-growers all over England, he said, and his master was not deterred from planting a whole lot more vines. Hamilton sold his 1753 vintage of white English Wine for 60 guineas a barrel, which Geneste told Marie was esteemed the richest wine of its kind ever seen.

When Geneste asked Hamilton for a rise, and was refused, he threatened to resign. But after tasting the 1755 vintage – five barrels of white wine and five of red, all from black grapes – Hamilton relented and offered his vigneron £15 a year rent free. Telling his sister that he had accepted the offer, he said if he had the good fortune to make a good harvest that year (1755) he hoped it would turn to his profit, since there were several other gentlemen considering planting vines in the vicinity, and he was the only one who could supply the stock. He now had 35,000 vines at Painshill, more than they had ever had at Beziat.

David Geneste was 63 in 1755, by which time he and Charles Hamilton had made such a success of the vine-growing and wine-making that critics were confounded, and the denigrators of English viticulture shamed. Apologists who peddled empty theories about its impracticability because of the unsuitability of the soil or mythical changes in the climate, were exposed as ignorant faint-hearts. In his *Observations Historical, Critical and Medical on the Wines of the Ancients and the Analogy between them and the Modern Wines* (1775) Sir Edward Barry held that Philip Miller, author of the 1747 *Gardener's Dictionary*, would have spoken with more certainty had he been acquainted with the success of Charles Hamilton. The lessons to be drawn from his achievement, said Barry, were self-evident. The fruits of any plantation could not afford that cheerful pleasure which gentlemen would receive from drinking fine wine of their own production.

After Sir John Parnell visited Painshill in 1763 he noted in his *Journal*:

From the terrace you descend a steep slope and mount as steep an hill through a Beech grove at the top of which you enter a walk which is continued along the side of a hill where a fine vineyard is planted, large enough to produce twelve hogshead a year.

On a second visit in 1769 he saw that a wooden bridge had been thrown over the high road which connected to his house 'a large piece of ground on the other side the road where I observed he [Hamilton] had planted some clumps of evergreen and made a new vineyard.' This will have been the second of the two places to which Richard Pococke referred.

I took notice that the grapes were kept Burgundy-fashion, near the ground as possible. They always cut all off to one shoot of this last year's growth, shortening it to but three eyes. The young shoots from it are what bear. They are let to run about three feet and a half high and are then headed. For next year they have three joints of this year's wood, but not what grows out of last year's, but out of the old wood. So the vines are never higher than about a foot of the old timber, many much lower . . . There are seven under gardeners and one head gardener kept.

A short time later a French visitor, Monsieur Grosley, saw Hamilton's vineyard 'properly exposed to the sun, where about half an acre of land is planted with Burgundian vines,' which was probably this second plot on the other side of the high road reached by the 'very pretty geometrical wooden bridge'. Earth thought to be suitable for vines had been brought into the vineyard 'which the owner is greatly attached to and upon which he spares neither care nor expence'.

When I saw these vineyards they had just fitted up the vineprops which were nothing else but pieces of the great poles used in hop-grounds. I told the vine-dresser my opinion of this bad method of propping up vines. In fact these poles by their size and their being set up so close to each other make a shade, which is most hurtful to the vine; and the juices which come from them, as they rot, mixing with those by which the vine is supported, totally weaken and destroy them. The vine-dresser listened attentively to my observations and promised to substitute in the place of the poles above mentioned the smallest rods that he could possibly procure. (A Tour of London; or New Observations on England and Its Inhabitants, translated by Thomas Nugent, 1772)

David Geneste would not have taken kindly to his methods being criticised by a fellow countryman, but the vine-dresser on this occasion will not have been him. By then he had handed over to another. He would have liked even less the opinion that Grosley passed on Painshill wine:

I have since tasted the wine, the product of that vineyard; to the eye it was a liquor of a darkish grey colour; to the palate it was like verjuice blended together by a bad taste of the soil.

The quality must have dropped with Geneste's departure, and with the erection in 1762 of the miniature Temple of Bacchus in which, according to John Hassell writing in 1818, 'was deposited the famous statue of Bacchus which was absolutely stolen from Rome and purchased by the Hon. Charles Hamilton for one thousand guineas'. It was later sold for £400 to William Beckford of Fonthill in Wiltshire on which estate in 1989 Messrs Craig-McFeely and Edginton have a 13½ acre vineyard of both white and red grapes from which they make 'Fonthill English Wine' of the highest quality. Perhaps that is where the stolen statue of Bacchus presides today?

Charles Hamilton was a rich man; that was evident from the way in which he lavished money on the development of Painshill. From 1743 to 1758 he held the lucrative post of Receiver General of Minorca, Britain's naval base in the Mediterranean, and the even more notoriously lucrative one of Deputy Paymaster General. But even so it seems that at one time he had to borrow £6,000 from an old friend, Henry Holland, and had agreed to pay him four per cent interest on the loan, which however he failed to do with any regularity. In 1773 Holland called the loan in and asked for repayment plus arrears of interest. Hamilton's fortune was in land and he was stumped for cash. There was nothing else for it but to sell Painshill, which he did that year to Benjamin Bond Hopkins for £25,000. Hopkins pulled down the modest residence which Hamilton had occupied all this time (all but a small part still standing), and built himself an altogether grander mansion. But he kept the 300-acre garden much as Hamilton had laid it out, including the vineyard. What the latter looked like at this time can be judged from the painting by George Barrett (1728–84) and Sawrey Gilpin (1733–1807) reproduced over the page, showing rows of vines running down to the water beside the ruined abbey and a gardener with a barrow full of grapes trundling along the footpath at the bottom. Another picture, painted by an unknown artist around 1780, shows the Painshill vineyard from a different angle. This painting is also reproduced on page 30.

Whether Hopkins retained David Geneste is not known, or when or where the Frenchman died – though perhaps it is to Claude Martin the owner of Geneste's manuscript letters. Charles Hamilton went to live in Bath where he died in 1786 at the age of 82. F. X. Vispré visited the vineyard in October of the cold and rainy year of 1782 and found the grapes were only just changing colour. They did not ripen at all. But 1785, he said, though very unfavourable to vines in Portugal, was so much better in England that the grapes in a small vineyard he saw in Chelsea were half-ripened by the second week in August. The vines at Painshill were then 40 years old and chilled by the damp air from the horse chestnut trees bordering the vineyard on the north side.

William Cobbett (1763–1835) visited the Painshill Vineyard as a boy. In *The English Gardener* (1829) he recollected,

> *The vines there were planted in rows and tied to stakes in just the same manner as the vineyards in France; and at the time when I saw the vineyard the vines were well loaded with a black-coloured grape.*

Benjamin Bond Hopkins kept Painshill going until his death in 1794, but there is no evidence that he made any wine. William Robertson saw the estate the year after his death, and in his unpublished travel diary (the manuscript is in the National Library of Dublin) he tells how,

> *directly under on the side of the Hill is the vineyard mentioned by Wheatly – with the Mole at its foot which runs by it at right angles to that at foot of terrace. The vineyard is now entirely neglected and the remnant only of it is to be seen.*

In *Picturesque Rides and Walks* John Hassell bears witness to the fact that in 1818 when the Earl of Carhampton was in possession, who as Colonel Luttrell had opposed John Wilkes in the famous Middlesex Election, the site was covered with firs. In his article in *Gardeners' Magazine* of 1829 J. Gale stated the vineyard enjoyed only two advantages, exposure and dryness; it lacked fertility and a loose and more porous subsoil.

'Painshill Vineyard and Ruined Abbey' by George Barrett RA (1728–1784) and Sawrey Gilpin (1733–1807).

Another contemporary painting of the eighteenth-century English vineyard at Painshill in Surrey by an unknown artist (c. 1780).

It was originally planted with white grapes procured from the neighbourhood of Paris, and a wine similar to champagne was made by confining the must or juice of the fruit in strong casks bound round with cords to prevent the force of fermentation from bursting the casks, until the cold of the autumn frosts checked the fermentation.

Where did all that take place? Norman Kitz who lives at Pains Hill and has done more research into Charles Hamilton's activities than most, and archivist Mavis Collier, have no clue as to the whereabouts of the 'Wine Barn' where the press was housed and David Geneste did his wine-making.

No one knows when the vineyard planted by Cistercian monks at Beaulieu Abbey in Hampshire in the thirteenth century was scrubbed. They arrived from Citeaux in France and started building the abbey in June 1204, but did not complete it until 1246. The vineyard may have been a going concern when King Henry III and his wife Eleanor of Provence attended the dedication of the abbey in June of that year, and had been maintained right up to April 1538 when Abbot Thomas Stevens surrendered the abbey to King Henry VIII, and the church, chapter house and cloisters were demolished. Did then Sir Thomas Wriothesley, later Earl of Southampton, who acquired the 8,000 acre estate in July for £1,340 6s 8d, see little point in demolishing the well-matured vineyard and dismissing the well-trained vine-keepers and wine-makers, and keep the whole exercise going?

There is no record that this was the case. What is known however – from receipts which have survived and can be seen in the archives at Beaulieu today – is that in 1736, 46-year-old John, second Duke of Montagu (1690–1749), who was a bit of a visionary, had the mediaeval vineyard re-planted on its old site. References to payments to Edward Raw for carting 7,000 vineyard stakes, and to James Pitt for cutting another 2,600 in Clobb Copice indicate a fairly large area. It would seem however that the Duke of Montagu had the grapes gathered and fermented but then distilled into *brandy* rather than left to become wine. William Mitchell was paid 19s in August 1739 for 'distilling ye grapes from ye vineyard ye last vintage 1738'; and again in February 1739 £1 8s for distilling 34 gallons of brandy which would fill about 18 dozen bottles. In 1988 Lord Montagu felt that it was more likely to be brandy than wine which was made in the disused Fulling Mill (of which the remains can still be seen) which for some time was mistakenly thought to have been the Wine Barn which housed a wine press.

It looks as if the second Duke of Montagu tired of the whole thing before he died in 1749, for there are no records of work being done in the vineyard after 1745. But the earlier accounts bear witness to its existence. None testify however to the vines planted at Whiteknights near Reading by George Spencer-Churchill, Marquess of Blandford, who had a passion for botany and plant collecting and moved there in 1766. In its heyday the garden at Whiteknights was famous for its rare plants, its temples and grottoes. When Mary

Russell Mitford visited it in 1817, the year George succeeded his father as fifth Duke of Marlborough, she wrote disapprovingly:

> *It is the very palace of False Taste – a bad French garden, with staring gravel walks, make-believe bridges, stunted vineyards, and vistas through which you see nothing.* (quoted in Mary Soames, The Profligate Duke, 1987)

But presumably once, like that at Painshill, the Whiteknights Vineyard had been well looked after, and who knows but that his lordship had indulged in the cheerful pleasure of producing Whiteknights White Wine from its grapes?

There was certainly English Wine being produced in the next door county, even though in his *Political Survey of Great Britain*, published in 1774, Dr John Campbell was not greatly impressed by its quality.

> *We have had vines in England in different places and in large quantities . . . If our wines in Hampshire may not reach that perfection which is requisite to please our palates or become fashionable here, they might possibly be exported with great profit to our plantations.*

Further west, in Somerset, Sir William Bassett annually produced several hogsheads of good-bodied and palatable wine however from his vineyard at Claverton a few miles to the east of Bath. Bassett was MP for Bath for many years until 1693.

There was also a vineyard at Bath itself at this time. It was on the face of a hill half a mile above the Abbey Church. H. M. Tod said that in 1718 it produced 63 hogsheads of wine which were sold at £10 each. There were vineyards in the Walcot area according to Tunstall's 1876 *Rambles About Bath*. Cultivation had ceased in 1730 however because of 'alterations in the climate'. By then only the name persisted, as did that of the old Domesday vineyard at Stonehouse in Gloucestershire still marked on a survey map of the manor of 1728. Viney Farm was all that remained of the vineyard at Mangotsfield which Sir David Blount divided into two in 1203. But in 1733 there were still grapes growing in the vineyard called the Sunns at Churchdown near Gloucester. A vineyard was being worked at Tortworth in Cromhall Park throughout the eighteenth century. A large plantation was said to have produced ten hogsheads of good wine in one year, according to Rudge's *Gloucestershire* (1803). Rudge added that it was 'discontinued or destroyed in consequence of a dispute with the rector on a claim of the tythes'.

In 1767 land known as The Vineyard at Benges in Hertfordshire near the old church of St Leonard was made into a vineyard by its owner Thomas Dimsdale. In the great vine-growing county of Essex a vineyard was known to have been at Gidea Hall near Romford, which was probably one of many. Charles Hamilton was not the only one to look to France for the viticultural experience which was lacking in England. In the seventeen eighties Sir Philip Cravenleigh planted a vineyard on his Shropshire estate after sending one of his sons to France to learn the art of planting and dressing vines.

The precise role of the Museum Rusticum which had spurred Samuel Pegge to action is far from clear, but it was this institution to which he referred his readers who wished to be informed of the quality of the burgundy made by his Grace the Duke of Norfolk at Arundel in Sussex. H. M. Tod stated that in 1763, 60 pipes of burgundy were made from the Duke's vineyard at Arundel Castle which were 'not equal to the best of Beaune but better than ordinary'. A 'pipe' was two hogsheads or 105 imperial gallons. Writing before Tod, Andrew Pettigrew, in 1884, also gave the year 1763 as the one in which the Duke of Norfolk's vineyard at Arundel produced excellent wine.

> *I remember some years ago having a conversation with the late Lord Howard of Glossop on vines and vineyards, and his lordship then informed me that his father remembered tasting some of the wine made from the vineyard at Arundel which he said was very good and resembled Burgundy. There were several hogsheads of it in the cellar at that time. The vineyard is not cultivated now [1884] but I believe some of the original vines were to be seen recently growing on the old site.*

That site of two acres 27 perches was clearly marked on maps of 1772 and 1804. It was within the castle precinct. But in the only detailed description of the pre-1800 castle which was partially or wholly rebuilt three times, there is no mention of the winepress where the 'burgundy' was made.

Today the site is outside the wall of Arundel Park and has never been built on. In 1970 Harry Evans acquired the land, planted vines on it once again, and the ground proved as fruitful as ever. When he first ploughed it he turned up a large number of old wine bottles which had obviously been in the ground a long time. So perhaps the Duke's winery of 1763 was beside the vineyard, like maybe Charles Hamilton's was, and not in one of the outhouses near the castle.

Thirty years after the Duke of Norfolk's venture in Sussex, in the adjoining county Edward Hasted was gathering material for his *History and Topical Survey of the County of Kent* published in 1797/9. He concluded that there was still a vineyard at Chart Sutton, and

> *in my memory there have been two exceeding fine vineyards in this county, one at Tunbridge-castle and the other in Hall-place, Barming near Maidstone, from which quantities of exceeding good and well-flavoured wine have been produced.*

As noted, Horace Walpole's attention was attracted by the vineyard at Tonbridge Castle.

OPEN-AIR VINES flourished in London in the eighteenth century as well as they had ever done, but since the Middle Ages the City had been widely built over, and metropolitan vines were now mostly single and the grapes for eating. There was little room in the centre for growing rows of wine-grapes, though there was more scope in 'Middlesex' – the West End and Greater London of today.

The land which James Lee and Lewis Kennedy turned into a nursery garden in Hammersmith in 1745 had once been a vineyard, which was why they called it The

Vineyard Nursery (not because they grew vines in it, which they did not). A cottage on the land in 1628 was called Vynehouse.

John Warner, the populariser of the Black Hamburg grape, is said to have restored the cultivation of the vine to a plot of land in East Lane, Rotherhithe in 1725. David Hughson said Warner had observed that Burgundy grapes ripened early and 'conceiving that they might be grown in England, obtained some cuttings which he planted here as standards'. His crop was so ample that he made at least 100 gallons of wine every year. Moreover he was able to supply cuttings of his vines for cultivation in many other parts of England. Richard Bradley, who became Professor of Botany at Cambridge University in 1724, described Warner in his book *The Vineyard* as a man of great curiosity 'who boasted he had made a pipe of wine from 120 vines in his Rotherhithe vineyard the first year of bearing and continued to make good wine for many years thereafter.'

Someone who may have bought 'Burgundy' vines from Warner was the Mr Rogers whose vineyard at Parsons Green was visited by Peter Collinson who noted in his diary on 18 October 1765 that 'all of the Burgundy grapes were seemingly perfectly ripe'.

I did not see a green half ripe grape in all this great quantity. He does not expect to make less than 14 hogsheads of wine. The branches and fruit are remarkably large and the vines are very strong.

English vineyards had by no means been eradicated by the eighteenth century as Francis Xavier Vispré had hinted. Compared with the Middle Ages they did not come so thickly on the ground, but they were as widely distributed over the English counties. No vineyard as big as those at Westbrook and Painshill had ever been seen in England before. However, since the making of English Wine no longer held a position at the centre of English life as once it had, the practice of viticulture and wine-making came to be regarded as eccentric. It suffered the fate of the dog which stood on one leg in front of Samuel Johnson and provoked the remark that the wonder was, not how well it did it, but that it could do it at all. It was a patronising attitude which died hard, and was that of the large majority, ignorant of its history, for many years to come.

GEORGE III'S WAR WITH the armies of revolutionary France led by General Bonaparte hindered English merchants from trading with the King's enemies but did not stop them. French wine was scarce in England but not unobtainable. The nobility and gentry, the rich tradesmen and professional men saw to it that the wine supply was maintained at whatever cost – which mounted every day. The stocks would have fallen even lower if it had not been for the cases of claret and burgundy captured at sea, and the even greater quantity brought to coves and beaches by smugglers.

In the year 1812, when Napoleon's humiliation at Moscow raised the hopes of the Allied Powers that the Disturber of Europe would finally be brought to heel, an English medical man demonstrated his irritation at the continuing high cost of wine from the Continent by issuing an *Invitation to the Inhabitants of England to the Manufacture of Wines from the Fruits of their Own Country*. Little doubt could be entertained, said Dr R. Worthington MD that 'in a well planted vineyard the grape would flourish with us and yield plentifully'. He held that if vineyards were again established under the improved system of cultivation and of gardening which was the characteristic of the new nineteenth century, the English vintage might on the average of years prove not only considerable but great. If only a few men of wealth and influence would sanction a well conducted trial in the South and Midlands, an English vintage could be expected to become general. Foreign compositions would be shoved aside, and the bottle of English grape would occupy the place of pride and honour on an English table. None but the man of comprehensive means could now, without ruinous expenditure, support the habit of drinking foreign wine.

He refused to be side-tracked by arguments about the English climate, and pointed out the mildness of English autumns,

> *the finest season of the English year, continuing not unfrequently soft and open to the middle of November . . . I have myself proved that grapes caught by the frost will make sound wine . . . There is more to be apprehended perhaps from foggy or wet weather than frost, but neither of them present any* real objection *against the establishment of vineyards in this kingdom. These existed and prospered centuries ago under the rude untutored hands by which they were cultivated. What therefore might not be hoped for under the present improved condition of natural science and of horticulture!*

If men whose example had influence came forward and asserted the powers of their soil and the science of cultivators Dr Worthington believed there could be an English Wine which required no 'adventitious help' from sugar or spirit. It would be a wine which the man of moderate income could store in his cellar at five-sixths less the cost of wine which was so adulterated and disguised as to have lost all flavour of the parent fruit, like foreign wines. A properly prepared English Wine conveying the full and agreeable flavour of the grape, might 'cheer a November day'.

In the following year (1813) the man of moderate income could even less afford French wine, for the British Government increased the duty on it to 19s 8d a gallon or three shillings a bottle.

The author of Phillip's *Pomarium Britannicum* (1820) had no doubts about the quality of the English Wine then in circulation.

> *The idea that we cannot make good wine from our grapes is erroneous. I have tasted it quite equal to Grave wines, and in some instances, where it has been kept for eight to ten years, it has been drunk as hock by the nicest judges.*

The Mr Middleton, who wrote *Agriculture in Middlesex* at this time, agreed with him.

> *It certainly is very possible to make a palatable and much more wholesome wine in England than what is generally imported. It is well known that wine may be made of the English sweet-water grape equal to Mountain [a type of Malaga wine].*

In spite of glowing testimonials such as these, wartime shortage of foreign wine did not revive any large scale interest in English Wine production. In fact viticulture in Britain was in the doldrums. As an agricultural industry which once gave occupation to a large body of labourers in the southern counties it had completely passed away, and could never return in its old form. In the introduction to his book *Vines and Vine Culture*, Archibald F. Barron, Head of Chiswick Garden, attributed the discontinuation of open-air vineyards to the marketing of cheap glass giving more satisfactory results.

This may have assisted in the demise of English viticulture as an agricultural industry, though dessert grape cultivation under glass never had any effect on growing wine-grapes vineyard-fashion, the tradition of which was never lost sight of. The knowledge *that it worked* was never forgotten. Charles Hamilton's operation at Painshill, which continued into the nineteenth century, was a success story within the memory of many who, now peace had returned, could indulge their fancies in a way impossible in wartime.

One such person was John Ward, a London merchant, who acquired an estate at Keston in Kent, some 14 miles south of London. The house, Holwood, had been the country residence of William Pitt. Ward pulled it down and replaced it with another which was completed in 1827. 'In the rear of Holwood' wrote William Hone in his *Every-Day Book and Table Book* (1841),

> *Mr Ward is forming a vineyard which, if conducted with the judgement and circumstance that mark the commencement, may prove that the climate of England is suited to the open culture of the grape. Mr Ward has imported ten sorts of vines, five black and five white, from different parts of the Rhine and Burgundy. They are planted on a slope towards the SSE.*

The author of the 'Home Grown Wine' chapter in *The Floral World and Garden Guide* of 1865 declared 'English vineyards are things of the past'. If anyone was tempted to do so now, he suggested they planted American vine varieties. 'We do not see why even to the Orkneys', he said, 'the American grape should not be found adaptable; for on their prairies and mountain slopes they have to endure severe winters, and they appear to be partial to a dry, poor, rocky soil.'

He never mentioned, because he never knew, the best reason for an English vigneron to plant American vines. In 1863 there appeared in Hammersmith a rare insect imported, unknowingly, from America which had a catastrophic effect on vine roots, the *phylloxera vastatrix*. The following year the killing disease Phylloxera broke out within the dense vineyards of the Department of the Gard in the South of France. Within 20 years it had spread to the whole country and very nearly wiped out its entire ancient wine industry. The insect had no effect on the roots of American vines because they had evolved a resistance and adapted to survive in spite of phylloxera. Vine roots in other countries which had evolved in phylloxera-free soil had no resistance to attacks by the insect, they just weakened and died. Thus the recommendation in *The Floral World* of 1865 that anyone starting an open-air vineyard in England should plant American vines was very apposite.

It was not advice taken however by the Marquess of Bute when he decided to embark on an ambitious scheme in South Wales.

JOHN PATRICK CRICHTON-STUART, third Marquess of Bute, was Scots. Born in 1847, he succeeded to the title when his father died the following year. In 1872 he married Gwendoline, daughter of Lord Howard of Glossop, a kinsman of the Duke of Norfolk whose vine-growing and wine-making activities at Arundel Castle have already been noted. He was immensely wealthy, the owner of some 117,000 acres of land, a London

John Patrick Crichton-Stuart, third Marquess of Bute, who was 26 when he planted his famous vineyard at Castell Coch near Cardiff in 1873.

house in Regents Park, Mountstuart in Rothesay, Dumfries House in Ayrshire, Falkland House in Fifeshire, Old Palace of Mochrum in Wigtownshire and Cardiff Castle. He was closely associated with the cultural life and commercial property of Cardiff, carrying on the work of his father 'the creator of modern Cardiff'.

The third Marquess engaged in a variety of activities ranging from translating the novels of Turgenev to investigating psychical phenomena. He worshipped the past and was fascinated by the ritual of guilds and orders, the heraldry and the dressing-up. He dreamt of reconstructing Cardiff Castle as it had been around the thirteenth century when it was built; and in 1865 he commissioned an imaginative architect William Burges to draw up plans for the no-expense-barred exercise in what the Italians call *scenografia*. Work began shortly after, but it was 20 years before the curtain rose on the finished transformation scene.

Also part of the Cardiff estate inherited from his father was the ruined Castell Coch – the Red Castle, so named because it had been constructed of unfaced red sandstone. It lay some five miles north of Cardiff near the tiny hamlet of Tongwynlais and commanded the plain of Cardiff to the south and the narrow gorge of the river Taff immediately below it. It had also been built at the end of the thirteenth century but had been uninhabited and neglected for 300 years. Here was obvious raw material for another flight of fancy, and in 1871, with the Cardiff Castle scheme under way, Lord Bute arranged for the ruins of Castell Coch to be cleared of undergrowth, and had Burges make a survey with a view to reconstructing it in all its mediaeval glory. The faithful architect had plans ready by the following year.

To be consistent, the surroundings as well as the castle itself, had to be mediaeval. Was there not a tradition that in this parish of Sully there had been a vineyard in the Middle Ages? To complete the scene, he must have one too. So one day in Scotland in 1873 the 26-year-old nobleman told his head gardener Andrew Pettigrew of his great plan to plant a vineyard at Castell Coch. He would leave the precise location to him. Some weeks later Pettigrew journeyed to South Wales, staked out a site which he considered the most suitable – to the west of the castle at a somewhat lower level with a gentle slope to the south. It was 150 feet above sea level and protected from the north by a large plantation, and from the east and west by hills. It lay open to the south overlooking the Bristol Channel some five miles away. The soil was two feet deep and of a light fibrous loam overlaying limestone.

Bute wrote to a number of his friends in France asking them to recommend an intelligent young man with experience of viticulture who would be ready to come to South Wales to help plant the vineyard, run it and make wine from its produce. But in spite of his generous terms 'we learned that it would be extremely difficult to induce a person of the class wanted to leave his home and friends to come here on any consideration'. So his lordship despatched Andrew Pettigrew on a tour of the principal vineyards of the Medoc and elsewhere to pick up what information he could. 'It was rather a perplexing duty to one totally unacquainted with the French language,' recalled the Scots gardener some years later. 'But furnished with letters of introduction to wine merchants and the principal vineyard proprietors in France and others, I set out in the latter end of September [1874] in time to see the vintage of the year.'

He visited vineyards around Paris, a large champagne manufactory at Chalons-sur-Marne, and around Bordeaux witnessed the vintage at Chateau Latour (103 acres), Chateau Lafitte (165 acres) and Margaux (197 acres). Back in Cardiff he told Lord Bute the vine-growers around Paris had recommended he planted the varieties known as Gamay Noir and Mille Blanch as being most likely to suit the climate of South Wales. They had a strong constitution, a reputation for producing fruit freely, and for making very good wine. Bute told Pettigrew to order what he wanted of these, and that winter they trenched and levelled a three-acre site in the chosen position. In March 1875 they planted the vine shoots from across the Channel 'on the French system', each three feet apart in north to south rows separated by three-foot gaps, and low on the ground.

The Castell Coch Vineyard, and Lord Bute's intention to make wine from it, was greeted with jeers in *Punch*. If ever wine was produced from Glamorgan, it said, it would take four men to drink it – the victim, two others to hold him down, and a fourth to force the wine down his throat. *Funny Folks* remarked that 'Lord Bute has, it appears, a Bute-iful vineyard at Castell Coch near Cardiff where it is hoped such wine will be produced that in future Hock will be superseded by Coch, and the unpronounceable vintages of the Taff. Coch-heimer is, as yet, a wine *in potentis*, but the vines are planted and the gardener, Mr Pettigrew, expects no petty growth.'

Grape pickers, at Lord Bute's vineyard at Castell Coch in the 1870s, pose in front of a horse-drawn cart laden with black grapes which were then taken to Cardiff Castle for pressing.

Pettigrew himself could only be sparingly optimistic. In an article in *The Gardener* for September 1875 he was able to tell readers that the 2,000 vines he had planted on 20 March the previous year had broken well considering the long journey they had had from France. He had propagated another 2,000 that spring from the eyes saved from the prunings which he would plant next spring. The correct name of the black grape variety he had planted was Gamais Noir, and of the white variety Le Miel Blanc. He agreed with Mr Fenn of Woodstock who had written to him to say, 'With myself there can be no question but that good home-made grape wine can be manufactured in England now as well as in former times.' But it was a matter of wait and see.

Over the first four years, each of which had a good summer, the vineyard consolidated itself. The vines grew well and made strong canes which ripened thoroughly, he told Cardiff Naturalists Society in 1884. Gardeners and others who came from a distance to see the vineyard were surprised at the luxuriance of the vines growing in the open air. They were growing vigorously and there was no sign of the dreaded phylloxera 'so common in many places in this country now'.

> *The sight about the end of July is a novel and interesting one. Long rows of vines, as straight as a line, in a curved slope down the hill, and the tops of the canes all neatly stopped at the height of four feet from the ground, with their large dark-green foliage almost meeting in the rows, was a sight not to be seen anywhere else in this country.*

Two years after planting they attempted to make some wine. There was nowhere for doing this at Castell Coch, and all the wine-making took place at Cardiff Castle, but no one knows just where. The crop of 1877 was not a heavy one, but they managed to make some 40 gallons of white wine which filled 240 bottles. They were stored in the Cart Shed Cellar, the Park Hall Cellar and the Mushroom House Cellar in Cardiff Castle. From the better crop of 1878 they made 300 bottles of wine. 'The vines broke well in 1879 and showed an abundance of fruit in the latter end of May, but with the cold and sunless wet summer that followed the fruit all dropped off, and we did not gather a bunch of grapes from the vineyard.' There was a total failure the next year too because the wood had not ripened the previous season. But a first-class white wine was made from the crop of 1881 which was sold at the Angel Hotel, Cardiff (which belonged to Lord Bute and faced the castle) for £3 a crate of 12 bottles. H. M. Tod drank a glass of the 1881 vintage at the Angel which he described as 'still champagne', which is what Charles Hamilton called his Painshill Wine. 'It was the palest in colour and the best,' added Tod. Every bottle of the 1881 wine was sold, except for a few dozen bottles which were salted away in the Cardiff Castle cellars – perhaps they are still there.

Archibald Barron, head of the Royal Horticultural Society's Chiswick Garden, included a chapter on the Castell Coch Vineyard in his book *Vines and Vine Culture* (1883). He mentioned the good crop of 1881 and stated 'the wine was of the best quality and pronounced by the Fruit Committee of the Royal Horticultural Society to resemble a first-class still champagne.'

Lord Bute's Castell Coch vineyard stretches behind a lone grape harvester shouldering a basket full of the large bunches of black grapes shown in the foreground.

Whereabouts in Cardiff Castle Lord Bute had his grapes pressed remains a mystery, but this contemporary photograph of wine-making in progress there should provide a clue.

It was the last Castell Coch Wine for two years. None was produced in the bad seasons of 1882 and 1883, but they made 1,500 bottles in 1884 and in 1885, and began selling it from the castle gardens as well as at the Angel. Lord Bute not only refused to be discouraged by another failure in 1886 but told Andrew Pettigrew to plant two more vineyards on other parts of the estate – another five acres at nearby Swanbridge within half a mile of the Bristol Channel, and a smaller one at St Quentins near Cowbridge. Swanbridge proved a good choice, but the vines were taken up at St Quentins after a few years' trial because the position was too windswept.

The summer of 1887 was one of high temperatures and light rain, and they made a record 3,600 bottles for Queen Victoria's Golden Jubilee. Archibald Barron reckoned they made 'nine hogsheads of excellent wine' that year. The crop was the largest and best ripened since the vines were planted, he said. The sturdiest variety was Gamay Noir.

Then the cycle repeated itself: two bad years and after them a third bumper year in 1890 with 2,000 bottles; but only 900 and 600 respectively in 1891 and 1892. Quantity may have been low but the quality was of the highest. The Mayor of Cardiff bought three dozen bottles of the 1885 vintage. Lord Bute noted in his diary that His Worship had considered it 'better (and I really think it is) than my Falernian here'. Someone whom Andrew Pettigrew described as 'a well-known chemist' tasted them and stated that they were 'most excellent as a British production, not only full of alcoholic strength but containing an agreeable amount of acid tartrate as well as aroma far in advance of grape wines generally manufactured in this country' – a reference no doubt to drinks like 'Onomosto' manufactured by Thos. Grant & Sons in Maidstone from imported grape juice and retailing at two shillings a bottle – an early 'British Wine'. Castell Coch White was in a different league. In 1893 the Birmingham wine merchants Ludlow, Roberts & Willes sold four and a half dozen bottles of the 1881 vintage, which cost £3 a dozen in that year, for £5 15s.

In 1893 Lord Bute decided to make some red wine too from his Gamay Noir. Tod thought 1893 was Castell Coch's finest year. The fine weather brought an enormous crop from which they made 40 hogsheads of must which produced 12,000 bottles of wine. A doctor who tried some at the Angel liked it so much he bought a dozen cases on the spot. He paid the usual 60s a dozen. When he died some years later the cases which he had not consumed were sold for 115s a dozen. This was an exceptionally high price. Searcy's wine list of 1886 was offering a Pommard at only 42s a dozen, and Chambertin at 66s; though Lafite 1874 cost 148s.

Tod thought Swanbridge was in the more favourable position. He paid regular visits to it up to 1897, and was flattered when Andrew Pettigrew invited him to suggest names for some of the Castell Coch wines. That presented a difficulty, confessed Tod, because of the want of definitiveness in style and character. Some were stronger than others and some reminded him of a mixture of incompatible sorts. When it came to the point, he was unable to think of anything peculiarly Welsh (or English) and could suggest nothing less derivative than 'Calcavella', the name of Portuguese white wine.

It was in 1897 too that Lord Bute made a serious attempt to promote the sale of Castell Coch Wine by appointing a well-known London wine merchant as the agency for its sale, Messrs Hatch, Mansfield & Co, established in 1802 of Cockspur Street, Trafalgar Square – still serving the public in 1989. In their 1897 catalogue they devoted two pages to WELSH WINES 'Canary Brand' – which showed that Tod's Portuguese suggestion had not gone unheeded. Under the sub-heading A NOVELTY, the Hatch Mansfield wine list stated that 'although the wines cannot yet be said to possess the delicate aroma and flavour of the best foreign wines, they are eminently honest and wholesome.' Eight sorts were listed with such descriptions as 'big soft wine, medium dry' and 'full rich wine'. Prices ranged from 48s a

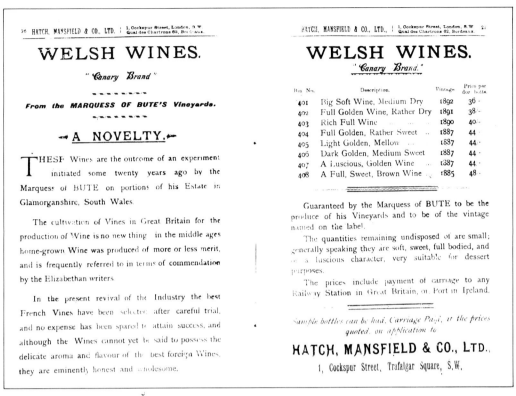

In 1897 Lord Bute appointed the old-established London wine merchant Hatch Mansfield as agent for his Castell Coch wine. In their wine list they called it 'Canary Brand'.

dozen for the 1885 vintage to 36s a dozen for the 1892 wine. Charming art deco labels were designed for the bottles, one for Swanbridge and one for Castell Coch wine.

Tod was inspired by the success of the Bute/Pettigrew venture to start growing vines vineyard-fashion at his own nursery at Wisley in 1891, 'and I found that I could ripen their grapes as well that way as on open walls'. The third Marquess of Bute died in 1900 and was succeeded by his 19-year-old son who took as much interest in the vineyard as his father. Tod paid a visit to the castle in 1905 and was amazed to find 63,000 vines in fruit. Owing to the impossibility of obtaining sugar for 'chaptalisation' during the Great War which broke out in 1914, no attempt was made at wine-making after that date. But the vines still grew both at Castell Coch and Swanbridge all through the war and were only finally uprooted in 1920 when his lordship decided to put the land to other uses. In the 45 years during which the vineyard flourished, as Andrew Pettigrew vouched in 1926, 'the late Marquess's interest in it never flagged, and no expense was spared by him or by the present Marquess that could in any way promote its success.'

The fourth Marquess of Bute disposed of the greater part of his South Wales estate in 1938. He died in 1947, and the following year Cardiff Castle was conveyed, with certain reservations, by way of gift to Cardiff Corporation for the benefit of the town's citizens. Castell Coch is now in the hands of the Department of the Environment and open to the public. The two vineyards are now council house estates. The twentieth century has taken over for good.

2

TWENTIETH-CENTURY REVIVAL

N 1911 WINE-MAKING STILL HAD three years to go at Castell Coch, but most people in Britain would have denied that grapes grown on British soil were capable of making wine. In that year H. M. Tod published his comprehensive work *Vine-Growing in England*, the first to deal with the subject historically on so large a scale. He named 2,265 types of vine in cultivation in various parts of the world, and gave the following list of vines grown in England for the purpose of making English Wine:

The Miller
Miller's Burgundy
Common or Royal Muscadine
Black Cluster
Experione
Cambridge Botanic Garden
Moore's Early

Ironclad
Duchess
Dutch Sweetwater
Brandt (which was of American
    origin and Tod claimed to have
    introduced to Britain in 1886)
Chasselas Vibert: white and red

Three years after the publication of Tod's book came the conflict which successfully sealed off the period that began in 1919 from what had become mythical times known as Before The War. Everything associated with the pre-1914 world became instantly old-fashioned and eccentric if not slightly bad taste. English Wine? You're not serious! Heard of it? *Actually*, no. Oh you mean that Elderberry stuff that Aunt May makes for the WI fete?

English Wine became unbelievable folklore. The word became irretrievably linked with the fruit wines, the made-wines, to which it was never related. Which was a pity, because in the nineteen-twenties and the nineteen-thirties the circumstances which had made possible the production of English Wine for 1,900 years did not change. The vine plants, if anyone had planted them, would have behaved in the same way as they had for the Roman officer who occupied the station villa at Vindomis, for Hamo, Bishop of Rochester at Halling, for King Richard at Windsor, Lord Salisbury at Hatfield, Charles Hamilton at Painshill. The soil was the same; the pattern of hills and valleys and rivers, the sea breezes, the summers, the autumns. The knowledge was there for anyone who had the urge to tap it, along with the potential vineyard sites. But sloth and ignorance prevented anyone from taking advantage of either. Perhaps there were some curious enough to have a go and risk being labelled eccentric; but unless they wrote a book about it, their vineyard and its wine went unchronicled. Certainly George Ordish planted a vineyard in the garden of his house in Yalding in Kent in 1939, and kept it going throughout the second conflict which started in that year.

Except for him and any others whose sites are unknown, it would seem without doubt that between the scrubbing of Castell Coch Vineyard in 1920 and the end of the Second World War in 1945 there was a 25-year gap in English viticulture of a kind which had never occurred before.

With English viticulture's period of suspended animation extended even further by the events of 1939–45, the time when there had been people making English Wine appeared even more remote. Seriously to contemplate applying oneself to anything so quaint, so un-English, in the cynical 'contemporary' Britain of what was left of the nineteen-forties, needed exceptional single-mindedness, fanatical drive and determination.

All three were the attributes of Ray Barrington Brock who up to 1938 had been a Senior Research Chemist in the Ilford photographic group, and in 1946 was managing director of one of the large instrument manufacturers. At his house in Oxted in Surrey he was delighted to see how well his peaches ripened out of doors without the aid of glass. If peaches, he asked himself, why not other fruit not normally associated with England – grapes for instance?

So in 1946, with no previous knowledge of viticulture or wine-making, without prejudices or inhibitions, he set himself a project: to discover which varieties of grape would grow and ripen in England in the open air. He plunged in with the methodical approach of a scientist who takes nothing at face value. He started by reading 24-year-old Francois de Castella's *Viticulture in the State of Victoria* which described how methods of cultivation changed according to climate. He visited viticultural research stations in France and Switzerland. He got in touch with Edward Hyams, one of Britain's most distinguished writers on garden matters who was doing research for a book on English viticulture.

Soon after the war Hyams planted a vineyard not far distant from Yalding where the vines which George Ordish had put down in 1939 had well matured. It was at Shottenden near Canterbury. At Wrotham Hyams found a vine which closely resembled the old Pinot Meunier or Dusty Miller type which he identified with the Roman *aminea lanata*. He took a cutting of his find and it became the father of the now famous Wrotham Pinot of which Ray Barrington Brock soon had a row for experimentation.

Edward Hyams published the book he was preparing in 1949. It had the title *The Grape Vine in England, The History and Practice of the cultivation of Vines in England*. The sub-title told readers it was an account of their origin and introduction, a guide to the plantation and care

Ray Barrington Brock, who in 1946 at his home in Oxted set out to discover which vine varieties would grow and ripen in the open air – 30 years' research which formed the base of an English Wine Revival.

of vineyards today (1949), a refutation of the notion that English weather was hostile to the vine, and a description of the way to make wine. It was the most comprehensive book on the subject since H. M. Tod's *Vine-Growing in England* of 1911, and played an important part as the propaganda arm of Ray Barrington Brock's scientific work at Oxted. To the new post-war generation it put English viticulture in its proper perspective, gave them reason for taking it seriously and pointed to its commercial potential. A main message of the book was that in his view the English climate had not changed for 1,000 years. It was still what it had always been, an island climate which distinguished it from parts of the continent of Europe on a similar latitude. The climate was temperate, humid and gentle, and because of this English Wine could claim the distinction of being an island wine with qualities of a different sort to that made from grapes grown on the Continent.

Barrington Brock invited continental research stations to send him cuttings of vine varieties which they thought were likely to grow and ripen in England. In the spring of 1946 with the help of E. G. Walker he planted a selection of these in his Oxted garden some 450 feet up on the North Downs which he called the Summerfield Vineyard, and later the Oxted Viticultural Research Station. In 1949 he published his first findings in *Outdoor Grapes in Cold Climates*. This with the three reports that followed, together with Edward Hyams's *The Grape Vine in England*, gave the English Wine revival its scientific basis. Barrington Brock started experimenting with wine-making in the underground winery he built at Oxted. To obtain independent judgements on the quality of the wine he made he invited members'of the Institute of Masters of Wine, which had just been formed, to pronounce on bottles of Oxted and continental wine labelled only by numbers. From the marking of the Masters it became evident, to Barrington Brock's delight, that he was beginning to make a liquor which matched, and was often better than, the average French product.

Similar experiments were being made at this time by Dr A. Pollards who planted a vineyard at Bakewell near Bristol, and by Mrs S. M. Tritton whose husband wrote a book in 1951 called *Grape Growing and Wine Making From Grapes and Other Fruits*. In his introduction Tritton justified his work insofar as 'in recent years much interest has been shown in the art of outdoor grape-growing and in wine-making'. More important was George Ordish's book *Wine Growing in England*, published in 1952, in which he described how he had been open-air vine-growing in Kent since 1939. His vines continued to flourish at Yalding until he moved to St Albans in the nineteen-sixties.

It was books such as these, and particularly that of Edward Hyams and the reports of Ray Barrington Brock, which inspired a vine-grower who, although a retired army man, was not going to regard the exercise as a retirement hobby but planned to follow in the footsteps of Lord Bute and Charles Hamilton and plant a vineyard from which he would make English Wine which *sold*.

WHEN IN 1952, AT THE instigation of his stepson, Major General Sir Guy Salisbury-Jones GCVO, CMG, CBE, MC, planted a vineyard at Hambledon in Hampshire, he set in train a sequence of events which stimulated interest in English viticulture on an unprecedented scale. On a one and a half acre site in front of his house at Hambledon he planted 4,000 French vines from Burgundy – mostly Seyve-Villard, but also *pour ajouter un peu de noblesse*, as his French suppliers put it, a few of the noble Chardonnay and Pinot Noir. He put down about 3,500 vines to the acre. He built himself a winery beside the house and on the door of it he had inscribed a passage from Duff Cooper's memoirs *Old Men Forget* in which he averred that to him wine had been a firm friend and wise counsellor. The press house cost him £6,000 but his total outlay was in the region of £15,200. The inaugural Hambledon Wine went on sale in 1955. It was the first commercially made English Wine to be produced since the final Castell Coch vintage of 1915. The 40-year gap had been bridged.

In his third report of 1961 Ray Barrington Brock pointed out that at Oxted he could not attempt to produce any wine commercially if he was to continue with his research. But with reference to the Salisbury-Jones exercise in Hampshire, he said:

It is naturally of tremendous interest that somebody should be doing this, and we are taking every step that we can to assist these commercial vineyards to get going . . . There is no longer any reason to doubt that the quality of the wine we can produce in southern England is excellent and can be compared safely with imported wine . . . [and this] has naturally been a factor in deciding people to start commercial vineyards as a serious experiment.

Sir Guy and Lady Salisbury-Jones at their Hambledon Vineyard, planted in 1952, the first of the English Wine Revival. On the left of the picture is Bill Carcary, the vineyard manager, who is still on the job.

Someone else who assisted the first commercial English vineyards to get going was Anton Massel who came to England the year after the first Hambledon Wine became available. He had just completed the two-year advanced course in *wein-chemie* at the old-established, state-run Hoehere Weinbau Institut at Geisenheim, the leading viticultural college in Germany. He was able to instruct the new generation of English Wine makers in the latest techniques. He played an important part in ensuring that the incipient wine-chemistry of England evolved on lines which were both professional and scientific. As Norman Cowderoy said in 1988 on the occasion of Massel leaving England to set up in Spain, 'with his departure for a kinder climate, one of the great pioneers of our early days goes ... Without the inspiration of people like Anton Massel today's English Wine industry would not exist.'

Massel visited Sir Guy Salisbury-Jones at Hambledon and was able to give him good advice, based on the outcome of the first vintage, on how to improve his vinification process and also on running his vineyard. He suggested for instance that to be properly commercial the plot should be at least three acres, and acting on this advice, Sir Guy enlarged the Hambledon Vineyard to four and a half acres.

Sir Guy's activity at Hambledon was a one-off operation which attracted the attention of the media because it came under the heading of 'Eccentric' and therefore 'News'. But no one else took any notice, let alone farmers or commercial fruit growers, let alone the wine trade or the Government. Sir Guy did not embark on his project to give a lead to others; he did it purely for his own enjoyment. There was no mastermind stimulating interest. Ray Barrington Brock was 'available' but took no positive steps to promote a revival of English viticulture or enlist revivalists.

When the revival came it was entirely haphazard, a happening not a movement. Moreover it arose behind the backs of 'the authorities', who only became aware of it many years later after it had acquired a dimension which even busy civil servants could not fail to notice, and then of course with suspicion. What low-powered momentum it gathered in the years following the opening of Hambledon came from people who found themselves with a piece of land and said 'Let's plant a vineyard!' The second lot were to say 'Let's plant a vineyard!' and then set out to find a suitable piece of land. But nothing as logical as that prompted Sir Guy Salisbury-Jones, one time Master of the Diplomatic Corps, or Mrs Margaret Gore-Browne who was second in the field.

Colonel and Mrs Robert Gore-Browne had spent most of their lives in Central Africa. They had seen the ill-fated Ground Nuts Scheme come and go, so they knew something about making the best use of 'unusable' land. On returning to England in 1956 they looked for a home, and one of the first they saw was a mansion on the Beaulieu estate in Hampshire. Mr Gore-Brown disliked the house. In any case what would they *do* there? And then, as they came out of the drive they noticed the name of the house written on the gate, The Vineyards. 'There' said Mrs Gore-Browne who was determined to buy the place, 'someone must have grown vines here at some time for it to have that name. So that's what we'll do. *We* will run a vineyard.'

The someone who had grown vines there was the thirteenth-century Abbot of Beaulieu Abbey – the first account book of 1269 refers to the vineyard and it is likely that it was planted before then, but there is nothing to show the actual date.

Mrs Margaret Gore-Brown with her godson, Lord Montagu's son Ralph, in the Beaulieu vineyard which she planted in 1958 – the next after Hambledon.

They bought The Vineyards and proceeded to clear, drain and deep-cultivate two acres at the bottom of the estate as a vineyard. Margaret Gore-Brown took advice from Ray Barrington Brock on what varieties to plant, and consulted Anton Massel on wine-making. In 1958 she planted four rows of Müller-Thurgau and Seyve-Villard, and persuaded Archangelo Lanza, a cousin of film star Mario Lanza, to leave his home in Southern Italy to be her vine-keeper and wine-maker, while his wife Santina did the cooking and helped run the house.

Their landlord, Lord Montagu of Beaulieu, offered to restore the ancient Fulling Mill which formed part of the abbey ruins where the Cistercians were once thought to have made wine 750 years before. In 1960 they built a well equipped winery at the end of the drive. The first pressing was in 1961 – a rosé.

Though set in motion by amateurs, these operations at Hambledon and Beaulieu were strictly commercial from the start, but the establishment of the third vineyard was even more calculated. This was the half-acre plot planted at Horam in East Sussex by someone whose influence on the revival of English viticulture was to be immense, J. L. Ward.

Returning from the Second World War at the age of 36, Jack Ward started making cider commercially with his neighbour Ian Howie. They bought a 50-year-old cider press and installed it in the garage of Jack's home near Rotherfield which was called Merrydown. The Merrydown Wine Company was soon producing fruit wines from fermented fruit juice as well as from apples, and became a major operator in this field. After the manor at Horam which they made their headquarters was destroyed by fire they built themselves new offices and plant. Sale of Merrydown made-wines and cider was widespread throughout Britain and overseas, and the next step was to experiment in the making of 'real' wine and the planting of an experimental vineyard. In time they added to the original half acre and in 1962 were growing Müller-Thurgau and some dozen other varieties from which they made small quantities of English Wine.

Jack Ward, chairman of the Merrydown Wine Company of Horam in Sussex, where he planted an experimental half acre of vines in 1958. He became the first chairman of the English Vineyards Association when it was formed in 1967.

Jack Ward and his like looked to the Oxted Viticultural Research Station for most of their information, but Anton Massel, Charles Wheatley of Wantage and N. F. J. Schembri, who had had experience of vineyards in Malta and operated from Reading, also contributed to the new data on which the new English viticulture could build. As a result many were spurred to jump on a wagon which had been lying forgotten all these years but was now on the move again, no longer a museum piece attracting the patronising attention only of folklorists and social historians but restored to the English way of life of which it had once been so familiar a part. In spite of Ray Barrington Brock's warnings against the danger of taking continental data at its face value, many based their vine-growing on continental practices and planted 3,000 vines to the acre and in rows so close that they could not use modern machinery. They learnt their lesson to their cost, but to the benefit of those who followed on.

Lord Bute and Andrew Pettigrew had laid out the South Wales vineyard 'on the French system' – low on the ground – at a time when communications were bad and means of exchanging information was undeveloped. In the nineteen-sixties however circumstances favoured the building up of a corpus of purely *English* viticultural experience which had no need to pay court to European practices or to the past. Gradually it became less amateur, less romantic, less the hoe and knapsack sprayer, more cost-conscious, profit-orientated, professional, commercial.

AN EARLY SUCCESSOR TO THE pioneers of Hambledon and Beaulieu was Philip Tyson-Woodcock who planted a vineyard at Broad Oak near Brede which he later sold to Derek Thorley. Another was Mrs P. Smith who in 1963 started a vineyard at Fletching Common. Both of these were in Sussex. In the same year Gillian Pearkes initiated trials in East Devon 'to see if I could ripen grapes satisfactorily that were too late in other well-tried vineyards'. Her vineyard was planted in an old walled garden which by tradition occupied the site of a nunnery dissolved by Henry VIII. It was in the grounds of her part-Tudor, part-William and Mary house on the site of an earlier Saxon manor in Hawkchurch, Axminster, half way up the valley of the river Axe with a south-westerly aspect. She planted most of the varieties which Barrington Brock had shown to be suited to English conditions, Müller-Thurgau (which used to be called Riesling-Sylvaner), Madeleine Sylvaner, Seyve-Villard 5/276, and Madeleine Angevine. She took her first crop in 1966.

The declared aim of Gillian Pearkes, who took to the pen to spread the word about the delights of running a vineyard in *Growing Grapes in Britain* (1969), was 'to produce fruit fitted to create a really good quality wine'. That was the aim too of wine merchant turned vigneron Alan Rook, similarly urged to demonstrate the joys of an activity by which more and more were being smitten, in *The Diary of an English Vineyard* (1969).

The family firm of Nottingham wine merchants, Skinner, Rook & Chambers was founded in 1847, the year Lord Bute was born. In 1964 Rook planted 2,500 vines in the walled one-and-a-quarter-acre kitchen garden at Stragglethorpe Hall near Lincoln, land which had once belonged to the Priory of Sempringham. It was at Lincoln that the Romans once had a vineyard. On the 53rd parallel Major Rook and the commander of the Ninth Legion shared the distinction of having the most northerly vineyard in the world.

Rook attended a one-day Fermentation and Wine-making Course at Anton Massel's Oenological Research Laboratories at Ockley, and Massel, whose firm supplied the equipment for the winery, came to help with the first vintage at the end of October 1967. They had 80 gallons of grape juice from which by June the following year they made 43½ dozen bottles of white English Wine which they called 'Lincoln Imperial' – after the imp which is in Lincoln's coat of arms, not the British Empire. 'The 1967 vintage was made at the end of a splendid summer,' wrote Alan Rook in his *Diary*,

> *and produced a wine better in every respect than I had allowed myself to hope for. In Lincolnshire we shall not produce a great wine. What we produced in 1967 was a wine which was dry, clean, golden, fruity and full of taste and character – in every way a serious, even a considerable wine.*

It convinced many of his friends, he said, that it was possible seriously to make wine in England, even as far north as Lincolnshire. If he had tasted the wine he made next year (1968) blind, he felt sure he would have placed it as from the Loire.

In Wales, where Andrew Pettigrew had been laughed at for his efforts at Castle Coch and Swanbridge, a number of vineyards were planted from 1964 onwards. George Jones, 'Jones the Grape', was the father of the revived Welsh viticulture. His vineyards at Wangara near Llanelli, and most particularly at Pembrey in Carmarthenshire, roused others to Wales's potential as a vine-growing area. He presented a bottle of Pembrey '67 to the Prince of Wales for laying down in the Buckingham Palace cellar against the day when he came of age in 1969. It was said to be like a Loire red wine. It reminded Michael Broadbent, Christie's Master of Wine, of a Bourgeuil to be drunk by itself rather than with a meal, chilled like young Beaujolais.

Dr Idris Thomas planted five varieties of vine at Werndeg, Llanarth in Cardiganshire; Lewis Mathias planted a two-and-a-half-acre vineyard at Lamphey Court in Pembrokeshire. Margaret Gore-Browne who came from Neath, and Anton Massel, tried to induce the Welsh Development Board to take an interest.

In England Graham Barrett and his wife Irene started growing a few vines in their garden at Hornchurch in Essex as a hobby. Then in 1965 he bought a plot at Cricks Green near Felsted to turn into a proper vineyard. The next spring the Barretts planted a quarter of an acre with 30 varieties for the propagation of stock, and the hobby was well on the way to becoming the prevailing passion of Graham Barrett's life.

A scientific approach to the selection of a site came from Kenneth Barlow, a research consultant on coffee, cotton and tobacco growing, whose first step was to make a thorough study to discover what part of the south of England received the most sunshine. His conclusions led him to the Isle of Wight, where in 1965 he planted what must have been the most southerly vineyard in Britain at Adgestone near Brading.

English Wine received its first recognition from the Continent when in 1966 the Belgian Academie du Vin gave a banquet in honour of Hambledon Wine. Commercial vineyards appeared in a number of counties. Joy and Trevor Bates planted 4,000 vines on a three-acre plot at Nettlestead in Kent; Robin Don, a Master of Wine, laid out an eighth of an acre at Dereham in Norfolk; Jack Furnace planted a vineyard at Bridgnorth in Shropshire; ex-barrister Jack Edgerley started one at Kelsale near Ipswich and Walter Cardy another at Pangbourne in Berkshire.

The English Wine movement was gathering pace at a rate that required control and steering; and in 1967 a body was registered called The English Vineyards Association (EVA) to present a combined front to government departments and to any body which could aid or thwart development of an activity which now represented a sizeable investment. The idea of an association had been discussed throughout 1965 by Anton Massel and Norman Cowderoy, a London shipbroker who grew outdoor vines on a two-and-a-half-acre plot near Haywards Heath in Sussex. They got the support of Jack Ward of Merrydown, and on 23 October 1965, at the invitation of Margaret Gore-Brown, called a first meeting of key persons at The Vineyards, Beaulieu to consider launching an association with the aim of 'promoting the intelligent cultivation of vines for commercial purposes in England'.

It took the Board of Trade a year to approve the title, and at the first annual general meeting on 17 January 1967 at Ockley in Surrey when Anton Massel had his viticultural equipment firm, Sir Guy Salisbury-Jones was elected President of the new association, Lady Montagu of Beaulieu Vice-President, Jack Ward Chairman, and Mrs Irene Barrett Secretary. The EVA was formally registered on 8 March 1967 when there were eight full members from Sussex, Kent, Berkshire, Somerset, Worcestershire, Middlesex, Notting-hamshire and Surrey.

In March 1966 Lewis Mathias and others formed a Welsh Vineyards Association, sponsored and encouraged by the Development Corporation of Wales. None of its half dozen members were producing commercially, and in course of time their numbers dropped. 'Efforts to encourage farmers and possibly other growers proved unsuccessful, as it was a new and strange venture, and the capital outlay for vines and winery equipment is very high', explained Lewis Mathias.

The pioneering work of the Oxted Viticultural Research Station was coming to an end. The circumstances which now favoured the formation of an association of enthusiasts were largely of Ray Barrington Brock's creation, and he saw it as a moment to make a planned withdrawal from a scene in which the excitement of the lone rider of 1946 establishing precedents on which others could build was no longer present. That his message had been received and understood by the leader of the new association was evident from the penultimate paragraph of Jack Ward's piece in the first EVA *Newsletter*: 'It should not be forgotten that the industry is new in this country, so that any advice coming from the Continent may have to be modified to suit our own peculiar conditions.'

Barrington Brock issued a fourth report *Starting A Vineyard* in 1964, and throughout the nineteen-seventies continued to issue price lists and sell vines which had proved their staying and ripening power in the Summerfield Vineyard. As N. F. J. Schembri said in his article 'The New Era of English Wines' in that same first *Newsletter* of the EVA:

The thinking behind the revival of English viticulture was Oxted's. So the ignorance which always accompanies any movement where fools rush in for reasons based largely on emotion and enthusiasm received a leavening from which the revival of English viticulture and the establishment of a British viticultural method, greatly benefited.

Few gained more from the research which Ray Barrington Brock did at Oxted than Margaret Gore-Brown who in 1967 gave her account of her pioneering exercise at Beaulieu in *Let's Plant a Vineyard*. She said that the late Alfred Langenbach had told her 'climatically you should make good wine; your chances depend purely on viticulture.' She died in August 1976, and left her vineyard to Lord Montagu's 15-year-old son Hon. Ralph Douglas-Scott-Montagu, and the winery to Lord Montagu, whose company Montagu Ventures had for some time been managing the vineyard.

Over the ten years from 1967 to 1977 the shape of English viticulture became firm in outline, and English Wine (which included Welsh Wine) re-emerged with the distinctive character impressed upon it by a non-continental, island ambience which in its 2,000 year history no other vine-growing area of the world has ever been able to capture.

Membership of the English Vineyards Association grew to 50 within a year of its inauguration in 1967, and by 1969 there were 83. In 1970 a South West Vinegrowers Association was formed after a meeting at Pilton Manor. The revival was acquiring a degree of cohesion but each vigneron hugged his patch and proudly proclaimed it on his label. European traditions of naming wine were adhered to in England. The name had to reflect where the wine was *made* – bottled – not where the grapes were grown. When Graham Barrett wanted to market the wine made from his Essex grapes he wanted to call it 'Felsted'. But as the Felsted grapes had been processed and bottled at Horam in Sussex he had to settle for the nondescript 'Felstar'. Ken Barlow's wine however, of which he made a first 6,000 bottles in 1969 and a further 30,000 in 1970, could be called 'Adgestone' because he made it in the Isle of Wight. Everyone avoided any name that might make the consumer think that English viticulture was just a branch of the continental wine industry, eschewing the eighteenth-century habit of describing English Wine as 'Rhenish' or 'Gascon'. The twentieth-century revivalists insisted that their produce should be judged as wholly *English*, not better or worse than the foreign product, but enjoyed for its own unique characteristics. It was impossible to stop comparisons however. Sir Guy Salisbury-Jones, who had engaged ex-Royal Military Policeman Bill Carcary as a full-time vineyard manager, found his 1969 Hambledon vintage described by an expert as outstanding 'with character between a delicate dry Vouvray and a first-class crisp Moselle'. Maybe it was flattering, but in a more enlightened vein another expert declared that in its gentle bouquet there was a sweet waft of English flowers.

By 1969 40 English and Welsh acres had been planted with open air vines yielding an average of 2,000 bottles of wine each. One of the largest to open that year was the six-acre site owned by Peter Baillie-Grohman at Hascombe near Godalming. Kenneth McAlpine planted eight and a half acres of his large farm at Lamberhurst in Kent with vines. Many regarded viticulture as a good investment, particularly as a hedge against loss from other less dependable agricultural activities. Bernard Theobald had 100 milking Friesian cows on his farm at Pangbourne where Walter Cardy had run a vineyard for many years. In 1970 Theobald added a vineyard in order to keep his farm going. He reckoned the 13 acres he would have under cultivation by 1974 would produce more gross profit in a year than his cows. He estimated his vines would bring in an annual £3,000 an acre, whereas each of his cows produced £250 worth of milk – £36,000 from wine against £25,000 from milk (both on 12 acres).

The cottage industry image was fading and the joke about Red Biddy from grapes on grandad's allotment was a less reliable generator of instant laughter. In August 1970 English Wine was the centre of attraction at a gathering of the International Wine and Food Society. Nine varieties of white and rosé wine, all made by members of the EVA, were selected to win recognition for the new race of English vignerons at the society's first-ever English Wine tasting. The press was invited and mockery was significantly absent from most of the next day's headlines. The tasters were 'clearly surprised with the quality, individuality and presentation of the wine', wrote the *Guardian* correspondent. There was general agreement, he said, that the wine was well above *vin ordinaire* standards. From 1970 the concept of English Wine was treated with considerably more respect. The news began to infiltrate the hotel and catering world, and lap the conservative stronghold of the wine trade and denizens of Vintners Hall.

Many growers sensibly felt that they should first get the viticulture right and graduate to the art of vinification later. To bridge this time gap, and give the vineyard owner a product by which to judge his grapes' suitability for wine-making, Jack Ward offered them the facilities of the Merrydown plant for co-operative wine-making. The vineyard owners harvested their grapes, piled the baskets on to a lorry and drove as fast as they could with them to Horam where they were pressed and processed into wine. The vine-keeper collected the majority of 'his' wine but left a proportion as payment to Merrydown who blended it along with the wine of other co-operative customers into what Ward called 'Anderida' Wine. Had it not been for the introduction in 1969 of the efficient co-operative processing scheme at Horam, many would doubtless have sheered away from viticulture for fear of having to grapple with the still less known wine-making operation. As it was the acreage of open air vines in Britain increased from 50 in 1970 to 200 in 1971. In that year a new wine press was installed at Merrydown which produced 18,000 bottles of wine.

It was the year Hugh Johnson devoted a whole page to 'England and Wales' in his *World Atlas of Wine* (1971). After stating that the idea of English Wine was usually greeted with mockery or disbelief, Johnson described the quality as 'satisfactory'. In 1971 The Wine Society with 7,000 buying members put Hambledon 69 on its list. Members took 600 bottles of it which, as Jack Ward remarked, could not have all been out of curiosity. Cunard offered Sir Guy's produce to the mainly American passengers on the ocean liner Queen Elizabeth II. A first English Vineyards Fair, organised by Greville Powney, was held at Botesdale Lodge, Diss in Norfolk. Initial planting was much bolder – Bill Greenwood planned to have

15 acres under cultivation at Purleigh in Essex by 1975 producing 20 tons of grapes; Gruff Reece planted ten acres at Gamlingay near St Neots; Ian Paget and his brother Andrew planted 10,000 vines at Singleton in Sussex and another nine thousand the following year, and in 1975 were picking 20 tons of grapes from their seven acres which Merrydown turned into 17,500 bottles of 'Chilsdown 75'.

Where were the Greenwoods, Reeces and Pagets going to sell all that amount? With all the publicity which English Wine was getting, several national wine merchants made up for lost time. Saccone and Speed became sole agents for 'Kentish Sovereign' from Joy and Trevor Bates's vineyard at Nettlestead Green in Kent; Deinhard & Co became agents for Kenneth Barlow's 'Adgestone' wine from the Isle of Wight. Many hotels and restaurants started to put English Wine on their wine lists.

It was getting reputation abroad too. Graham Barrett's 'Felstar', of which he made 10,000 gallons in 1971, was exhibited at the Stuttgart Trade Fair. The next year 'Felstar' was one of three English Wines at the wine tasting after a reception given in Stuttgart by the Praesidium Des Deutschen Weinbauverbandes and attended by personalities from wine-producing countries of five continents. The other two were Sir Guy's Hambledon and Nigel Godden's Shepton Mallet wine. One of those present commented that they could be classified half way up the German 'Kabinett Wein' quality. A buyer from Atlanta bought the whole of the Barretts' Riesling-Sylvaner 'Felstar' 72.

The bad weather of 1972 had no effect on the numbers who hastened to order vines by the thousand. There were now 300 EVA members with 250 acres planted, though not all bearing. David Carr Taylor planted the whole of his 21-acre farm at Westfield near Hastings in Sussex. 'I found that vines would give the best return for agricultural investment,' he said, 'partly because wine is one of the few agricultural products you can control the selling price.' The first civic vineyard appeared in Lincoln, consisting of vines presented to the City by its twin town of Neustadt in Germany to mark the 900th anniversary of Lincoln Cathedral. Kevin Fitzgerald and James White had plans for their Suffolk Vineyards Limited to run a seven-acre vineyard at Cratfield and build a winery to handle 250,000 bottles a year.

The publicity given to English Wine rubbed off on English vineyards. Sir Guy's August and September Open Days attracted 12,000 visitors to Hambledon in 1972. It was the least costly way of marketing English Wine to sell it at the vineyard gate where the maker received retail and not wholesale prices. The charges for a guided tour helped with the overheads which were very considerable, and with no help from the Government. But absence of a grant did not deter a man like Kenneth McAlpine from extending his Lamberhurst vineyard in 1974 from eight to 30 acres. At nearby Biddenden Richard Barnes extended the vineyard first planted in 1970 to ten acres, and formed Biddenden Vineyards Limited, which was now the prudent *modus operandi*.

A warning of how expensive and capital intensive a business viticulture had become was given by C. D. Walker, National Fruit Adviser at the East Malling Research Station at the Ministry of Agriculture's Development and Advisory Service (ADAS) at the Wine Production Conference at the Royal Show site at Stoneleigh in Warwickshire in February 1975. Before the vineyard owner had his wine safely in bottles awaiting sale, he said, it would be quite easy to spend £4,000 an acre. 'It is all too easy to be taken in by romantic ideas of sunny vineyards and ignore the many cultural problems that lie between planting the vines and selling your first bottle of wine.'

Be that as it may, what the Ministry of Agriculture called 'the explosion of interest in the cultivation of outdoor grapes' had already occurred. It had captured the imagination of horticulturists and fruit farmers all over the country, and was unlikely to keep hold of it in spite of the would-be alarming statistics. In the introduction to the first List of English and Welsh Vineyards published jointly by the Ministry of Agriculture and the English Vineyards Association in 1974 was the statement that the number of English vineyards now in existence and the acreage that was known to have been planted since the war more than outstripped the legendary sites of the Middle Ages. But who were aware of them?

The sudden renaissance of English viticulture has enjoyed a generous measure of publicity, but in spite of this few people are able to buy English Wine from the shops. As a result the consumer is quite unaware of the recent developments which have done much to revive this ancient husbandry in our somewhat wayward climate.

There were 107 names on the list, and the area under vines was optimistically estimated at 380 acres. But it was not enough for English Wine to make any real impact on British wine drinkers. The small amount of English Wine made each year in the nineteen-seventies, selling at between £1.50 and £2 a bottle, found a ready market. The need was to make more of it. So it was little help to the nascent English Wine industry, suffering from under-production, to find itself bracketed with fellow members of the European Community in having to comply with measures to reduce the effects of their *over-production*, and the 'structural surplus' they called the Wine Lake. The purpose of this however was very laudable – to turn attention away from quantity to quality. Britain's membership of the EEC caused the British Government to take a strict stand on the maintenance of wine quality. Overnight a 'Wine Standards Board' came into being under the Ministry of Agriculture, with inspectors recruited through the Vintners Company.

English wine-makers aimed eventually to achieve the status of what the French called *vins de qualité produits dans regions delimités (VQPRD)*, the Germans *qualitätswein* and the English 'quality wines produced in specific regions' or simply Quality Wine. To qualify for a Quality Wine rating an English vigneron had to be prepared to limit the quantity of grapes harvested from an acre of vines. The idea was to produce a small number of grapes rich in sugar content rather than a large number weak in sugar, and to do that, they said, the root of a vine required a specific area of earth in which to grow. In 1976 English Wine, however fine its maker considered it to be, could not be rated anything more than Table Wine, the grade below Quality Wine. In Germany the word was *tafelwein*, in France *vin de table*. The label of every bottle of English Wine had to carry the words 'Table Wine'.

The phenomenally hot summers of 1975 and 1976 gave England and Wales and the Channel Islands continental timing and a vintage which promised to equal the quantity of Germany but owing to the heavy September rain, not the quality. On the same area of ground and from the same number of vines, the tonnage of wine-grapes gathered from English vineyards in 1976, compared with 1975, trebled. But the wine made from them was nothing more than Table Wine. The biggest crop of wine-grapes per acre England had ever seen meant low sugar readings. The more bunches, and the bigger bunches per vine, meant less sugar went into each grape. The September rain reduced the sugar content even further. But at that stage in the revival of English viticulture the trebling of output in 1976 was a godsend because it was more important to increase quantity than to raise quality.

In the first decade of the century, Europe increased her average output of wine-grapes per acre from two to five and a half tons. On average Germany produced six tons an acre, Luxembourg eight. On the Continent the Müller-Thurgau vine, the variety which represented 56 per cent of all the vines then planted in England, had an average yield of 900 to 1,300 gallons of juice an acre which signified a harvest of up to eight tons an acre. Yet in England in 1976 there were commercial vignerons who were unable to produce two tons of Müller-Thurgau an acre – though there were eminent exceptions like Nigel Godden who consistently produced five tons of grapes an acre from the four and a half he had at Pilton Manor in Somerset.

Two hot years in succession, at a time when viticulture was being considered as a potential activity by so many farmers, fruit growers and others with money and energy to invest, were providential. Large numbers of them were young people prepared to devote the rest of their working lives to English Wine and hand the enterprise on to their children. A series of bad summers and bad crops would have deterred many would-be venturers and given them reason to join the ranks of the unsuitable climate brigade. As it was, the Ministry of Agriculture Survey of November 1976 recorded 196 hectares (485 acres) 'down to vines' compared with 21.5 hectares (53 acres) in 1971. Eighty-five per cent of the vineyards were in East and South East England, which was reflected in the huge interest shown in the Third Festival of English Grape Vines and Vineyards which Christopher Ann of Drusillas organised at Seaford in Sussex in September 1977.

Not only warmer but wealthier? Bernard Theobald, who wrote to the Queen urging her to plant vines at Windsor again and at Sandringham too, never ceased to warn anyone contemplating viticulture that survival depended on sufficient capital. 'The time is ripe for real investment in English Wine,' he told Derek Cooper of *The Observer* in 1980. 'I'm talking about a million quid. Growing vines is a capitalist enterprise. It's no good crying woe woe! because you have three bad years in succession.

> *We need lots more investment, more professionalism. Wine-making isn't all that difficult; there are thousands of peasants all over Europe making very good wine. Far too many growers here are befuddled and betwitched by European mythology, and they won't use their brains. Given the right site, right vines, proper skill and a high regard for integrity and quality, we can produce not imitations of the Rhine or Alsace or the Loire, but the finest wines in the world.*

And given a little help from the Government? Peter Walker, the Minister of Agriculture, saw a deputation from the English Vineyards Association in 1981 and had personally to account for the absence of Government support for the struggling English Wine Industry. Why could not HMG recognise viticulture and wine-making as an agricultural occupation so that winery rating and agricultural grants were allowed without question? It would seem, they said, that what they called 'wine-growing' was now accepted – but of course wine did not grow in the fields any more than Ribena or Syrup of Figs, only the raw material which then had to be processed in what was not an agricultural operation.

When they remonstrated against the Ministry rating 'British Wines' lower for Excise Duty than English Wine, Walker made it clear that 'for political reasons he could not change this'. However, 'he thought he could help us with financial aid to support our efforts in marketing.'

They were going to want all the help they could get with marketing the 1984 vintage, since the 1983 grape crop was 'the vintage of the century'. There were going to be three million bottles of English Wine to dispose of. David Carr Taylor's 21-acre vineyard at Hastings yielded 15 tons of grapes an acre, four times the average. He had only made 56,000 bottles in 1983, so installed three more 23,000-litre vats to cope with what he expected to be a yield of 200,000 bottles.

But like everyone else he felt leant upon by the Government to whom he had to pay some 45p a bottle VAT and Excise Duty of 85p which in 1984 would amount to £250,000, payable before he sold the wine and had therefore to be borrowed at interest, which put a further 7p on the price of a bottle. Because of what he had to add to his retail price, his wine was cheaper in France than England – £3.24 a bottle compared with £3.80.

Like everyone else Carr-Taylor was irritated too by the Government's reluctance to differentiate between English Wine and 'British Wines', a matter which was raised in an adjournment debate in the House of Commons in February 1984. British Wines, said Anthony Steen MP for South Hams who is retained by the EVA as their political adviser, were made of concentrate, must or syrup imported into Britain from Italy, Greece and France, 'often the worst end of their wine', and from Argentina and Chile. 'The only thing that is British about British Wines is the water that dilutes the syrup and the people who put it in the bottle.' Hugh Dykes, MP for Harrow East, who said he was parliamentary adviser to the National Association of British Wine Producers, said no concentrated grape juice was currently being imported from South America. But that was beside the point, which was what Steen described as 'the deliberate misrepresentation of bottle names by the British Wine producers – 'Rougemont Castle', 'Exeter Castle', 'Carrow Prior' and the rest with labels carrying pictures and wording designed to deceive and mislead the public. 'The manufacturers are attempting to misrepresent the area from which their product comes.' The labels on bottles of British Wine carried the line, 'Produced from imported grape concentrate' but not in large enough type.

In raising the matter in the House of Lords, Lord Montagu of Beaulieu said that hitherto British Wines had been made sweet and strong to appeal to those looking for a cheaper alternative to port and sherry. But the new phenomenon was the British Table Wine for which the manufacturers negotiated for themselves a special low-strength duty enabling them to retail their product in 1981 at around £1.30 a bottle.

It was in no way due to competition from British Wines however that after the bumper harvest of 1984 only some 653,000 litres of English Wine were produced in 1985 – less than half that of the previous year. Not all the vineyard owners from whose grapes this wine was made were members of the English Vineyards Association, and it was part of the brief of Commander Geoffrey L. Bond, MBE, RN (ret'd), who was appointed its first full-time, paid Chief Executive in 1985, to try and persuade non-members owning some 300 acres of vineyard to join the fold and contribute to its funding – through an English Wine Levy Board maybe? All of them for instance had reason to be grateful to the EVA for obtaining the allowance for home consumption and samples of 1,100 litres duty free. Kenneth McAlpine, who as Secretary had administered the association so efficiently with the help of Diana Hibling from Lamberhurst for so long, became Secretary/Treasurer.

English vignerons had occasion to be mindful of what they owed the EVA with the death in 1986, at the age of 77, of its first chairman Jack Ward. As Colin Gillespie who succeeded him observed, Jack Ward shaped the English Vineyards Association and saw it safely through the penniless years. 'He forged our good relations with the wine trade and he negotiated single handed with the Customs and Excise and various government ministries. With foresight he saw the need for a Seal of Quality and he spent five years deeply enmeshed in the process of bringing the Trade Mark regulations to fruition.'

He wrote a scholarly book *Growing Vines in England* which was published in 1984; and for his services to viticulture in England he was awarded the OBE in 1977. It would not perhaps be too much to say that without Jack Ward and the EVA which Anton Massel and Norman Cowderoy conceived, there would be no English Wine industry in 1989.

ASTE THE INE

ODAY

⊰ 3 ⊱

THE ENGLISH WINE PRODUCERS

ACK WARD KNEW OF, BUT did not live to see published, the second Survey of English Wine conducted by the Ministry of Agriculture with the support of the EVA. This showed that in January 1986 the total area under vines in England was 488 hectares or 1,206 acres consisting of 323 vineyards, 134 of which (356 hectares/880 acres) were producing wine which amounted to 653,000 litres.

In 1988 the Ministry published a third survey which showed that the total area under vines in January of that year was 546 hectares or 1,349 acres, of which 382 hectares (944 acres) were in production and had made some 411,000 litres of English Wine.

Of the 12 counties named, most of the wine – 103,000 litres – was made in Kent from 50 hectares (124 acres), and the second most from Somerset – 53,000 litres – from 22 hectares (54 acres). Though East Sussex had the largest area in production – 62 hectares (153 acres) – it produced the third largest amount of wine, 51,000 litres.

The actual statistics looked like this:

SURVEY OF ENGLISH WINE – 29 JANUARY 1988

(Small areas and amounts of production on
vineyards of less than 0.05 hectares are excluded)

TABLE 1   AREAS AND PRODUCTION – ENGLAND AND WALES

	1986 Hectares	1988 Hectares
Total area of vines	488	546
Area in production	356	382
Area not yet in production	132	164
	'000 litres	'000 litres
Quantity of wine produced	653	411

THE ENGLISH WINE PRODUCERS

TABLE 2   AREAS AND PRODUCTION BY COUNTY

* Figures for counties with a large and predominant producer are not shown separately, but included in 'Other counties'.
* Production for some counties includes that from grapes grown in others and 'bought in'.
* Figures for counties and thus their year-on-year comparisons may be relatively less accurate than those for the whole country.
* Totals may not necessarily agree with the sum of their components due to rounding.

County	Area of vines (hectares)			Quantity of wine produced ('000 litres)
	In production	Not yet in production	Total area	
England				
Kent	50	27	77	103
Somerset	22	3	25	53
East Sussex	62	20	82	51
Isle of Wight	14	13	27	42
Gloucester	13	1	14	24
Hampshire	34	20	54	21
Berkshire	13	2	15	18
Essex	23	7	30	9
Cambridge	15	–	15	8
Devon	6	4	9	6
Other counties	128	66	194	78
Total	380	163	544	411
Wales	2	–	2	–
England and Wales	382	163	546	411

TABLE 3   MAIN VARIETIES OF VINE GROWN

* Figures by main varieties, and thus their year-on-year comparisons, may be relatively less accurate than the total figures shown.
* (a) includes varieties too small to analyse separately, as well as mixed and experimental areas.
* Totals may not necessarily agree with the sum of their components due to rounding.

Variety of vines	Area of vines (hectares)						Quantity of wine produced ('000 litres)	
	In production		Not yet in production		Total area			
	1986	1988	1986	1988	1986	1988	1986	1988
Müller-Thurgau	138	125	17	20	155	146	185	85
Reichensteiner	36	47	19	15	55	62	55	48
Seyval Blanc	35	39	10	14	45	53	79	50
Schönburger	13	16	14	18	27	34	25	21
Madeleine Angevine	19	17	7	6	26	24	19	19
Huxelrebe	15	23	10	7	26	30	28	12
Bacchus	6	14	8	20	14	34	8	4
Pinot Noir	11	13	2	3	13	16	13	6
Kerner	7	11	4	7	11	17	11	5
All other varieties see note (a)	75	77	41	54	116	131	233	161
Total	356	382	132	164	488	546	653	411

Apart from enlarging vineyards and starting new ones which, as the survey shows, has resulted in a net increase in the acreage under vines (allowing for annual scrubbing of vines) over the last two years, a number of established vineyards, as always, have changed hands. In 1988 two big vineyards, Chilsdown and Barnsgate, were put up for sale as going concerns – though by the summer Ian Paget had withdrawn the former. Abbotts Countrywide were asking £375,000 for the smaller Mersea Island Vineyard off the Essex Coast which at five feet above sea level was considered England's lowest. Derek and Janine Game had built it up into a popular tourist attraction.

The Ministry's survey was of course of quantity only, not quality which can never be analysed so neatly, if at all. Quality, particularly of something like wine, is necessarily subjective, of which Christopher Fielden, Master of Wine, the chairman of the panel judging the EVA's English Wine of the Year Competition was made aware when he announced the prize winners for 1987. The panel consisted of Masters of Wine, wine buyers of London, and Bristol wine and spirit merchants, and Dr Gabor Sellyei, director of Monimpex the Hungarian State Wine Importers. In the panel, said Fielden, there was a divergence of opinion as to the style that was preferred. The rather aggressive vegetal style (as of Sancerre) was much liked by two Masters of Wine, while more delicacy was appreciated by most of the other judges.

There is nothing like a genuine 'blind tasting' to throw up affectation-free likes and dislikes, and the one organised by *Decanter* in June 1986 showed a degree of attachment to the Union Jack welcomed by those who had been enraged by Robin Young's articles in that magazine which urged readers 'Don't Drink the Flag'. In having to place the contents of ten unmarked bottles of English Wine and ten from others parts of the world in order of preference, wine-writer tasters Jane McQuitty of the *Sunday Times*, Elizabeth Berry MW, Stephen Spurrier and Don Hewittson, put three of the English brands in the top five. The Alsace Gewurtztraminer was placed at no. 1; the Barton Manor and Carr Taylor Gutenborner at no. 2 and no. 3; the Carr Taylor Reichensteiner at no. 5. When in December 1987 Conal Gregory MW, MP for York, staged one in the House of Commons for MPs, several of whom had never tasted English Wine before, he was pleasantly surprised to find that the latter took the first five of the ten places.

WHAT THEN WAS THE English Wine which these expert wine writers and inexpert legislators preferred to French, German, Italian and Spanish wine? Who in 1988 were growing the grapes in the open air for the product which had so deep-rooted a tradition? Where could it be bought and drunk? Would the sellers and servers know as much about it as continental wine? Was anyone bothering to educate them? Where was it being promoted? What chance was there of being able to see around an English vineyard? Above all, what future was there for English Wine?

ALL BOTTLES CONTAINING English Wine are today labelled 'Table Wine'. When the UK joined the European Economic Community in 1973 it had to conform to the regulations of the Council of Ministers' Wine Working Group on which every Member State is represented. From 1973 English Wine had to take its place on the ladder of wine classification as drawn up by the committee. It was one way of giving consumers an indication of what they were buying. The first rung on the EEC wine ladder was (in English) 'Table Wine', the second 'Quality Wine'.

In the latter the word 'quality' does not have the meaning given it in the Oxford English Dictionary. No drinker should infer that wine that is not labelled 'Quality Wine' is of less than good quality. 'Quality Wine' status in the EEC sense is based mainly on which of the many wine-grape varieties the wine is made from – but not entirely. It is also determined by the method employed to cultivate the vines from whose grapes the wine is made, the method of wine-making, the wine's minimum natural alcoholic strength, yield per hectare, 'delimitation of production zone' (the spacing of vines), and 'organoleptic properties' (what it tastes like). There is however no agreed Community definition which incorporates all these factors, since the relevant regulation on 823/87 essentially endorses the different national legislation currently in force. The regulations governing the French *Appellation d'Origine Contrôlée (AOC)* are significantly different from the German *Qualitätswein*.

English Wine is 'Table Wine' in 1989 not because the EEC classified it as such in 1973 for a ten-year 'proving period' as some believe, but because there is not in England a quality wine scheme akin to the French *AOC* or the German *Qualitätswein*. It has always been open to the British Government to put a case to the EEC Wine Management Committee for the recognition of a quality wine scheme in the UK, but so far wine growers in England have not asked the Ministry to do so.

All the other factors apart, it is unlikely that the EEC would allow any English Wine to be classified as Quality Wine in 1989 if it was made from a hybrid vine, valued by some growers for tolerance of cool climates but which EEC Members see as tending to produce high yields and in some cases poor quality. In the UK however there is one hybrid on the EEC list of varieties authorised for cultivation and that is the Seyval. There are other hybrids on the authorised varieties list of other Member States. Germany particularly is anxious to develop new varieties and has been lobbying the EEC to permit the production of Quality Wine from certain experimental hybrid varieties grown on limited areas for a trial period.

Seyval wine-grapes.

In 1988 up to 20 per cent of England's vineyard acreage was planted with varieties not yet on the UK List of EEC Authorised or Recommended grape varieties. The area planted with such varieties, which may or may not be hybrids, could be as little as 12 to 15 per cent of the total. No one knows for certain. In theory any vine planted in 1972 or earlier, which is not on the EEC approved list, must be grubbed up before it is 25 years old – by 1997. And it must not be re-planted. Before then, however the Ministry of Agriculture hopes to get most, if not all of the currently unauthorised non-approved vines approved. It aims to hold trials of these varieties with a view to demonstrating their suitability for cultivation in the UK so they can go to the EEC Wine Management Committee with a proposal for an amended list. In the meantime they are turning a blind eye to the planting of unapproved varieties. There is in any case no record of who is planting what. But with Britain on the verge of being seen to be growing more than 500 hectares (1,236 acres) of vines, the situation is about to change. For when Britain has more than that acreage it will be compelled to draw up a Vineyard Register, like every other Member State, which among other things will show what varieties are being grown. The Ministry are therefore stirring themselves to find a solution to the problem acceptable to the English Wine industry before an unacceptable one is imposed on it. Technically the Ministry has six years in which to complete the register, but they aim to do so in four or five years time, using the Wine Standards Board as their agent.

In theory at any rate, right now and irrespective of whether there is or is not a register, any wine made from a grape variety not on the authorised or recommended list has to be exported, converted into vinegar or consumed by the producer's family. If the vigneron is not prepared to do any of these things he must turn his wine into undrinkable pure alcohol – 'obligatory distillation'.

In the context of the small English Wine industry all that would be ludicrous. Be that as it may, Britain would be in serious trouble if Brussels found out that she was defying EEC regulations and allowing wine to be made from grape varieties they had ruled out of court (see Appendix 1).

The Ministry is working hard to make sure that the non-approved vines *do* get on to the EEC Approved List as soon as possible and at least by 1997. To set the inevitably long process in motion they have formed the inevitable committee consisting of their own representative David Harbourne of Alcoholic Drinks Division; Sheila Baxter, the vine specialist on their Agricultural Development and Advisory Service; and a representative of the English Vineyards Association. This committee will supervise trials of the varieties which Britain wishes to have approved, the reports of which will form the basis of Britain's case. Since most of the vines in question have long been grown commercially in England, the Ministry is hopeful of getting them approved quite rapidly.

So there is little need for panic. The 'unapproved' vines growing on 15 per cent of England's vine-growing acreage have little chance of ever being uprooted. Even so Gillian Pearkes is appalled by what it all might signify for English Wine and insists that England must have separate categorisation and individually tailored regulations. 'Being an island above the recognised northern wine growing limit, the 50th parallel, underlines our differences in the UK very distinctly.' Her concern is shared by many.

What is the criterion for this life-giving approval? What pleases the EEC Wine Management Committee? What displeases them? In 1988 the ground rules had yet to be formulated. But it would appear that for the time being the Ministry is aiming to seek approval for any variety which an English Wine producer finds has been commercially viable for him. And it believes that that is the criterion which Member States will accept.

As soon as the United Kingdom has an up-dated list of approved varieties, it will be much easier to attain the coveted 'Quality Wine' status for the English Wine 'brands' that deserve it, and have for so long deserved it. In their efforts to persuade the EEC to give English vignerons the option of calling some or all of the wine they produce 'Quality Wine' – and not all of them wish to go to the bother of having their operations confined by the very strict rules – the Ministry feels it has an acceptable basis in the ten-year-old 'Seal of Quality'

This was the name the English Vineyards Association (EVA) gave to the Certification Trade Mark which in 1978 – thanks to a large extent to Jack Ward – the Department of Trade and Industry (as it is now called) agreed could be assigned to batches of English Wines in the same way as it was to cheese and other provisions, indicating that the named produce of a named manufacturer was of a certain character, which was defined. It was the Government (the DTI), not the EVA, certifying that a particular stock of a particular type of English Wine, with such and such a description made in such and such a year (or maybe a blend of several years' wine), had been made to the standard required by *its* rules – not the EVA's. Certification was not confined to members of the EVA. It did not automatically denote that that batch was of high quality, just that it had attained a certain grade of excellence. It was a guarantee for both producer, distributor and consumer that the batch of wine to which it referred was both properly made and palatable. In 1979 nine batches qualified out of the 17 submitted; in 1980 15 out of 28, of which five were from Lamberhurst Vineyards and three from Carr Taylor Vineyards.

The status of the Seal of Quality is national. It carries with it independent endorsement of objectively defined 'quality'. The Department of Trade and Industry entrust the operation of the scheme to the EVA. For the most part certification is sought by the producer of the wine – the vine-grower and vineyard proprietor whose name is on the wine bottle label. He may make the wine himself or may have it made for him by a wine-maker in a winery at another vineyard. In this case the certificate or seal is not given to the wine-maker but to the wine producer who organises the whole of the two-tier process of horticulture-cum-chemistry. But there is no restriction on who may apply for a Seal. He may be only the seller of the wine. What is important is that all the people involved in the chain of producing wine – the owner of the vineyard and the owner of the grapes (who may not be the same), the maker of the wine and the owner of the wine – have all complied with the regulations.

Certification trials take place twice a year in May and September. They are for a specific and defined batch of wine, a particular wine, not for the wine of that name as such and applying to it without further application from year to year, nor for the output of the winery or vineyard as a whole, nor for the winery, the vineyard, the vineyard owner or the wine-maker. The DTI have laid down the strictest rules – some say too strict. Anyone wishing to enter must apply for a Declaration of Stock form and give the EVA Notice of Intention by 1 August, which does not commit him however in any way. After he has harvested his grapes in November he must write particulars of the wine he wishes to be considered for certification on the form. It can have been made in any year, not necessarily in the previous year. In May he has to send four bottles of it to the EVA who pass two of them to an analyst appointed by the DTI.

The person who does the analysing only does the job for a year, or maybe two or three years, and is chosen from those who apply by tender. He may charge the applicant around £40 a bottle, perhaps less. He will apply the series of tests specified by the DTI and apportion marks according to a scheme of their devising. He is not required to comment or grade, merely to pronounce whether the wine has passed his tests or failed them. The analyst sometimes has to be sent another bottle. If one bottle fails and a second one passes, it is necessary to test a third bottle. If that passes, then the wine is declared OK, but if it fails then the wine is deemed to have failed.

In ten years some ten per cent of entries on average have failed to pass the analytical tests each year. Two bottles of wine which have passed go for a blind tasting organised by the chairman of the EVA and undertaken by three Masters of Wine who change each year and volunteer to declare those which in their collective opinion reach the desired standard and those which do not. The bottles are wrapped in aluminium foil which completely covers the labels, and the capsules are entirely removed.

An official letter notifies those whose wine has satisfied the tasters, followed by a DTI certificate which they can frame and hang on their wall. Finally they apply and pay for, say, 20,000 paper seals at 1½p each plus VAT to stick on the bottles of the newly certified batch. The quantity of seals applied for is checked against that given in the Declaration of Stock. Sticking seals only on the bottles containing the wine which has been certified is, of course, a matter of trust, but it is as well not to have too many surplus Seals of Quality lying around.

English Wine's Seal of Quality.

Any producer whose wine fails to pass either the chemical tests or the blind tasting can, according to the DTI rules, appeal to the Registrar of Trade Marks at the Patent Office. He may send another four bottles to the EVA for testing by a different laboratory selected by the association, the cost of which he will be asked to pay. In rejecting a wine at the May tasting, the Masters of Wine may withhold out-and-out rejection and make it known that they would like to see it in October when they might revise their opinion if the producer chose to re-enter this wine. Otherwise no comment is called for from the tasters, though the chairman of EVA will at his discretion probably hand on any comment to a producer whose wine has failed to be certified.

STIMULATING MEMBERS TO ASPIRE to even higher standards of vine-growing and wine-making is the English Vineyards Association's English Wine of the Year Competition. A panel of judges allot gold, silver and bronze awards to full members who must show they have a large stock of the wine they submit (at least 1,500 litres) and to both full and associate members (under half an acre) who have less than 1,500 litres but more than a hundred. Those in the first category are the serious, commercial producers; the others are mostly amateurs doing it as a hobby, or potential commercial operators starting small and discovering whether they can cope.

Lord Montagu of Beaulieu (centre), President of the English Vineyards Association, makes the first presentation of the Jack Ward Memorial Salver, given in her husband's memory by his widow Betty Ward (right), in 1987. The recipient is Tom Day of Three Choirs Vineyard.

Apart from the awards in nine classes of white, rosé, red and sparkling wine, the Presidents Cup is given to the producer of the most outstanding wine in the low quantity section; the Jack Ward Memorial Salver to the maker of the best wine in the high quantity section in whatever year it was made; and the Gore-Brown Trophy to the producer of the best wine of the previous year's vintage (with more than 1,500 litres of it), either white, rosé or red. The latter was inaugurated in 1974 and won in that year by Brede Riesling Sylvaner 1972. Subsequent winners have been the producers of Pilton Manor (twice), Pulham (twice), Kelsale, Adgestone, Tenterden, Wootton, Lamberhurst (twice) and Barton Manor. In 1987 the Gore-Brown Trophy was awarded to Richard Barnes for his Biddenden Ortega, and in 1988 to David Ealand of Chiltern Valley for his 'Old Luxters 1987'. In recent years the presentation has taken place at the invitation of Lord Montagu of Beaulieu, the association's President, on the terrace of the House of Lords. The trophy itself went on a tour of West Germany in 1987 to draw attention to the high quality of English Wine.

David and Fiona Ealand of Chiltern Valley whose 'Old Luxters' 1987 won the Gore Brown Trophy in the EVA's English Wine of the Year Competition 1988.

A regular member of the judging panel has been the noted wine writer Hugh Johnson. Tasting the 70 or so samples of English Wine entered for the Gore-Browne Trophy in 1981 gave him a greater respect and admiration than ever for the English Wine producers, he said. The 1979 and 1980 vintages showed surprisingly little signs of the problems their makers must have encountered. It was the third time he had taken part in the competition as a judge, and more and more each year he found that determination was backed up by experience and technical competence. 'No one can hope to make excellent wine the first time he tries, even in ideal conditions. But there is a consistency of quality among the finalists this year which make it hard to come up with an outright winner.'

English Wine is and always will be a light, refreshing, slightly tart summer drink. It comes into its own in the gardens of the country houses and farmhouses that make it, or sleepy sunlit lawns or over the well mannered malice of a game of croquet. The qualities we look for are floweriness, delicate fruitiness and a crisp clean freshness. We hope to find the acidity well matched with a gentle sweetness; total dryness is unappealing without a certain 'body' to back it up. The very positive flavours of some of the new German grape varieties can also easily be overdone in light wines for refreshment. A little tingling 'spritz' is often a plus.

Most regional associations hold their own English Wine of the Year Competition for which many enter who are not members of the EVA. Ian Berwick of Bruisyard's entry was the first to be designated East Anglian Wine of the Year when the East Anglian Wine Growers Association started a competition in 1987. It was designed, said Sam Alper the association's chairman, to encourage high standards in East Anglian vineyards and their products, and to draw attention to the quality of the wine of the region. By inviting expert independent judges of the highest reputation to assess the entries, they hoped to achieve both those aims. It was significant, he said, that the judges had been sparing with their awards – only one gold out of a possible ten. 'With standards like that an award really means something to grower and buyer alike.' The association's members exhibiting in their marquee at the summertime Suffolk Show also compete for the Macrae East Anglian Wine Challenge Salver for the best dry and medium wine, the winner of which in 1988 was 'Bruisyard St Peter 1987'.

Eight wines were selected from the 18 submitted for the third South East Wine of the Year Competition of 1988, and at the final tasting in Leeds Castle the judges, chaired by Christopher Tatham MW, declared the winner to be 'Downers 1985 Müller-Thurgau Dry' from Ted Downer's Henfield vineyard. Michael Bache's 'Astley Kerner 1986' was judged South West Wine of the Year 1987 in the competition that takes place each September, and Tom Day's 'Three Choirs Medium 1985' won the South West Challenge Cup.

After a three-day tasting of the contents of 180 bottles, the Wessex Vineyards Association (late Central Southern Vineyards Association) presents the awards to winners of their annual competition at a dinner in Ringwood in November. Before announcing the winners in 1987 John Avery said the judging had been far from simple, since tasting was necessarily subjective and every judge's opinion would differ slightly from his fellows. His own criteria were basic: bronze was awarded to the wine which was well made and sound but lacking in distinctive character, silver to the one that showed distinctive character and gold for an exceptional character. Of the possible 20 points which could be awarded, ten were given for taste, seven for bouquet and three for appearance. He was pleased that the wine which received the Gold, 'Barton Manor Medium Dry 1986', was dry, since it was much harder to make an excellent dry* wine from Germanic varieties.

ARE JUDGES AND WINE WRITERS all looking for the same thing? Is there a norm which attracts commendation, deviations which they frown upon? Is English Wine, for instance, essentially dryish or sweetish?

To raise the alcohol content during fermentation, most English Wine makers add sugar (the 'chaptalisation' which Andrew Pettigrew of Castell Coch resented). Others will give it extra sweetness by adding, when the fermentation has died down, what is called *Sussreserve*, unfermented grape juice, often from grapes which have not been grown in England which, for that reason, many regard as cheating. In his *Sainsbury's Book of Wine*, Oz Clarke says he thinks doing so makes 'a wonderful drink at only a year old and in *no way* inferior to the rather more purist wines of the "dry" school.'

Clarke considered that in Germany, in places like Baden and the Rheinpfalz, German vines ripened too fast to develop the interesting personality which John Avery awarded in those English Wine competitions. In England the German early varieties ripened very slowly and would be just ripe enough to make wine as winter closed in.

> And instead of the burnt-out dull tastes of much cheap, overripe southern German wine, all the essential acids and perfumes are only just coming to the fore when the grapes are finally picked.

The most important thing in English Wine's favour, he asserted in the England & Wales section of his *Websters Wine Guide*, as adapted by Joanna Simon for the *Sunday Times Handbook of Wine*, was that it was different. It really did have a style of its own. Despite the monumental obstacle of the British weather, standards of wine-making in England and Wales were high 'and the wines *are* good'. The wine-makers produced white wine with breathtaking acidity.

> But it is acidity balanced by fresh fruit flavours and flowery, aromatic smells. All sorts of fruit creep into English wine-tasting notes – apples, pears, gooseberries, lychees, peaches, you name it – but the only real give-away is grapefruit, not just tart and mouth-puckering but sharp, sweet and deliciously refreshing.

Medium Dry and Medium Sweet is certainly the choice of most English white wine drinkers in 1989, but English Wine maker Kit Lindlar believes that a taste is developing for wine that is dry and what he prefers to call 'Off-dry' (as in Off-white) though not as

---

* The 1988 EEC definition of 'dry' is 'where residual sugar is not more than four grams per litre, or nine grams per litre where the level of total acidity expressed as tartaric acid does not fall more than two grams per litre below the residual sugar level.'

raspingly dry as Chablis which is an acquired taste. The English preference for sweeter wine, he says, is largely due to marketing men and cost accountants who have applied marketing principles which work for soap flakes – 'pile it high and sell it cheap' appealing to the lowest common denominator – to English Wine. He acclaims Master of Wine Christopher Tatham's dictum: 'Today's mediocrity is tomorrow's standard of quality.' Give Jo Public a chance to try the drier wine being made in 1989, and Kit believes he will recognise its quality and be happy to pay good money for it. He will be ready to be persuaded that it is what he *should* like – drier, that is, than the marketing men assert the Man and Woman in the Street normally likes.

> *Everyone has aspirations; everyone likes to have their lifestyle elevated. These aspirations have a role to play in the kind of wine which we English Wine makers make. Because we do not have cost accountants looking over our shoulders, we can take a gamble to produce wine, not of the kind people think they like but wine they should like, which is marvellous and delicious and a snip at five pounds a bottle.*

English Wine in 1989 is relatively light, fresh and fragrant, with an alcohol content between 10 and 11 per cent, which to implement EEC legislation has to be shown on the label of every bottle of wine. It is a far cry from the heady, block-busting wine from the Latin areas of Europe with an alcoholic strength of between 12 and 14 per cent. Lindlar thinks English Wine has enough alcohol in terms of balance and flavour, so a little is fun to drink without fear of being stopped by the police.

'The authorities' in the person of the Parliamentary Secretary at the Ministry of Agriculture, Donald Thompson MP not only gave their blessing to English Wine but their commendation. 'I am impressed by the high standard of wines made by English and Welsh wine producers,' he said after visiting Kent vineyards in March 1988. 'The emphasis on quality in English and Welsh wine-making is first rate because there is a good market for quality wines at home and overseas. I would like to take the opportunity to wish the English Vineyards Association and the English and Welsh wine industry a profitable and successful 1988.'

For Lord Montagu of Beaulieu, President of the English Vineyards Association, the quality of English Wine had improved quite dramatically since Mrs Margaret Gore-Brown re-planted the vineyard in the grounds of his Palace House. The public were now accepting as very drinkable what had then been considered a gimmick. It was because then very little was known about which vines would grow and ripen here. Since then the wine-makers had gained that much more experience and become that much more professional. And more of them were seeing it as no loss of face, no diminution in the role of vigneron, so often over-romantically conceived, to delegate the wine-making part of the operation to someone who, by taking the time to be taught the far from simple techniques by experienced practitioners, was alone qualified to call himself truly professional. It might be romantic to grow the grapes and make the wine, but in too many cases it resulted in a botched-up product or certainly wine whose quality belied the quality of the grapes. More English vignerons in 1989 were seeing the merit of at least consulting people like Kit Lindlar, Kit Morris, Mike Thompson and Stephen Skelton, if not actually handing over their harvest to them for vinification.

When in 1986 Stephen Skelton sold Tenterden Vineyards at Spots Farm in Kent which he had established in 1977, he contracted to operate its winery for the new owners and became one of the small band of elite freelance wine-makers and consultants to whom the higher quality of today's English Wine is so largely due. In 1975 and 1976 he worked at Schloss Schönborn in the Rheingau and then spent a year studying at the Geisenheim Institute. He ascribes much of the dramatic improvement in the quality of English Wine, to which Lord Montagu refers, to the greater readiness of English wine-makers to ensure they are using the right equipment. Mercifully they were abandoning the impetuous, 'anything-goes' attitude to the tools of the trade which had retarded progress for so long, born of ignorance and a reluctance to take the trouble to find out what was needed – the inertia to which writers like Samuel Hartlib attributed the small output of English Wine in the eighteenth century. Skelton believes:

> To a certain extent it is like cookery. If you have the right equipment, the right ingredients, the right temperatures, you will turn out a product that is acceptable. If, in making a cup of tea, instead of boiling the water in a kettle you boil it in a frying pan and make tea in a baking tin instead of a teapot, you'll make a hash of it. The right equipment helps – to say the least – to make the right product. Fifteen years ago people were trying to make wine with equipment that was not suitable for our type of grapes. They bought French and Italian equipment entirely unfitted for English Wine production – bottling equipment incapable of being sterilised, tanks of the wrong size, plant designed for making red wine instead of white, or for making wine on a scale that no English Wine maker was attempting, too small or too big.

People who invested in such equipment were not giving themselves a chance. People with small crops who had bought huge tanks second-hand from London firms who bottled millions of bottles a year, were at last realising their mistake, selling them off and replacing them with tanks more suited to their smaller scale of operation. With wine-making going into second gear, there was very much less really bad English Wine about. The best of ten years ago was equal to the best of 1988; but the worst of 1988 was far superior to the worst of 1978. The Seal of Quality and the national and regional competitions had done wonders.

> People who make bad English Wine today are shown up. Wine which is not up to scratch will not get mentioned in the Press – or worse, will get lambasted and scorned. It won't be liked and no one will buy it. People can afford to be choosey these days. They go from vineyard to vineyard, and compare one wine with another.

In 1989 they can taste the wine at more than a hundred vineyards spread right across southern England from East Anglia to the West Country. They lie just above the 50° latitude where, as Sam Hartlib remarked 'a hundred miles more or less can set little alteration in heat or cold, and some advantages which we have will supply that defect'.

'If you have the right equipment, ingredients and temperatures, you will turn out an acceptable product' – Stephen Skelton. Here is some right equipment: fermentation tanks at Penshurst (above) and Chilford Hundred (centre); a crusher at Wootton (below).

Some say that the chalky soil of East Anglia gives all the wine made there a taste which distinguishes it from that made from vines grown on the clay soil of Kent and Sussex. Others cannot find any distinctive taste in East Anglian wine, or indeed in the English Wine from any region. East Anglia might be expected to produce wine that differed from that of other regions through being so close to the northern limits for viticulture, seen roughly as a line from the Mersey to the Wash. The 40 members of the East Anglian Wine Growers' Association in Norfolk, Suffolk, Cambridge, Essex, Hertfordshire, and Bedfordshire (who pay a £25 annual subscription) enjoy longer hours of sunshine than the warmer south and, thanks to clearer skies, better sunshine than the West Country. Such conditions are ideal for the slower maturing of fruit which Kit Lindlar pointed out gives the wine a fuller flavour. The Association hold that their conditions produce English Wines from their 28 commercial vineyards which have a variety of flavours but that all of them have a fruitiness with a flinty crisp character. H.P.B. Dow, the Queens Counsel who has been running the six-and-a-half-acre Brandeston Priory Vineyard near Woodbridge since 1975, goes so far

as to claim that Suffolk, with its light but persistent summer breezes, 'offers the best hope for the survival of English Wine'. He takes pride in his 'Brandeston Priory' wine being estate-bottled with its own provenance, which would not be found in wine made from the grapes from a number of different vineyards. The label on his bottle however is less cheery than its contents. It depicts the 90-year-old Rev John Lowes, vicar of Brandeston, hanging from gallows to which he was condemned by Matthew Hopkin, Cromwell's Witchfinder General, in 1646.

London businessman Ian Hutcheson has Robert Hemphill to manage his Shawsgate Vineyard at Framlingham – 13 acres of Müller-Thurgau – where another five acres were planted in the spring of 1988 with Bacchus, Reichensteiner and Seyval. There was no crop in 1987, but in 1986 they produced single variety Müller-Thurgau and Seyval wines which they were still selling from the vineyard shop in 1988 – Seyval made from grapes bought in. The first 'Shawsgate' wine from their modern new wine press, made with the help of Karl-Heinz Johner in 1988 was the same two single varieties plus a blend of the two.

After many years as a member of a wine society, Basil Ambrose came to the conclusion that the real challenge would be whether he could grow the stuff. Late though it was for him to have a go, he spent 1971 laying his plans and the following year planted a Suffolk vineyard in the Stour Valley at Nether Hall, Cavendish near Sudbury, a village where the Ambrose family had lived for 300 years. Despite the atrocious summer and autumn weather of 1974, his first wine won him a trophy. Now grown to ten acres, the vineyard is

maintained with the help of vineyard Master W. G. Stearne. 'Cavendish Manor' wine is light and delicate. In Basil Ambrose's own words, it has 'an enchanting freshness combined with a lingering gentle bouquet, and aims to qualify as an excellent aperitif, as a stimulant to the appetite during one's meal or as a satisfying drink by itself.'

Maureen and Robin Aikman spent 18 months choosing the plot of land on which to plant the vineyard they had set their hearts on. In 1970 they settled for Holly Farm at Heywood near Diss on the Suffolk-Norfolk border, a flat two-acre site well sheltered by trees and hedges. The 'Heywood' white wine which Peter Cook makes from their grapes at nearby Pulham is, in the Aikman's description 'a fresh tasting, fairly dry quality white wine with a full flavour and a delicious bouquet'. Peter Cook who makes his own 'Pulham' wine learnt the art in Luxembourg.

Ian Berwick had just completed 28 years in tropical agriculture, the last five years as manager of a 3,000-acre plantation and factory, when in 1974 he planted five acres of sandy clay loam at Bruisyard near Saxmundham in Suffolk with 7,500 Müller-Thurgau vines. The next year he planted another 6,500 of the same variety to make up the ten-acre vineyard of today. It is a hundred feet up, but none the worse for that. Nestling in the Alde Valley it is protected from the worst of the weather, with trees set round to prevent the wind blowing the warmth away. Ian and his wife Eleanor are in the business together. He makes the fine 'Bruisyard St Peter' on the up-to-date plant in his own winery, and provides a wine-making service for other grape growers in the area.

The 'Elmham Park' wine which Robin Don MW makes at Dereham in Norfolk was at one time also exclusively Müller-Thurgau, but he is gradually replacing the plants with Madeleine Angevine which 20 years have shown to be the best for the climate of central Norfolk. He has also added Kerner and Huxelrebe.

He planted his first vines experimentally in 1966 but, with encouraging results in 1970 and 1971, he established three sites for commercial cultivation covering six acres, Little Heath, Cathedral Vineyard

and Bells Vineyard. He made his first 'commercial' wine in 1974. He already knew a fair amount about wine since he had joined the wine trade in 1958 and spent eight years with John Harvey & Sons, served on their Wine Buying Committee and started their museum. He became a Master of Wine in 1965, and the following year formed his own firm of wine merchants Hicks & Don. He supervises the making of 'Elmham Park' wine by his manager and wine-maker in the winery he installed in a fine old, pantiled eighteenth-century building of mellow red brick which stands across one side of the courtyard of Elmham House. The press is in the old harness room where the pegs can still be seen on which the harness for the coach horses once hung. 'With its modern stainless steel horizontal wine press and glass fibre fermentation tanks,' says Robin, 'it is better equipped to make fine wine than many a winery of comparable size in France or Italy.' 'Elmham Park' Dry is a crisp, fresh, very dry white wine with a pronounced fruity nose and a real taste of the grape. He also makes a Medium Dry. The attractive label, showing the church, vineyard and dovecote, is designed by Elisa Trimby.

Old farm buildings house the winery in which dry and medium dry 'Chilford Hundred' wine is made by Sam Alper MW at Linton in Cambridgeshire. He planted the vineyard, which has now grown to 22 acres, in 1972. He chose Müller-Thurgau, Ortega, Huxelrebe, Siegerrebe and Schönburger varieties for their hardiness and early ripening. He tastes the wine made from each four months after harvesting and decides which will constitute the blend of that year. He describes his wine as 'good, clear, fragrant nose, fruity body with good acidity'. Peatling & Cawdron, the wine department of brewer Greene King, said the Huxelrebe-Schönburger blend of 1983 on sale in 1987 was 'pale yellow almost water white', and the Müller-Thurgau-Ortega blend clean and dry with a hint of yeast.

Bill Greenwood of Purleigh near Chelmsford in Essex designates all his 'New Hall' wine 'estate bottled single variety'. It is made from grape juice, he says, which has only travelled yards, rather than miles, to the winery. It is all medium dry. He grows the white Huxelrebe, Müller-Thurgau and Bacchus, and the red Pinot Noir and Austrian Zweigeltrebe on his 22 acres which began as a one-acre plot in 1970. From each of the white grapes he makes a 'New Hall Essex Huxelrebe' etc.; a light red 'Essex Zweigeltrebe'; a light red 'Essex

Zweigeltrebe/Pinot Noir; and from his Pinot Noir and Chardonnay a 'New Hall Vineyards English Sparkling Wine, Méthode Champenoise (Fermented in the Bottle)'.

Pinot Noir grapes, along with Müller-Thurgau and Huxelrebe, are the ingredients too of the wine which Hon. Patrick Fisher makes in his modern winery at Highwaymans Vineyard at Heath Barn Farm, Risby, near Bury St Edmunds in Suffolk. He took over the vineyard from Miss Merry Macrae whose niece he married. The vines were first planted here in 1974. Now the 24 acres incorporate the site of the mediaeval vineyard of the abbey of Bury St Edmunds. This was where the English barons gathered in 1214 to pledge unity over the articles of Magna Carta which the following year they presented to King John at Runnymede. Patrick Fisher's 'St Edmund' medium dry wine is a blend of the two white varieties, and is stocked by the Tesco supermarket chain who have now taken 14,000 cases of it and retail it at £2.59. From the Pinot Noir he makes a 'St Edmund' rosé.

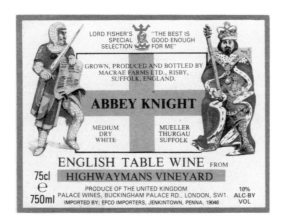 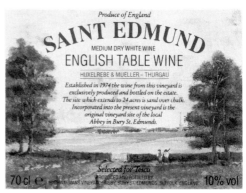

The location, if not the actual site, of the vineyard at Leeds Castle near Maidstone in Kent is also that of a mediaeval one, the '2 arpents of vines' planted by or for Bishop Odo of Bayeux, brother of William the Conqueror. It was recorded in the 1086 Domesday Book, as seen. The revived two-and-a-half-acre vineyard established by the Trustees of the Leeds Castle Foundation in 1980 produced its first crop in 1983 and was opened by Peter Walker MP, Minister of Agriculture. In 1984 the first 7,700 bottles of wine were made from a blend of the vineyard's Müller-Thurgau and Seyval-Blanc – 'light, crisp, medium dry'. It was not for public sale but kept for guests attending the conferences and other events for which this first Norman, stone-structured castle is now used.

THE ENGLISH WINE PRODUCERS

The owners of the 50 commercial vineyards who belong to the Weald and Downland Vineyards Association (formed in 1978), of whom the Leeds Castle Foundation are one, claim that South East England – Kent, Sussex and Surrey – is 'the premier wine producing area in the United Kingdom'. The infinitely varied landscape from the Downs of Surrey and Sussex to the Kentish Weald (the Garden of England) was at the hub of the vibrant renaissance of vine-growing in England.

> *Our diversity of soils and varieties, coupled with the lack of the rigid local restrictions that European producers have to work to, means that wine from the South East region cannot be categorised in the same way as one would say 'it is like Mosel wine' or 'it is like Chablis'. It is 'English Wine', different, and bursting with freshness and flavour.*

The association's commercial members account for nearly half the national acreage under vines and have never received less than half of the awards in national competition. One Kent grower, however, has no pretensions to commercial status, and that is Peter Springall who since 1982 has grown vines on his allotment in the Kent House Leisure Garden in Beckenham on the warm southern slopes of Crystal Palace. He came to appreciate wine when he was with the British Army in Cyprus. He persuaded his fellow allotment holders to follow his example, and now each of them grows enough grapes to make around 170 bottles of wine a year. In his shed in 1987 Peter Springall made 300.

Highly professional on the other hand is the operation started, as seen, by Stephen Skelton at Spots Farm, Small Hythe, Kent, in 1977. Tenterden Vineyards are today owned by Bill Garner and Derek Todd who in 1988 were offering a blend of Seyval-Blanc and Müller-Thurgau called 'Tenterden 1984'; 'Spots Farm Müller-Thurgau 1985'; 'Tenterden Special Reserve 1986', a more expensive wine aged in Limousin oak casks; and a 'Tenterden Rosé' made from Pinot Noir and the deep coloured Dunkelfelder. Stephen Skelton makes these personally in the newly designed winery opened in 1987.

At nearby High Halden, Susan and Laurence Williams claim that the site of their Harbourne Vineyard, 15 metres up but well protected from cold north winds, enables their largely Müller-Thurgau vines to take advantage of that part of the Garden of England's beneficial climate. Started as half an acre in 1980, it now covers three. 'The long growing season allows the grapes to assimilate the delicate flavours that are the hallmark of Harbourne wine,' they say. To add extra depth of flavour and perfect balance they add Seyval-Blanc to the blend, say, for piquancy, Reichensteiner for sugar, and Madeleine Angevine for body. They grow Regner and Ortega too, and red Pinot Meunier and Blue Portuguese.

'Harbourne' wine comes dry, 'with a lovely flowery bouquet and crisp clean finish'; medium dry, 'very fruity with a fine bouquet and a long finish'; and medium dry rosé, 'a delicate pink with an elegant taste and bouquet with just a hint of tannin in the finish'. The varieties which go into the blends vary from year to year. 'The weather may favour one variety over another in any given year, so we make our wine to a consistent style as much as the weather permits.'

We make our wine very carefully using as little machinery and chemicals as possible. We realise that in a modern world there is little place for traditional methods, but we try to combine the best of the old ways with modern knowledge – making, we hope, a better wine. Our wine-maker, trained in France, using continental grape varieties, produces superb wine which is totally English! We use old-fashioned basket hand-presses, glass fibre tanks and cold sterile bottling. The end product is 'Unqiue handmade wine from Harbourne'.

'No bubbles but bags of flavour and fruit with a dry finish,' is how Bill Ash describes the dry 1986 'Staple St James' Müller-Thurgau, single variety wine he was selling in 1988 along with a dry 'Staple St James' Reichensteiner 1987 and the slightly 'spritzig' medium dry 'Staple St James' Müller-Thurgau 1985. This estate-bottled wine is from his seven-acre Staple Vineyards near Canterbury. Bill reckons his wine can be drunk within a few months of bottling, but that it reaches its best after about 18 months to two years from the vintage date. The best characteristics decline after four or five years.

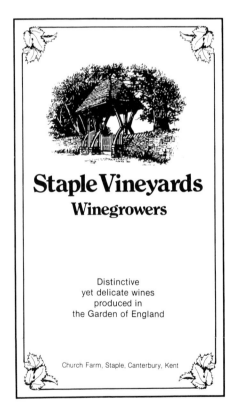

H. B. Smith and I. Winter, who in 1987 took over the two-and-a-half-acre Bardingley Vineyard at Hawkenbury which the late Harold Turner planted in 1979, offered a 1986 dry 'Bardingley Blend' of four varieties, Huxelrebe, Zweigelrebe, Reichensteiner and Seyval-

Blanc, but the other three white wines on sale in 1988 were all single varieties of the previous year, Seyval (medium), Huxelrebe (medium dry) and Zweigelrebe (medium dry). With Seibel and Pinot Noir they made 'Bardingley Estate Rosé', and with Leon Millot and Triomphe d'Alsace a 'Bardingley Blend Red', both 1987.

Jonathan Abbs produces a red wine from the Zweigelrebe grapes he grows on the Syndale Valley Vineyards he planted with Müller-Thurgau in 1977 at Newnham near Faversham, where there were all those ecclesiastical vineyards in the Middle Ages. He was not offering it for sale in 1988, but instead was selling his medium dry 'blush-coloured' Rosé blend, two medium dry single varieties Müller/Thurgau (1983 and 1986) and a 1986 medium dry Ortega/Wurzer blend. Not much Wurzer is grown in England, but even less Regner and Chasselas which Julia Bridgwater chose for the dry 'Conghurst' 1985 (medium dry) and 1986 and 1987 (dry) from her small vineyard near Hawkhurst. Her Müller-Thurgau/ Madeleine Angevine blend 1984 was medium dry.

'A taste of local luxury', is how Charles (ex-Army) and Jan (ex-WRNS) Galbraith describe the 'Tricorne Fine English White Wine' they produce from the three-and-a-half-acre Three Corners Vineyard they planted at Woodnesborough two miles from Sandwich in 1980. 'We did a lot of diligent research to find grape varieties which would make a fine wine slightly different from that available elsewhere', says Charles. Their brands are: 'Tricorne Siegerrebe', a connoisseur's dry wine of character; 'Tricorne Trocken', a blend of Reichensteiner and Siegerrebe, crisp and dry; and 'Tricorne Melange' a medium dry blend. James and Pat Wilkinson too claim that their Müller-Thurgau and Schönburger 'St Nicholas' wine which they make at their St Nicholas Vineyard at Ash near Canterbury has an appealing flowery bouquet not obtainable in hotter climates. 'Although the vines are German', says Pat, 'our pruning and training methods are French, as we feel that our climate is close to that of Champagne. Future plantings will include Pinot Noir and Pinot Meunier – most appropriate since

TRICORNE
FINE ENGLISH WHITE WINES

from

THREE CORNERS
VINEYARD

Canterbury is twinned with Rheims!' Their modern winery is housed in a charming old, slate-roofed barn.

Larger and older is the vineyard which Richard Barnes keeps at Little Whatmans, Biddenden near Ashford. Planted on a third-of-an-acre site in 1969, it now covers 22 acres in a shallow sheltered valley which were once apple orchards. He built himself a winery in 1975, and when Jack Ward decided to discontinue Merrydown's contract wine-making service at Horam, he took it over and ran it until recently with Kit Lindlar in charge, when they made some 120,000 bottles of other people's wine every year. He still has a few customers for wine-making however, such as H. I. H. Grant of Headcorn Flowers who has a 12-acre vineyard and produced a first 'Headcorn' wine in 1987.

On a five-year average Richard Barnes makes 36,000 bottles of his own 'Biddenden' wine each year in seven single variety, medium dry styles from his mainly Müller-Thurgau and Ortega but also Reichensteiner and Huxelrebe vines. He produces too a medium dry rosé; and what he calls 'a cheaper alternative to our varietal wine' and labels 'Biddenden Table Wine'. The label on the neck of his bottles shows the famous twelfth-century Siamese Twins Eliza and Mary Chulkhurst who, legend has it, lived in Biddenden village from 1100 to 1134. Less of a legend is the vineyard which according to parish records seems to have been kept on a piece of land at Biddenden close to Three Chimneys.

When the Gore-Brown Trophy toured Berlin, Hamburg, Frankfurt and Cologne in 1987 it was accompanied by bottles of 'Biddenden Ortega 1986' and others of Richard Barnes's making imported by Wolfgang Lehmann, Weinkontor of Nauheim, who organised this highly successful English Wine promotion tour.

For David Westphal of Penshurst Vineyards the German connection is not just commercial but ancestral. His great grandfather was a German who left home at the turn of the century, went to Australia, started making wine in the Hunter Valley and his grandfather became a much sought-after judge of wine for competitions. David's father Bob Westphal came to England with the Royal Australian Air Force in 1943 and became joint managing director of the pest control firm Rentokil. He bought The Grove at Penshurst in 1971 and when he retired the following year he planted two acres of Müller-Thurgau in the grounds, from which he had a first vintage of 200 bottles in 1975. With 14,000 bottles from a three-acre vineyard in 1976 he 'went commercial'. David, who had trained on the 50-acre family vineyard at Muswellbrook in Australia, took over Penshurst Vineyards from his father in 1979. He expanded them to 12 acres and added Reichensteiner, Scheureber, Seyval and Ehrenfelser vines from which he makes five or six single variety wines. They are compatible and could be blended, but since 1982 only varietal wines have been produced. Though none are 'sparkling' (which attracts more Excise Duty), a couple of 'Penshurst' wines have a slight 'spritz'. The scene on his wine label is from a 150-year-old print of Penshurst village, known widely as the location of the famous home of the Sidneys, Penshurst Place, looking down Rogues Hill. Hidden somewhere in the label is an Australian wallaby.

In 1981 David Westphal built his own winery at Penshurst and was able to put into practice the wine-making techniques he had been taught by Karl-Heinz Johner at Lamberhurst Vineyards.

Karl-Heinz Johner, for 12½ years wine maker at Lamberhurst Vineyards, who in June 1988 set up his own English Wine consultancy in Tenterden.

When Johner took over wine-making from Robert Reeves at Lamberhurst in 1975, Kenneth McAlpine had extended the eight and a half acres he had planted at Ridge Farm in 1969 to 30 acres. Lamberhurst Vineyards had established itself as a leader in English Wine production.

Johner's parents and grandparents were in wine. They had an eight-acre vineyard in Baden in which he had helped as a boy. If he had not had his pelvis broken by a run-away vineyard tractor, he had hoped to get away from wine and become a stockbroker. But after the accident he opted for an apprenticeship in viticulture. He spent three years at Geisenheim, followed by courses at the Baden and Weinsberg viticultural institutes. He was studying for ten years non-stop. He married and fathered two children. While waiting to hear the results of his final exams he met Reeves, who was on a viticultural study visit to Germany and told him of the English Wine exercise in Kent. English Wine? He could not resist going to have a look for himself. He could not speak a word of English but went to Lamberhurst for what was intended to be a three-month stay helping Reeves with the vintage and returning to Germany. But he was so intrigued by the potential of what he saw, with its impressive scale and patently ample resources, that when Kenneth McAlpine invited him to take up residence he accepted at once.

For him the secret of producing a drinkable wine, even in a miserable vineyard year, is to get the timing right. But, having got that right and then rushing the process can spoil any wine. The biggest killer is oxygen. If a vat is not filled to the top, air will attack the surface of the wine with fatal results. Conducting the process at the wrong temperatures can ruin the best grape juice. Most destructive of all is the wine-maker doing too much. 'Leave the stuff alone! That is what wine wants.'

In June 1988 Johner left Lamberhurst, where he had been wine maker for 12½ years, to set up his own consultancy in Tenterden. He soon secured contracts with Penshurst, Shawsgate and St George's Vineyards, and the new Piltdown and Wellow operations. 'English vineyards have come of age,' he said. 'England is now an established wine-making country. We can hold our heads high alongside the world's leading vineyards, and I see a great future for English Wine. More than ever before English vignerons are looking for world-class wine-making expertise and I feel that I am in a unqiue position to provide this service.' The latter includes inviting clients to visit his winery and vineyard in Baden where they can take part in the harvesting and wine-making under his supervision.

Stephen Skelton has taken over at Lamberhurst where Kenneth McAlpine now has the capacity to produce 500,000 bottles a year. Jon Alexander is still in charge of the vineyard, the consultancy and vineyard management service and the sale of vines and machinery. McAlpine produces 'Lamberhurst' wine from the grapes he grows at the Ridge Farm vineyard, now with 60 acres, and from grapes grown by others under his supervision, which he purchases by contract. The amount of wine produced each year varies from the 60,000 litres of 1987 to the 700,000 of 1983. In 1988 annual production was reckoned to be 250,000 bottles a year. In addition he does contract processing for a fee of grapes from other vineyards, whose owners take the wine, either in bottles or in bulk, bottle it themselves, and

Stephen Skelton, who in 1977 started Tenterden Vineyards at Spots Farm, and in 1988 took over as wine maker at Lamberhurst Vineyards.

Kenneth McAlpine, whose Lamberhurst Vineyards near Tunbridge Wells cover some 60 acres.

market it as their own brand with their name and the name of their wine on the label. He supplies 'own label' wine – as for the National Trust Ightham Mote Appeal and The Mary Rose Trust.

Lamberhurst Vineyards produce dry and medium dry white, single variety wine (which EEC regulations allow to be so called even if only 85 per cent of it is the single variety named on the label, and the other 15 per cent is something else). In a good year when there were plenty of grapes to press, they used to make a blend, which sold quickly, but in 1988 they were offering three 1986 dry Huxelrebe, Müller-Thurgau and Seyval-Blanc, and four medium dry of the latter plus Schönburger which is a cross between Pinot Noir and Pirovano 1, and Reichensteiner, a cross between Müller-Thurgau and Madeleine Angevine x Calabreser-Frohlich. In addition they were selling a medium dry rosé made from Pinot Noir and Seibel grapes having a 'lingering flavour with a hint of oak in the palate', and the 'Lamberhurst Brut' traditional method quality sparkling wine which has been developing for three years.

One of the first wines made by contract at Lamberhurst was for Peter Hall who in 1976

Breaky Bottom

Dry White Table Wine

Estate grown and bottled by Peter Hall
Breaky Bottom Vineyard, Rodmell, Sussex

Produce of United Kingdom

e 72cl

had a first crop from his six-acre Breaky Bottom vineyard at Northease near Lewes in the neighbouring county of East Sussex. He grows not only Müller-Thurgau, Seyval and Reichensteiner but some Loire grape varieties and a little Chardonnay.

Peter Hall now makes the wine himself in his own small winery, and puts it into distinctive Alsace-type bottles. David Allcorn, who runs Vats Wine Bar in Lambs Conduit Street in London and once headed The English Wine Centre at Alfriston, thinks 'Breaky Bottom' the best English Wine there is. Its excellence, he says, has much to do with Hall picking his fruit not on sugar levels but on acidity levels.

Ian and Andrew Paget planted some 5,000 Chardonnay vines as early as 1973 in the 13-acre vineyard, 250 feet up on Chills Down at Singleton near Chichester in West Sussex which they had opened, as seen, two years before. They scrubbed them however in 1979. The Müller-Thurgau and Reichensteiner survived, and Ian Paget's 'Chilsdown' wines for sale in 1988 were both white blends, the 1984 and 1986 vintages. Ian had put the vineyard on the market but then decided not to sell it after all. By 1988 there had been no buyers either for the 20-acre

Barnsgate Manor Vineyard, 500 feet up at Herons Ghyll near Uckfield, which had a lively acre of Chardonnay, since Pieroth Ltd put it up for sale in 1985. Ferdinand Pieroth of Burg Layen near Bingen in Germany bought the four-year-old vineyard from Willy Ross who had just brought his vines to maturity. After a grand re-opening, Barnsgate traded profitably from July 1980, but then domestic difficulties forced them to realise what assets they could and they tried to sell the whole estate for £750,000. While they waited for a buyer they recovered their position at home and lowered the asking price to £600,000. Richard Evans, their manager, decided to move elsewhere, and Pieroth appointed Martin Hoare. The hurricane destroyed their 1987 crop, but wine was made from the 1988 harvest.

In 1988 Pieroth were marketing 'Barnsgate Manor Vineyards Medium Sweet' 1985 and 1986 made with Chardonnay and 'Barnsgate Manor Vineyards Kerner 1983', a single variety dry wine which they billed as 'Our Wine of the Year'. The most expensive was 'Medium Oak Aged 1985' which had been six months in oak casks. The two 1984 blends of six grape varieties came medium dry and medium.

1983
BARNSGATE MANOR VINEYARDS
ENGLISH TABLE WINE
Estate produced and bottled at
BARNSGATE MANOR VINEYARDS at
Barnsgate Herons-Ghyll, nr. Uckfield, East Sussex 70 cl

Commander and Mrs E. G. Downer played safe with the well-tried Müller-Thurgau at Downers Vineyard in Fulking at the foot of the South Downs near Henfield. They planted three acres of it in 1976 and another three in 1977. So 'Downers' wine is willy-nilly single variety, and the 1985 vintage was so good it won the South East Wine of the Year Award of the Weald and Downland Vineyards Association. In 1988 they were selling this as well as the 1983 vintage which was dry and the 1984 which was slightly sweeter. Further along the South Downs under Ditchling Beacon, six miles from Brighton and 250 feet above the sea, lies the five-acre vineyard which David and Ann Mills planted in 1979 with Müller-

Thurgau, Reichensteiner and Ortega. They had their first wine in 1981 and are now making around 15,000 bottles a year, dry to medium dry and single variety.

The captain of a *Concorde* supersonic airliner Hector McMullen and his wife Beryl planted Seymours Vineyard on the edge of St Leonards Forest, Horsham's first, in 1981 with Seyval Blanc. They later added Kerner and Schönburger. Just before his retirement in 1985 Hector commanded the World Record Flight to Sydney and back, celebrating the achievement at Sydney airport with a bottle of 'Seymours Seyval'. The deer of their label is symbolic of the wild herds which still roam nearby St Leonards Forest.

'Berwick Glebe' and 'Alfriston Glebe' are the names of the estate grown quality wines which J. D. Broster and D. A. Birks produce from their two-acre Berwick Glebe Vineyard some seven miles from Eastbourne. They put down 2,000 Reichensteiner in 1980, but mostly Müller-Thurgau. A much larger operation, started a year earlier, takes place at the 14-acre Nutbourne Manor Vineyard which J. J. Sanger and David Shaw keep near Pulborough. They make four 'Nutbourne Manor' wines, single variety Müller-Thurgau, Reichensteiner, Huxelrebe and Schönburger.

Production of much of this Downland English Wine was doubtless inspired by the activities of Christopher Ann who planted The English Wine Centre Vineyard at Drusillas, Alfriston, in 1973 which today provides some of the grapes, along with others grown in Sussex, which go into the making of the medium dry 'Sussex County' wine. The grapes for his own 'Cuckmere' wine come from a single nearby vineyard whose entire crop he buys each year for this purpose.

The English Wine Centre

Still an inspiration to others too, both in Sussex and further afield, is Norman Cowderoy's five-acre Rock Lodge Vineyard at Scaynes Hill near Haywards Heath in the district famed for its Leveller Gooseberries. This evolved from a trial plot of 50 grape varieties in 1961 and the decision to plant 1,000 Müller-Thurgau in 1965. The first 'Rock Lodge' wine was made by a co-operative in 1970, and in 1976 Cowderoy had a winery built for himself. In 1988 he took over Ditchling Vineyard which also has five acres of established vines. Many of the early post-war English Wine exercises recorded in *A Tradition of English Wine* are, for a variety of reasons, no longer in existence to-day. But in spite of losing all his grapes in 1972 from a combination of wicked weather and vicious birds, Cowderoy has not only kept his vineyard and winery going but, after a quarter of a century, is still exploring new ways of making even better wine:

> *The latest stage in our continuing trials of different vine cultivars is the planting of some 25 white varieites and five red. These include some classic grape types which have not so far succeeded in England. We also have under trial some of the latest pruning techniques with a view to improving fruit quality and yield. In our winery we are concentrating on further development of wine with a distinctively English character by experimenting with different vinification methods. Our findings will be made available to other growers on a consultancy basis.*

In 1988 the Cowderoys' stock consisted of a medium dry 'Rock Lodge Müller-Thurgau 1986' and a dry 1985, a dry 'Rock Lodge Special Reserve 1986' and the 1987 medium dry Müller-Thurgau, awarded a bronze medal in the 1988 International Wine and Spirit Competition. Cowderoy could not have done what he has without the help of his wife Jennifer and his son David who, with a B.Sc. in Soil Science and Plant Nutrition from Wye College, went off to Australia and obtained a post-graduate diploma in viticulture and vinification at Roseworthy, the country's leading wine college. Bob Bryant, who came to Rock Lodge as Vine Dresser in 1967, still makes as big a contribution as ever. Adrian and James Cowderoy help too.

Not as old, but larger is John Sax's 35-acre Leeford Vineyards which he planted in 1982 at Whatlington near Battle. Sixteen acres of them were in full production in 1988 when he was producing his 'Saxon Valley' blend of Reichensteiner, Kerner and Huxelrebe. In 1989 he also had a 'Saxon Valley' dry, single variety Schönburger.

Such operations are no less professional for being family. At the centre of them is almost always a husband-and-wife team like Moira and William Gammell who run the Swiftsden Vineyard just outside Ticehurst – though property developer William's time, unlike retired shipbroker Norman Cowderoy's, is fully occupied elsewhere in the week. With only three and a half acres, which began as a row of 200 Müller-Thurgau at the top of the field in 1979, Moira sold Tesco the idea of stocking 'Swiftsden' as a second own-label English Wine in support of the Müller-Thurgau/Huxelrebe blend of which they had a reliable supply from the 24-acre Highwaymans Vineyard at Bury St Edmunds (of which they sold 30,000 bottles in 1987). Tesco took 400 cases (4,800 bottles) of 'Swiftsden' medium dry Müller-Thurgau/Reichensteiner blend in 1986. When their customers went for it with unexpected vigour, they came back for more – as much as the small vineyard could supply. That was erratic, to say the least. It produced 132,000 bottles in 1984, but only 1,200 in 1987. But the mostly female shoppers all over Britain had seen 'Swiftsden' alongside 'St Edmund' on the shelves of some 50 of the larger branches of the famous supermarket chain – more than half of it – and the demand for it has never fallen off. How did they come to select this English Wine from Sussex? Through a combination of tasting and being satisfied with the quality, said Claire Gordon-Brown, the firm's Wine Buying Executive.

Swiftsden Vineyard now produces two-thirds Müller-Thurgau and one-third Reichensteiner, with the gaps filled in with Schönburger and Huxelrebe. Moira also sells what wine she can to local shopkeepers and local publicans like Trevor and Shane Steed of *The Salehurst Halt* at Robertsbridge to supplement the 'Hackwood' Müller-Thurgau/Seyval blend they make from the nearby vineyard owned by John and Juliet Bidwell; and to Sheila Mitchell-Sadd of *Fuller's Arms* at Brightling who (before she sold up in May 1988) made a speciality of selling English Wine across the counter, both by the glass and bottle, such as Rosanne Sternberg's 'Bodiam Castle' which she produces from the Frenchay Farm vines.

But there is rarely much left over after she has fulfilled the fat 'central buying' order from Tesco's head office in Harlow – which Gay Biddlecombe of St George's Vineyard, Waldron, however, believes is not the market English Wine producers should aim for.

'I don't need to look for supermarket and pub business', says Mrs Biddlecombe. 'Not that I look down on either. But most publicans look for a quaffing wine for customers to drink with a Ploughman's Lunch of bread and cheese, not a top quality one like ours.'

> *I prefer to trade in more up-market establishments. I have created a rarity value for 'St George's' wine – a snob value, if you like. Exclusivity. I intend to continue that. The fact that you can't buy my wine in Tesco is to me a good point. I don't sell in thousands of bottles.*

She liked it when the *Financial Times* called her Müller-Thurgau 1984 'the quality end of the market', and the *Daily Telegraph* 'an English Wine worth shouting about.'

Gay Biddlecombe and her husband form another family team, though Peter Biddlecombe is away in the week running his PR consultancy in London, and the main burden of running the English Wine business falls on his wife, sister-in-law Ruth Robertson and an all-female band of helpers. The Biddlecombes were London journalists when they purchased the picturesque estate near Heathfield, 49 miles south of London, in 1979 and planted five acres with vines. They planted another 15 acres in 1985. 'Some people thought I was mad. I had saddled myself with a 15-hour day, seven days a week.' She was not a fruit farmer diversifying into viticulture. She had bought Cross Farm with its well preserved, eleventh-century tithe barn with the specific purpose of making a vineyard out of it, and she never allowed herself to be detracted. There are now 20 acres covered with 24,000 vines.

She stressed the Englishness of her wine by calling it 'St George's'. When she came to produce a pink wine with a slight sparkle from her Pinot Noir, Seibel and Black Hamburg red grapes matured in oak she called it 'Tudor Rose' – none of that rosé/rosay French nonsense! *Decanter* called it 'certainly better than any Anjou Rosé'.

She does not produce plonk, she says, but full-bodied wine with no artificial additives to destroy the natural flavours. Up to 1988 she had it made for her elsewhere, but in that year her purpose-built winery – the most modern in Britain? – was inaugurated on site and

A pony-trap drive around St George's Vineyard for a VIP visitor.

produced the 'St George's' 1989 vintage. She plans to extend her own acreage to feed the new winery's capacity, and to buy in grapes from other vineyards, as they do in France. She already 'manages' – that is, helps and advises – two other vineyards in Sussex and Kent, whose crops she buys, so long as they match the quality of her own grapes.

In 1988, apart from her Tudor Rose and the 'Domesday English Wine' which continued to be marketed after the 900th anniversary celebration, she was selling in her vineyard shop and elsewhere a medium dry Reichensteiner and two Müller-Thurgau 'St George's' wines, a dry and a medium dry.

A number of English vignerons eschew chemical fertilisers, weedkillers, fungicides and pesticides, and rely on FYM (farmyard manure). Roy and Irma Cook planted England's first organic vineyard in 1979 – Pine Ridge now called Sedlescombe Vineyard in East Sussex. Its seven acres today produce 5,000 bottles of wine a year. David Chapman has one of the same size near Wadhurst, Bewl Valley Vineyard. Peter and Michel Cleary started Spilsteads Vineyard near Sedlescombe on organic lines in 1984, and it will soon be 16 acres. Cultivation is done through WWOOF (Working Weekends on Organic Farms).

Müller-Thurgau was conspicuous by its absence on the shopping list of David and Linda Carr Taylor, another enduring husband and wife team, when they cautiously entered the

David and Linda Carr Taylor.

English Wine scene in 1971. Carr Taylor's father was an engineering tea planter in India in the nineteen-twenties. When he returned to England in 1947 he set up a heating and ventilating firm and purchased a Victorian mansion at Westfield near Hastings where his son was brought up. At the end of the nineteen-sixties, now a qualified engineer and running his father's business, Carr Taylor was concerned that no better use was being made of the 21 acres of farmland at Westfield. He lost money on growing wheat, contemplated garlic, mushrooms, roses and sugar beet, but was persuaded by German viticulturist Hermut Becker to make them into a vineyard.

Make English Wine you mean?

Most Europeans were warning people off. 'You can't do it in England, *mon vieux*. You have neither the climate nor the expertise. Why bother?'

But bothering had been the secret of his success with the family firm, and he saw in intensive, sustained bothering the only hope of surmounting the real and assumed obstacles that everyone told him in 1971 lay in the way of anyone fool enough to think he could make money out of English Wine. Hence the caution. Before he engaged top gear he embarked on a four-year trial to discover which vines to plant. Not just a dozen or so but 57 different German and French varieties.

Making English Wine in the 1980s is sophisticated and professional, and uses the latest equipment, representing a big investment – typical crushing (above) and bottling (centre) plant at the Carr Taylor winery, and (below) Clement Novak from Epernay making the vineyard's sparkling wine.

I consider myself a new style of commercial English Wine maker. It was my engineer's approach to problem-solving that made me realise that you start with the end product, then work out how to get there. The mistake that so many made was to concentrate on the agricultural side without defining the end product.

For him most of the Müller-Thurgau English Wine he tasted was much too dull. Fifteen years after the first proper planting of 1973 he has some 15 varieties to handle, both from his own 21 acres and from the 180 acres of grapes grown by farmers under contract as an alternative crop on spare land within 30 miles of Westfield. But he is only just getting into his stride.

I want to extend into other varieties which will grow perfectly well in southern England, such as Chardonnay. There will soon be a whole range of generic styles of English Wine with different floral tastes – 'mangoish', 'elder-flowerish'. At Carr Taylor Vineyards we are trying to introduce a bit of style into wine. We have been fed for many decades by austere, neutral French wine, very woody and very alcoholic. What I want to try and break away into is rather delicate, subtle flavours and essences with an appealing, individual style not found on the Continent but peculiar to England. We now know what we are doing. We can do what the Europeans so long said we could never do. Even in 1986 and 1987, when we had perhaps two of the worst winters and summers ever, we have survived and produced economic crops.

The Europeans are regretting their hasty prognostications. The international sales manager of Miguel Torres of Barcelona, 'wine-growers since the seventeenth century', put the bottle of Carr Taylor wine which David sent them into a blind tasting. In February 1988 he sent a letter of congratulation. None of his tasting panel had guessed it had been made in England. In the palate they thought it 'gentle, fruity, good, citric, well balanced, silky, mango, pleasantly light bitter after taste'. France took 2,000 cases of 'Carr Taylor' wine in 1986; Germany 1,000 cases; Canada 1,000.

On sale in England in 1988 were a dry, a medium dry and a medium single variety Schönburger, Gutenborner and Reichen-steiner; a dry Kerner Huxel blend; a medium blend of five grape varieties from the Westfield vineyard 'Hastings Table Wine', and a medium dry blend 'Sussex County'. He also offered for the fourth year in succession his pink 'Carr Taylor Sparkling Wine', described as 'a carefully selected blend, bottle-fermented in the traditional *méthode champenoise*' of which, with the help of Clement Nowak of Fleurie-la-Riviere, Epernay, he made 30,000 bottles. 'It looks like champagne,

it smells like champagne,' said the *Daily Express* of the first vintage, 'and by golly it even tastes like the stuff!'

Fine tasting wine deserves tasteful presentation.

A flowery style of the kind David and Linda Carr Taylor are developing in Sussex is also the aim of Michael and Betty Bache of Astley Vineyards at The Crundels near Stourport-on-Severn in Worcestershire. After experimenting with 15 varieties on half an acre between 1971 and 1975 they planted five acres in 1979 on three sites some 180 feet up. They had two single variety wines on sale in 1988, a medium dry 'Astley Kerner 1984', probably the first from this new-to-England grape, and a dry 'Astley Madeleine Angevine 1985' – 'reminiscent of a fine Gewürztraminer'. In addition there were two blends, a medium 'Astley Severn Vale 1984' and a medium 'Astley Huxelvaner 1986' which is from Huxelrebe and Müller-Thurgau. The Bache family produced 23,000 bottles in 1984, a bumper year.

John Wingfield Digby reckons his yield has averaged 5,000 bottles a year from his three-acre vineyard which is part of his 750-acre corn and dairy farm at Wake Court, Bishops Caundle near Sherborne in Dorset. He and his wife grow seven varieties of grape and produce two dry white wines, both blends, 'Wake Court Bacchus Reichensteiner' and 'Wake Court Schönburger Seyval'. From their Pinot Noir grapes they produce a sparkling wine and from their Leon Millot a red wine, but these are for their own consumption.

One-time naval officer Bernard Theobald markets all the red wine he makes from the

Michael and Betty Bache in the centre of their Astley Vineyards near Stourport in Worcestershire.

Pinot Noir he grows at his Westbury Vineyard at Purley near Reading in Berkshire. When he brought it out in 1975 he claimed it to be the first commercial red wine to be made in England since 1914. The 'Westbury Pinot Noir 1984' was not on his 1988 list however, though he still had the lower yield 1986 vintage which produced 'a superior wine, fit to walk in exalted company' priced at £7.50. Alongside this, at a modest £2.30 was what he called 'Purley Red Non-Vintage', made from a blend of red grapes, and 1985 rosé at £2.95. The twelve other wines on his 1988 list were white, four single variety – Reichensteiner 1983, Müller-Thurgau 1985 and 1986, and Seyval 1986 – and four blends of two of these.

Bernard Theobald started Westbury Vineyard in 1970 as part of a 200-acre dairy farm, now covering 16 acres, a third of which are planted with red grapes. He produced 100,000 bottles of red and white in 1983 and 70,000 in 1984. Because of his resilience and the aid he gets from Helen Tarry his wine maker, Simon Parker and the band of helpers known as Theobald's Casual Women, the amount of English Wine that emerges from Westbury Vineyard each year is maintained at a high level.

Cliff Sentance's worry is not physique, but foxes who eat his grapes and deer who nibble his vine shoots. Otherwise his vineyard at Lymington on the Hampshire coast is well protected from all other enemies of viticulture, being only 50 feet above sea level and, as he

Bernard Theobald with his 'Casual Women', harvesting the crop at Westbury Vineyard near Reading in Berkshire.

says, 'bathed in reflected light from the sea'. He planted it in 1979 on ground where the previous owner had grazed old and sick donkeys and known as the Donkey Field. He now has six acres of grapes from which he produces an excellent 'Lymington' wine. A few miles further inland visitors to Beaulieu Palace and Abbey can buy bottles of the 'Beaulieu' wine produced by Lord Montagu from the vineyard in the grounds tended by Alan Baker. In 1979 he renewed the older half of the six-acre vineyard over the next four years. It now consists of 60 per cent Müller-Thurgau with Reichensteiner and Huxelrebe and a small amount of Seyval Blanc and red varieties Seibel and Zweigeltrebe. Almost all the wine is bought by visitors, or at local hotels.

Most of the wine produced by the other Hampshire operation, Hambledon Vineyard, goes to the new proprietor John Patterson's Drinks Wine Bar in Abingdon Road, Kensington, although some of it is exported. The vineyard which was no. 1 in 1951 in the English Wine Revival, to be followed by the Beaulieu Vineyard planted by Margaret Gore-Brown, was sold by Lady Salisbury-Jones and her son Raymond in 1986. Patterson, who runs Dateline, a computer 'dating' agency, doubled the size of the vineyard to 15 acres, and with the aid of Bill Carcary (and his wife Vicky), whom Sir Guy engaged as vineyard manager in 1966, produces about 10,000 bottles of 'Hambledon' dry white wine in his brand new winery every year. It is a blend of Pinot Noir, Pinot Meunier, Chardonnay and Seyval. In 1982 Sir Guy planted an area of Auxerrois.

Hambledon – The Home of English Wine and the Cradle of Cricket 1777

England's first commercial vineyard was planted at Hambledon in 1951. The chalky soil there is similar to that of the Champagne region and produces a light, dry wine from a blend of Chardonnay, Pinot Meunier and Seyval grapes.

Sir Guy Salisbury-Jones's Hambledon Vineyard, planted in 1952, is still producing a crop under new ownership in the shadow of the famous eighteenth-century Hambledon Cricket Club on the other side of the valley.

Pinot Meunier and Zweigeltrebe go into the 'Hillgrove' rosé and Triomphe d'Alsace into the 'Hillgrove' red wine made in his own winery by Christopher Hartley of Meon Valley Vineyard at Swanmore near Southampton. He planted his first vines in 1977 on a plot used for growing early strawberries. He had had training in cider making at Long Ashton Research Station in Bristol and made his first wine in 1982. Apart from the red and rosé, the 'Hillgrove' range of white wines of 1988 were a 1983 medium dry blend of Müller-Thurgau, Madeleine Angevine and Seyval-Blanc; a 1984 medium dry blend of Müller-Thurgau and Seyval-Blanc only, and a 1984 blend of Pinot Meunier and Chardonnay. There were also three single variety wines, a dry Müller-Thurgau and a dry Madeleine Angevine, both 1984, and a medium Seyval Blanc of 1985.

Robert Kinnison called the two-acre vineyard he planted in 1973 at South Gorley near Fordingbridge 'Four Kings' after England's four Norman-French rulers who owned the New Forest which it abuts. His 'Four Kings' medium dry white wine however is made from three German or Swiss grapes, Reichensteiner, Huxelrebe and Müller-Thurgau. Müller-Thurgau grapes from their vineyard at Ringwood are the main variety which Michael and Wendy Baerselman put into their 'Aldermoor' medium dry and medium white wine. They planted a trial one and three quarter acres in 1975, and today Aldermoor Vineyards cover five acres. They added a few Reichensteiner to make a blend. The same two are blended to form the dry 'Court Lane Vineyard' white wine produced by S. A. Flook at Ropley near Alresford. From the vines he planted in 1979 on two sites, he had his first vintage in 1983.

He also grows Huxelrebe which he blends with Reichensteiner to make a second white wine which is medium dry.

Many followed in the footsteps of Kenneth Barlow and have benefited from his 1965 research which told him the Isle of Wight was the sunniest place in southern England. He made his first commercial vintage of 30,000 bottles, as seen, in 1970, and in a good year now makes 70,000 bottles of his 'Adgestone' English Estate Bottled White Wine from his 28 acres of Reichensteiner, Huxelrebe and Müller-Thurgau at Sandown near the remains of the Roman villa at Brading. 'Adgestone' is a blend of all three. Anyone who has never had the opportunity to visit the Isle of Wight can always order a bottle when next dining at The Savoy – or the refurbished Dorchester when it re-opens.

Ken Barlow goes grape harvesting astride his tractor at his 28-acre vineyard on the Isle of Wight, where he has been producing 'Adgestone' wine since 1970.

Anthony and Alix Goddard took themselves to the Isle of Wight ten years after Ken Barlow had settled into Adgestone. In 1976 they acquired ancient Barton Manor at Whippingham, East Cowes, noted in the Domesday Survey of 1086, and the following year planted a six-acre vineyard which in 1988 had grown to ten acres with another five planned. From the winery they had built in rehabilitated outbuildings, they were soon producing an average of 20,000 bottles of a wine which was to be ordered for the table of Buckingham Palace and the royal yacht *Britannia*. They grew the well-tried quartet of Müller-Thurgau, Seyval-Blanc, Huxelrebe and Reichensteiner, plus Gewürztraminer (from 1982) and Schönburger. In 1988 blends of these constituted the two 1986 white wines on sale. When the demand for 'Barton Manor' wine began to outstrip production, Goddard bought the output of two of the Isle of Wight's other vineyards and was able to offer in addition a medium 'Wight Wine'. His medium rosé with a raspberry flavour is made from Zweigeltrebe and Seyval.

Currently chairman of the English Vineyards Association, having taken over from Colin Gillespie in 1987, 41-year-old Anthony Goddard is an accountant and the Treasurer of the Wine Guild of the United Kingdom.

The single acre vineyard 450 feet high which C. P. M. Craig-McFeely and J. F. Edginton planted on the mainland at Fonthill Gifford near Tisbury in Wiltshire in 1975 has grown to 13½ acres on a regular programme of development. To the familiar trio of German white varieties, they added five less than familiar red grapes: Dunkelfelder, Seibel, Leon Millot, Zweigeltrebe and Maréchal Foch. They believe they have 8,200 white grape vines and 1,200 red ones, from which they produce a dry single variety 'Fonthill' Seyval, a medium dry and a medium blend of the trio and a 'Fonthill' rosé, a blend of all the red and white grapes.

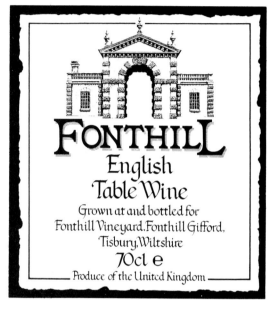

For the wine of another Wiltshire vineyard, Douglas Mann and Mark Thompson blend Müller-Thurgau with Bacchus grapes which, they say, results in 'a rich, complex wine with a buttery nose and a fresh appley taste'. These two began planting the vines of the Chalkhill Vineyard by the village of Bowerchalke in the Chalke Valley near Salisbury between 1980 and 1982. They now cover six and a half acres. Their single variety 'Chalkhill Bacchus 1984' on sale in 1988 has a strong Sauvignon-like bouquet, they say, and a sharp gooseberry flavour. Their 1988 list includes a single variety 'Chalkhill Müller-Thurgau 1984' and 'Chalkhill Chalke Valley', a blended wine.

Mark Thompson is steering Chalkhill Wines, the partnership he formed with Douglas Mann in 1986, in a very definite direction:

The trend in wine consumption today is towards light white wine showing good fruit character balancing dryness. The further up the market in terms of price, the more sharply defined these features are. Though there is the potential to produce such wine in England, it is not always possible to do so. So the producer has to settle for a higher volume, lower priced 'branded' wine, aimed at the middle market which looks for easy-drinking, medium-dry wine. This creates a premium for higher priced dry wine, the 'wine for the connoisseur' whose label never carries the give-away medium sweet or medium dry definition which identifies it as a Table Wine.

Mark Thompson's father is a Master of Wine; Mark himself has a Ph.D. degree from Bath University in Plant Biochemistry and took a three months' course in wine-making in California. As the wine maker of Chalkhill Wines he is anxious to make it clear that all 'English Wine' is not of one quality, to harden the somewhat blurred line between high quality and not-so-high quality English Wine. He aims to make it plain by stating on the label that the former is single variety, dry, estate-bottled (that is *made* in the vineyard's own winery) – 'Chalkhill Estate-Bottled Bacchus' at £4 – and the latter a regional, medium dry blend (in the way the Germans offer a Nahrsteiner or a Rheinstessen) labelled 'Wessex English Table Wine'. This would be made from the grapes grown in half a dozen vineyards in West Hampshire, South Wiltshire and East Dorset. It would make no bones about being less-than-high quality and for that reason being sold at less-than-high price, but thoroughly drinkable. The regional blend makes it suitable for being bottled for specific customers who would put their own label on it – like, for instance, the Bath Festival.

In all this Mark's thinking is in line with Christopher Ann's of Drusillas who makes it clear that his 'Cuckmere' is superior to Table Wine in so far as it is made of grapes of a single variety from a single vineyard, and his 'Sussex English Wine' is a blend of Sussex grapes which costs less. For Mark the danger lies in English Wine which has won itself a certain credibility in the eyes of the Wine Trade losing that credibility because of producers' inability to maintain not only the quantity of supply but consistent quality, and their liability to raise prices to maintain their income when there is a bad grape crop.

Given that irregular cropping will always be a feature of viticulture in England, any successful producer must be able to show the ability to regulate stock levels and cash flow through co-ordinated marketing. I see the pattern of production eventually changing in this country to a number of established large producers supplementing their own crop by buying in grapes from smaller growers who do not wish to compete in the market, or are unable to do so.

With many newly planted vineyards coming into production in the next few years, the total amount of English Wine on the market will continue to increase even if we have a succession of poor summers. To ensure credibility the larger producers should encourage the move towards the system widely practised on the Continent of grape growers supplying these producers.

That would prevent a multitude of new labels appearing on the market, and giving consumers an even more confused image of English Wine.

Dr Kit Morris has similar views. In charge of wine-making at Tom Day's Three Choirs Vineyards, Rhyle House, Newent in Gloucestershire, he too appreciates the need to produce and identify two qualities. His only dry wine on sale in 1988, however, was a blend, 'Three Choirs Seyval Reichensteiner 1984'. With a 'crisp gooseberry/apple tang', it is £10 more expensive per case than his 'Three Choirs' medium (1985) and medium dry (1986) blends. The other high quality 'Three Choirs Huxelrebe Late Harvest 1984' is single variety 'intense, rich honey nose with powerful melon palate', but labelled medium and not dry because the grapes were affected by Noble Rot and gave a rare concentration of fruity flavour and sweetness. The fifth 'Three Choirs' wine on sale in 1988, and the least expensive, was the blend they called 'Winemasters Selection 1984' available in dry and medium ('redolent of lush ripe melons').

Kit Morris says that by bottling his wine cold in March he gives it the pleasing prickle on the tongue which he calls 'a slight petillance'. Be that as it may, in 1987 the South West Vineyards Association made him the best wine maker of the year by awarding him their Eric Coates Trophy.

'"Three Choirs" and other people's English Wine are sometimes regarded as rather expensive,' says Tom Day, who is managing director of Three Choirs Vineyards Limited.

That is because they are quality wine. All of them are highly individual, made with great patience, care and attention to quality control. As quality wine it does not set out to compete with mass-produced wine like Liebfraumilch. Rather, English Wine should be judged against estate-bottled wine from Alsace or the Loire or Moselle, with which they compare favourably in price and quality.

Tom Day, who makes 'Three Choirs' wine at Newent in Gloucestershire, which is said to have all the exuberance of Chaucer and the elegance of Elgar.

Day is an apple man from Kent, whom one time racing car driver Alan McKechnie in 1973 engaged to manage his Newent apple farm and replace half an acre of it with vines. More and more apple trees were replaced until today the vineyard covers 20 acres. The name 'Three Choirs' reflects the vineyard's proximity to Gloucester, Hereford and Worcester in one of whose cathedrals takes place the famous annual Three Choirs musical festival. It once inspired a local newspaper to describe its wine as possessing 'all the exuberance of Chaucer yet with the elegance of Elgar'.

When Alan McKechnie put his farm, vineyard and winery up for sale in 1984, Tom Day formed a consortium to buy it. Most of his vines are Müller-Thurgau and Reichensteiner, but he is also growing Huxelrebe, Seyval-Blanc, Schönburger and Bacchus. With his Pinot Noir he has produced an 'Onion Skin' tinted rosé.

Keith James is one of those who concentrates on producing a dry wine from his mainly Reichensteiner grapes at the Broadfield Court Vineyard he has at Bodenham in Herefordshire. Bodenham wine matures well in the bottle, he says. After a few months it settles down and develops over a number of years. 'Vintages of the early eighties are still drinking well which says much for their fundamental quality.' He thinks his dry wine should be compared with French wine from the Loire Valley, and not the sweeter wine from Germany. He also produces medium dry wine with its own distinctive flavour and quality 'reflecting the wonderful site and soil at Broadfield'.

I started Broadfield for fun in 1971 with 50 vines, but with the general decline in farming the vineyard has become a very important department. I now grow vines on 12 acres and in the coming years it is likely to gather pace. We seem to have a unique site where the micro-climate yields fully ripe grapes even in the poorest summer. The drawback is that the grapes are extremely small, so our wine yield is proportionately reduced. It is because of this consistent ripening that we have concentrated on the production of genuinely dry wine – Reichensteiner and Huxelrebe – and only recently expanded to medium dry – a blend 'Bodenham Vintage Selection' and a single variety 'Bodenham Seyve Villard'.

In a *Decanter* magazine competition 'Bodenham Reichensteiner Dry 1983' was judged second out of 60 entries. Justerini & Brooks stock it, as well as the medium Seyve Villard.

Mark Capper gets a dry fresh wine from his 11 acres of Müller-Thurgau at his Stocks Vineyard at Suckley in Worcestershire which he planted in 1972. Since 1975 he has produced around 30,000 bottles a year. The 'Croffta' wine which John Bevan produces from the Müller-Thurgau and Seyval-Blanc grapes he grows at his vineyard in Wales is also dry. Croffta Vineyard is at Groes-Faen, Pontyclun in mid-Glamorgan near where Andrew Pettigrew and Lord Bute had their vineyard outside Cardiff at Castle Coch. He planted two acres in 1975 and subsequently added some Madeleine Angevine.

David and Fiona Ealand regard the Romans as their predecessors in the Hambleden Valley at Henley-on-Thames in Oxfordshire where they planted what had been a three-acre wheat field with vines in 1982. They chose vines in preference to pick-your-own vegetables and fruit which had been suggested but which they considered too labour-intensive and unexciting. Livestock was too risky; tulips were fun but disliked the chalky soil; rhubarb was potentially profitable but too much of a marketing headache. 'So we thought if the Romans saw fit to grow vines on the Chiltern slopes overlooking the Thames Valley nearly 2000 years ago,' said David Ealand, 'we would do the same.'

> *I read every book I could find on the subject; talked to as many people I could find who were making English Wine and tasted their product. I went off to Germany and spoke to the experts at the Geisenheim Institute, saw Davis in California and people in the Institute of Oenology in Bordeaux. I tested the soil to make sure it was compatible with vine rootstock. We were 538 feet up. Would the weather tell against us? Local weather reports of the last 25 years told us 'no'. The field was well drained. So that was that. I put in a row of Italian alder as a windbreak and erected a deer fence in the autumn of 1981 and the next spring planted the first Bacchus, Reichensteiner and Madeleine Angevine. Old Luxters Vineyard was in business.*

David Ealand continued his full-time activity in London as the partner in a City law practice in international maritime law, but managed to set up his own winery and bottling plant in time to handle the first 'Chiltern Valley' vintage in 1984. They sold 8,000 bottles of it with little difficulty. Despite the bad summers of 1986 and 1987 Old Luxters Vineyard produced 40,000 bottles in each of those years, luckily harvesting just a week before the hurricane of the latter year.

An 'own label' design by David Ealand for the Victoria and Albert Museum.

Since then we have expanded the winery to a present throughput of some 90,000 bottles a year. Our temperature-controlled bottle store can now take around a quarter of a million. After the 8,000 bottles of 1984 and again in 1985, which were sold out within six months, production has increased annually to approximately 35,000 to 45,000 bottles, with a scheduled increase on present acreage to around 200,000 bottles annually. Since 1984 we have been wholly or substantially responsible for the establishment of some 15 other vineyards in the locality totalling about 50 acres, most of which is or will be grown for us.

In 1988 Old Luxters Vineyard of Hambleden were offering four types of their 1986 vintage: 'Chiltern Valley Special Cuvée', medium sweet; 'Chiltern Valley Medium Dry'; 'Chiltern Valley Dry'; and the more expensive 'Old Luxters Reserve' of 1987 described as 'dryish' and put in the new 75-centilitre bottle as all English Wine now has to be. In view of his weektime work in London, David Ealand has been unable to pursue an active marketing campaign, but he has been approached by Justerini & Brooks and Corney & Barrow who for two years now have marketed 'Chiltern Valley' and several others nationally.

Barnsgate and Old Luxters have flourished in spite of both being more than 500 feet above sea level, but Anthony Skuriat has matured grapes successfully at his Eglantine Vineyard at Costock in Nottinghamshire though he believes it to be 'the most northerly producing commerical vineyard in the world'. When Dr R. Smart heard of his wine he asked for samples of it to be sent to a tasting at the Second International Symposium for Cool Climate Viticulture and Oenology in New Zealand. Eglantine Vineyard was planted as half an acre in 1980 and has since been expanded to 3.3 acres. It has Madeleine Sylvaner, Siegerrebe, Seyval, Müller-Thurgau, Seibel and Triomphe D'Alsace vines. 'In addition', says Anthony, 'we have more than 80 different varieties imported from far-away places including Ontario, New York, British Columbia and even Japan.'

Being 300 feet high has been no handicap to Christopher Woosnam Mills, once a tea planter in Ceylon, who started what is now the five-and-a-half-acre Castle Cary vineyard in Somerset in 1979. 'Castle Cary Madeleine Angevine 1986' and his Müller-Thurgau/Seyval blends of 1984, 1985 and 1986, though not on the Waitrose central buying list, are to be found in several of that group's West Country stores, and at the London Hilton.

When Michael Jopling MP, Minister of Agriculture, attended the meeting of European Community Agricultural Ministers in Cumbria in 1986, he was presented with a case of dry 'Wootton Seyval 1985'.

The gift of the English Vineyards Asociation, it had won the gold medal in their English Wine of the Year competition. In accepting it Mr Jopling said the wine was an example of the high quality of production at the 250 or so commercial vineyards in England and Wales.

When my colleagues taste it they will realise that the English Wine industry has been going through a renaissance in the past few years, and is now able to produce wine of a very high standard. I think the emphasis on quality in English and Welsh wine-making is very commendable as there is a good market for high quality wine in this country and overseas.

Major Colin Gillespie planted his vineyard at North Wootton, Shepton Mallet, in the foothills of the Mendips in Somerset in 1971, as seen. No vines had ever grown there before. The risk, as he saw it, was not only in the uncertainty whether the vines would ripen the grapes but whether the soil would produce wine of character. 'After several vintages it became clear that the ground and local microclimate produced a delicious, high quality wine.' He increased the area to six acres. He makes the wine himself. He started slowly in 1971 by buying grapes from abroad and making wine from them a ton at a time to get used to handling them. He had Angelo Pizzi the wine maker at nearby Pilton Manor explain the rudiments to him; he talked to all and sundry who had had any experience in it; he read every book on the subject he could lay his hands on. He agrees with those who say let Nature take over, but 'you have to know when things don't look right'. A wine maker has to

The Manor House, Pilton   Griffin '73

know what he is doing when handling sulphur dioxide, and make sure he has the right yeast working for him.

Colin Gillespie has gained a wealth of experience from making wine with a large variety of grapes sent to him by some 15 other vineyards. He once thought of doing it all on a co-operative basis with local farmers providing him with the grapes. He dreamt of setting up a full-blown, French-style winemaking co-operative, but the local farming community showed no interest whatsoever. 'They produce milk, cheese and butter in Somerset, and the thought that God should have provided fields for anything other than cows is anathema.'

Colin Gillespie's vineyard which he planted at North Wootton, Shepton Mallet, in the foothills of the Mendips in Somerset in 1971.

In 1988 the Wootton range of English Wine on sale consisted of: a medium dry 'Wootton Müller-Thurgau 1984' (full flavoured spicy); and a medium 'Wootton Müller-Thurgau 1986' (strong bouquet, long aftertaste). He also sold what little remained of his 'Wootton Seyval 1986' which he considered a worthy successor to the prize-winning 1985 vintage.

Angelo Pizzi to whom Colin Gillespie went for instruction on wine-making had been engaged by Nigel de Marsac Godden two years after he purchased Pilton Manor, also in Shepton Mallet, in 1964. From 1966 to 1968, on the site of the twelfth-century vineyard of the monks of Glastonbury, Nigel planted Müller-Thurgau and Seyval-Blanc vines over an area which has since grown to 22 acres. Pizzi made a pale dry, single variety Müller-Thurgau in 1969 which was given the Gold Seal of Quality at an international wine tasting for the Best English Wine. The consensus of opinion was that it could not be a French wine in that it did not have the crisp and flinty characteristics of a Chablis. It could not possibly be an Alsace because it did not have the heaviness and fruitiness characteristic of the area. They thought it closest to a Moselle but it seemed to have more body and fruit than expected of the area. But they all pronounced it excellent.

Even drier than this was his pale, slightly scented Seyval-Blanc. From Pilton Manor in 1975 came the first English Sparkling Wine, a blend of Müller-Thurgau and Seyval Blanc, which Godden called 'De Marsac' after his great grandmother Marguerite Comtesse de Marsac who was the lover of Frederick Prince of Wales who died before he was able to succeed his father George II on the throne of England.

Nigel Godden sold the Pilton Manor Vineyard in January 1987 to J. M. Dowling who in 1988 offered three wines: a 1986 single variety 'Pilton Manor Müller-Thurgau' both 1985 and 1986; and a medium 'Pilton Manor Non-Vintage Blend'.

Midway between Glastonbury and Bridgwater below the Polden Hills, Tom Rees of Moorlynch Vineyard, Somerset's largest, makes two not-so-common single variety wines 'Moorlynch Wurzer' and 'Moorlynch Schönburger'. Tom and Judith Rees planted their first vines in 1981 and today they have 12 varieties of white and two of red grape (Blauberger and Cabernet Sauvignon) over 12 acres. In white, apart from Müller, Reichensteiner, Seyval, Huxelrebe and Madeleine Angevine, they grow Wurzer, Schönburger, Faber, Findling, Optima, Bacchus and Regner. In 1988 they started planting another four acres of Findling and Seyval.

They still had a few bottles of the 'Moorlynch Medium Dry White 1984' at the end of 1987, as well as their medium sweet and their dry of 1985. These were blends of Madeleine Angevine, Müller-Thurgau and Seyval. On sale in 1988 too were five 1986 vintages, medium, medium-dry and dry blends; and two single varieties, a medium-dry Schönburger and a new dry Faber.

Gallows feature for the second time on an English Wine label for 'Manstree' wine which Mr and Mrs Gerry Symons produce at Shillingford St George at Haldon Hill near Exeter.

On blasted heath and brackened bank
　Where sheep were wont to graze:
By where the gallows used to clank
　Now grape's the crop to raise.

Once high above the close cropped grass
　A dead man danced on air,
Where now through ordered rows men pass
　To reap a harvest rare.

No longer from the manstree's bough
   There droops the hangman's noose:
A sweeter sign is hanging now,
   With wines for all to choose.

Lie lads they hanged for stealing sheep
   In those unhallowed fields,
And from the plot where they now sleep
   The vine its amber yields.

Since loathsome lag and lightfoot land
   To dust alike must pass,
Such resurrection makes me glad;
   Both end up in the glass!!

JO HUNT

Jo Hunt, President of the Housman Society thus adapted a verse from *A Shropshire Lad* – Gerry Symons is A. E. Housman's great nephew. A 30-acre field still called Manstree was where they once hanged sheep stealers. From Manstree Vineyard today comes a fruity, medium dry 'Manstree' white wine, and a dry version. The varieties which they blend for these include the regulars plus Chardonnay, and soon they will be able to put in some Bacchus and Schönburger.

Most of Devon's vineyards are small, but all are thriving and adventurous. On his four-acre Loddiswell Vineyard at Kingsbridge, planted in 1977, R. H. Sampson produces 12 tons of grapes most years which give him 12,000 bottles of wine blended from Müller-Thurgau, Reichensteiner and Huxelrebe, plus Siegerrebe and Bacchus. Triomphe d'Alsace and Leon Millot were planted by Richard and Ann Trussell along with Madeleine Angevine and a few Reichensteiner in the vineyard they created at Whitmoor House in the Culm Valley at Ashill near Cullompton. They now make a medium dry blend from their two-and-a-half-acre site first planted in 1981 at half that size. Even smaller are Whitstone Vineyards at Bovey Tracey which two Americans established in 1974 on the edge of Dartmoor. Laura and George Barclay have been living in England now for 20 years. They made 24 bottles of wine in 1978 from their Müller-Thurgau and Madeleine Angevine grapes, but picked 12 tons of grapes in 1984 and made 12,000 bottles. All the wine they had to sell in 1988 was dry, two single variety Müller-Thurgau 1985 and 1987; two single variety Madeleine Angevine, 1985 and 1987; and a 1986 blend of the two.

The annual wine contests for which most of these Devon vignerons enter are organised for the South West Vineyards Association by its secretary, one of the most experienced operators in the English Wine scene, Gillian Pearkes, who laid out her own Yearlstone Vineyard at Chilverton near Coldridge, Crediton, in 1976. She makes two single variety white wines, a 'Yearlstone Madeleine Angevine' 'with a bouquet that can be likened to wild

THE VINEYARDS OF ENGLAND'S WEST COUNTRY

THE SOUTH WEST VINEYARDS ASSOCIATION

spring flowers', and a 'Yearlstone Siege-rrebe' which is medium dry 'with a bouquet like fresh peaches'. She has a limited supply of 'Yearlstone Special Reserve Chardonnay'. 'The discovery of two old, early ripening French vine varieties producing black grapes,' says Gillian without revealing what they are, 'has enabled a red wine to be grown and produced in Devon, a rare indeed unique product of England, made possible by a superb vineyard site.' After a single pressing the wine is matured in new French Troncais oak casks until bottling at a year old. This gives it a deep garnet colour and a mellow flavour similar to a Cabernet Sauvignon. She charges £8 a bottle retail for this 'Yearlstone Red Deer', and £6 for the Special Reserve.

Conditions for growing vines in the Channel Islands, so far south and so close to France, might be expected to be better than in England, but that is not that experience of Robert Blayney of La Mare Vineyards at St Mary, Jersey. 'I find that we are much the same for growing conditions as the Isle of Wight. However I find that our grapes mature better. Our consultant who has many clients in the UK is struck by the better ripeness we achieve. Our Seyval produces much more sugar than comparable UK sites.'

Robert Blayney is a Liveryman of the Vintners Company and a Freeman of the City of London. In 1968 he and his wife Anne bought the old farm of La Mare, built by the de Gruchys in 1797, and began to convert a traditional Jersey farm into a wine estate, La Mare Vineyards. Their 'Clos de la Mare' is principally from Reichensteiner grapes grown in the Devant Vineyard on the south of the house, blended with Scheurebe. 'Clos de Seyval' is from that variety. From particularly favourable vintages they make 'Clos de la Mare Blayney Special Reserve' which requires a large proportion of Huxelrebe. It was first made to celebrate the Silver Jubilee, and the 1984 vintage was made to celebrate the 40th anniversary of Jersey's liberation from the German occupying forces on 9 May, 1945.

4

BEYOND COMPARE

FROM THIS 'TAKEN-AT-RANDOM-LOOK' at Britain's commercial vineyards in 1988, and the wine they have for sale, from Norfolk to Devon, from mid-Glamorgan and Worcestershire to the Channel Islands, from 50 to 2½ acres, well matured and only just coming on stream, it is clear there is no fear as yet of an English Table Wine Lake.

Across the Channel they are turning out 34 million more hectolitres of Table Wine in a year than they are able to sell. Under the EEC regulation which applies to any country producing more than two and a half million hectolitres, this Surplus to Demand Table Wine is subject to Obligatory Distillation, the penalty for over-production. Only 8,000 hectolitres of English Table Wine were made in 1986, and 5,000 in 1987. 'Make more!' is the appeal to English Wine producers, not 'Make Less!'.

There is no question of the production of English Wine, all of which at the moment is Table Wine, being surplus to demand. Almost all of it is consumed just as soon as it is fit to drink by casual and regular visitors to the vineyard whose grapes were the raw material, buying a bottle or two at the vineyard shop mostly during the visiting season between May and September, but all the year round when the shops if not the vineyards remain open.

For the English Wine producer it is eminently satisfactory and effortlessly profitable, requiring nothing that could remotely resemble marketing expertise. No bother with parcels and postage, no outlay apart from the stall and, most attractive of all, instant collection of the full retail price. The easy way, the lazy way. Charge visitors £1.50 a head for walking round and that will cover any small overheads which selling at the vineyard gate involves.

Good in the short-term interest of the individual under-capitalised producer dependent on immediate cash flow to pay the winemakers' charges, for the bottles, the labels and fancy packs, the advance Excise Duty and Value Added Tax, *and* earn the living that buys groceries, electricity, petrol, new pairs of shoes.

But will it be ever thus? Should it – in the long term interest of English Wine? For how long will English vignerons go on avoiding the market place, wholesale and export? In England the problem is raising demand not lowering it. Greater demand should stimulate higher production.

Most English Wine is sold at the vineyard gate – Brenda Day has a fine display of wines to sell
visitors to Three Choirs Vineyard.

But for most, 'marketing' has a frightening ring about it. It is unknown territory. Selling
English Wine wider than the immediate area round the vineyard means a salaried sales
force, even if it is only the two travelling salesmen whom Lamberhurst Vineyards employ,
or Elizabeth Brooks who, for five years up to June 1988 (when Rachel Foster took over)
was Marketing Manager at Carr Taylor Vineyards – French and well poised for overseas as
well as home sales. For David Carr Taylor marketing is the key that opens all other doors.

*We split our marketing into five sections. A fifth goes to export; a fifth into the big supermarkets;
a fifth into specialist wine shops; a fifth into hotels and restaurants; a fifth at the vineyard gate.
We keep a close balance on the first three that they do not overstep our production. We have a
fairly wide spread geographically for our 11 products. It is about time that agriculture and
viticulture came into the twenty-first century and realised that any fool can actually produce
the goods. It is the person who can process his product and market it in line with normal
industry that has a chance of making it work. I regard myself not as Agriculture but Industry. I
have got a mediocre raw material. I am processing it, packaging it and I spend a lot of time
marketing it so I get my full price. At the beginning of the year I say 'How much am I going to*

spend on marketing?' I bill that into my price. 'How much profit do I want out of my business?'
'What am I going to earn this year?' I put that into the price and I make darn sure I get it.

He is of course a man with big resources; but he only got that way by the means he advocates and practised from the start. Many, if not most, however prefer to stay as they are and shrink in horror at the thought of adopting industrial marketing tactics, let alone allowing someone else to apply them to 'their' wine. So long as English vignerons cling to the notion which they regard as so romantic – and probably spurred them to plant a vineyard in the first place – of growing grapes and selling 'their' wine at the vineyard gate, it is unlikely that English Wine will ever emerge from the primaeval stage.

Grow grapes, send them to a wine maker, have the wine back and sell it yourself. That's the fun of the thing, old boy!

For these individualists the fun would go out of it if they had to sink their individuality into a co-operative whole, which would be another way of putting more English Wine into the market place and stimulating demand. Kit Lindlar is one of many who deplore England's lagging behind in this regard.

We revel in being out of step with the rest of Europe, indeed the rest of the world, where the man who grows grapes is by no means invariably the man who sells the end product. In California, New Zealand, and Australia there is a very clear dividing line between the people who grow grapes and those who make and market it. Two separate disciplines. In Europe the trend is reflected by the Co-operative Movement where the growers sell their grapes to an organisation of which they are the shareholders, which makes the wine and sells it for them.

Kit sees little chance of English growers adopting such a scheme for a long time yet. Until there were more large growers consistently producing more wine than they could sell at the vineyard gate, drink themselves and give to their friends and relations, the pattern of 1989 would remain much the same. However when, as might well happen in the next decade, English Wine production swelled into a huge industry, resembling the 'ranching' envisaged by David Carr Taylor, many of the smaller individual vineyard owners might well not *want* to compete, and would see the merit of joining with others in a collective operation. They would *welcome* the opportunity of being relieved of the task of getting people to buy their wine, which in the new circumstances, had become a new ball game and altogether more sophisticated.

Maybe the activity will be clustered round the larger wineries already established. One might find a group of growers getting together and saying they had enough wine to sell to their friends and relations, and to locals, but their vineyards were producing more grapes than they could comfortably sell. 'Let us enter into an agreement as a group with a winery and a marketing man, and say we would like you to make all our wine, but we would like some of it back to sell ourselves. However we want to make a deal by which the rest of the grapes are processed and marketed collectively in a way that relieves us of that responsibility.'

Christopher Lindlar, leading viti-vinicultural consultant of Tenterden, with pronounced views on English Wine production, who advises a large number of English vignerons on the processing of their grapes.

For Kit Lindlar the wine maker and the marketing man performed two services: for the market in general in making English Wine more widely available and by providing a service to the grape grower, and to the English Wine industry at large by relieving him of the marketing responsibility and marketing in a collective way wine which would otherwise be in small parcels and be a drag on the market. It would give a role to the two-and-a-half-acre man who would otherwise get trodden on in the crush. In volume, ten two-and-a-half-acre vineyards add up to a lot; on their own they would only be a nuisance to themselves and to everyone else.

It is against nature for so many brand names of English Wine to be marketed when only such small quantities are available. If English Wine is to proceed and get away from vineyard gate sales, then there must be more consistency, more continuity and slightly more homogeneity.

There is a role for the one-man-band. His day has not gone. But the industry of which he is a part is already very much larger than it was ten years ago, and is all the while getting larger still. All I say is, let him be aware of that and make preparations well in advance for adapting himself to what it portends.

A move in the direction of collective production of English Wine has already been made by people like Christopher Ann of The English Wine Centre and Mark Thompson of Chalkhill Wines who advocate marketing regional wine labelled 'Wealden' or 'Wessex', and within the region a County Wine.

Christopher Ann sees 'Wealden' English Wine as a blend of grapes (or wine) from Kent, Sussex and Surrey or any combination of two or three. This would mean that if there was a glut the producer of 'Wealden' could buy in grapes from small vineyards in the region and use them in the blend. A regional product would be the bottom step of a structuring of English Wine of the Chateau-bottled/Medoc/Bordeaux kind – single vineyard/county/region with the price rising with each step up. 'Wealden' would be less expensive than 'Sussex' or 'Kent', which in its turn would be less expensive than, say, 'Rock Lodge' or 'Swiftsden'. Structuring gives price differential its raison d'être. In his Autumn 1987 English Wine Centre Wine List Christopher Ann had two regional wines 'Wealden' and 'Drusillas' priced at £32.35 a case. 'Sussex County' was £36.71 a case, and the nine Müller-Thurgau single variety/single vineyard wines ranged from £38.13 to £50.32. There were three single variety Reichensteiners from £40.87 to £50.32; two Seyvals at £41.56 and £47.75; a Huxelrebe at £46.27; a Gutenborner at £40.74; a Rivana at £43.49. There were six blends from £38.13 to £54.80.

The difference of price has, of course, to reflect difference of quality. 'Wealden' was likely to be a wine which had had a greater blending, explained Christopher Ann, and so a broader appeal. 'When you go up to a County wine you rightly expect it to be marginally more distinctive and more representative of a smaller area; and then at the top is the single vineyard wine, which may or may not be of a single variety or indeed perhaps a blend, specific in its style and with a Seal of Quality.'

Not everyone goes along with the Regional and County Wine idea. 'If you can make an absolutely distinctive wine in a particular county which is immediately recognisable and tastes quite different from that of another county, that would be OK,' says Lord Montagu. 'Otherwise I can't see much point in it'. Colin Gillespie of Wootton Vineyards at Shepton Mallet believes that though there may be distinctive vineyard tastes there are no distinctive county tastes: 'I certainly cannot distinguish East Anglia wine from Somerset wine, though I have no doubt that small hotels round here would stock bottles labelled "Somerset Wine" without naming a specific vineyard.' Cecil Paynter of the Wine Standards Board thinks it is something that might come with time. 'It is a matter of evolution – like deer in certain parks becoming an almost different breed. Over, say, 25 years, a Sussex or Kent wine might develop a recognisable individuality.' The English Vineyards Association took County Wine to be a new category of Table Wine and, in view of the EEC labelling regulations, thought introduction of another description in a wine label's fine print would only confuse the buying public and impede the progress they were making in persuading the authorities to grant English Wine 'quality wine' status.

DEMAND WILL BE STIMULATED not only by what is in the bottle and how it tastes, but by the bottle itself and how it looks. The visual appeal of English Wine will determine to perhaps a regrettably great extent the amount of it that the public buy. Lord Montagu thinks English Wine should be instantly recognisable by the distinctive shape and colour of the English Wine bottle, in the same way that Chianti is inseparably associated with its straw-based bulbous flask – take away the flat base and it will not stand up which is a fiasco. With the aid of a Government development grant, the English Vineyards Association and the Design Council coaxed by Barry Whitehorn, bottle designer turned bottle merchant, invited designs for a 75-centilitre English Wine bottle. Out of 20 submitted, reduced to a short list of five, they recommended a tall slim Mosel shape in 'Autumn Leaf' green. Producing it will take money – some £12,000 for the moulds alone. Persuading English vignerons collectively to place the initial bulk purchase order for at least 500,000 bottles which a manufacturer would require, will take time.

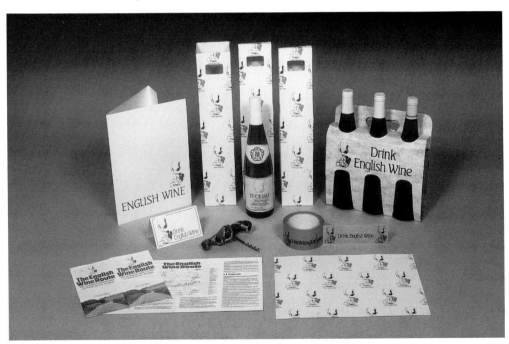

Making English Wine more attractive on the shelves demands well-designed and easily identified packs, and colourful sales promotion material.

Whatever the shape or colour of the bottle, the design and appeal of the label will turn more eyes towards it on the shelf than to the bottle with the lack-lustre, vulgar piece of printing that probably quite erroneously damns its contents unworthy of a second glance. To encourage good design the EVA hold an annual competition. Out of 37 entries the 1988 winner of the Anthony Steen Trophy was Nutbourne Manor – see page 94.

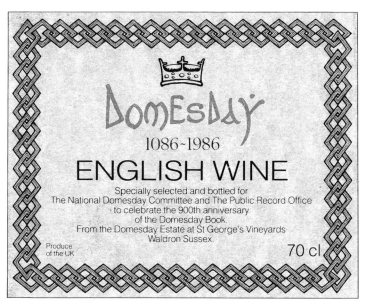

A typical St George's Vineyard 'own label'.

Gay Biddlecombe claims that her St George's Vineyards at Waldron were the first to introduce 'own label' English Wine, special blends made for a specific customer for a special occasion as those she created for The Royal St George's Golf Club, the House of Commons, the Speaker of the House, the Royal Observatory at Herstmonceux Castle, the Domesday Book 900th Aniversary, the Esperanto Centenary, the 400th Anniversary of the Defeat of the Armada in 1988, and the Caravan Club. She will have her calligrapher draw personalised labels to put on bottles of wine which companies will present to their employees and suppliers for Christmas, and to customers who want to give a different gift for the same old occasion – 'Happy Birthday Janie', 'Happy Wedding Anniversary Joe and Silvia'. She may not make a big profit on the three cases of 'Welcome Home Arnold' wine, but it pays dividends in terms of promotion. It is hard work, but it works. Word of mouth recommendation is the best advertisement. The people who attended Arnold's party tell their friends of Arnold's Wine, and they and he go to Waldron for more.

Gay realised early on that it was not merely a matter of marketing 'St George's' but promoting it – and not with unaffordable press, let alone television, advertising but with good presentation, newsworthy editorial publicity and imaginative ploys which attracted attention because of their novelty. She sells a lot of 'St Georges' at the vineyard gate, but even more on the phone.

> *Originally I never sold through wine merchants, as I knew eventually they would come to me. I now get wine merchants ringing me up saying 'someone has recommended your wine, someone has read about your wine, could you send us details?' I do all the selling. I decided to approach the general public and institutions like the British Museum and banks, direct. As a result the wine merchants began to sit up. 'Here is a wine we cannot ignore any more.' They may only order a case or perhaps six to start with. But they come back.*

The small volume which each of them was able to offer buyers was the problem too of each of the four vineyard owners who in March 1986 pooled their output in a combined marketing company they called 'Wines (UK) Limited'.

Colin Gillespie's Wootton, Michael Bache's Astley, Kenneth Barlow's Adgestone and Raymond Lock's Wickenden vineyards handle their run-of-the-mill domestic sales direct for the most part, but Wines UK have procured a good customer for them in Government Hospitality and several foreign embassies. Their company concentrates mainly in securing orders for their high quality, single variety wine from overseas buyers – 1,000 cases from Singapore and 2,000 from Japan. In May 1988 Sales Director Raymond Salisbury-Jones, whose office is in Regent Street, London, was hoping for orders from Eastern Seaboard USA despite the strong pound. All the wine he has to offer – all 8,000 cases of it – has won an award or been given the Seal of Quality. The bottles carry a special consortium label with the name of the particular vineyard whose wine it is.

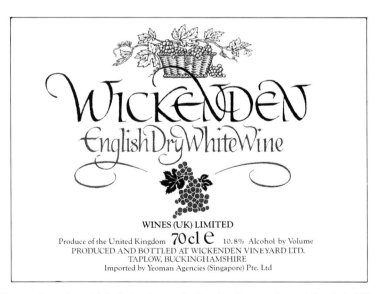

Wines (UK) Limited produced labels in this style for the four makes of English Wine which they began to market in 1976 – one of the four: Raymond Lock's 'Wickenden' wine.

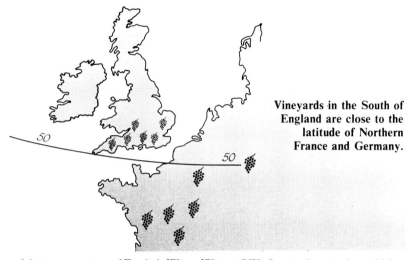

Vineyards in the South of
England are close to the
latitude of Northern
France and Germany.

As part of their promotion of English Wine, Wines (UK) Limited remind would-be purchasers that the vineyards of England are not all that distant from those on the Continent.

'We set ourselves a target of making available from the four of us 10,000 cases a year, but so far we have not managed as many as that,' says Colin Gillespie.

> *The trouble with America is that they all want to buy at the bottom price, whereas Japan has accepted our price. We did a tasting for a group of sophisticated Chinese living in London at their embassy. They all smiled and said they liked it, particularly the dry wine. They happily downed the lot – but there were no orders. I doubt if we shall ever sell any English Wine to China, or to Hong Kong. But we have hopes that our Chinese salesmen will sell some to North Vietnam.*

They intend to keep Wines UK to the original four. But as they made the market they would let anyone join them who wanted to sell abroad. Exporting English Wine, even of high quality, has not proved easy, as Raymond Salisbury-Jones admits:

> *I had already had many years previous exporting experience, including some from our family vineyard at Hambledon. We at Wines UK have not only to bridge the yawning education gap*

and overseas prejudice where English viticulture is concerned, but also to justify a relatively high price without assurance of adequate supply from any one vineyard. In retrospect, we might have made faster progress with a quality blend. *But blends, at anything over supermarket price, have yet to win acceptance in overseas mrkets. The overseas market potential is almost limitless in terms of sheer size. But our resources are too small to take advantage of it, or even to conduct the necessary and thorough market research before committing ourselves to a particular territory.*

Using her direct approach tactics Gay Biddlecombe has managed to sell 400 cases of 'St George's' wine to the Mitsukoshi department store, which is the Harrods of Tokyo, for an English Goods promotion fortnight; to the Mandarin Hotel in Hong Kong; to an American department store; and to customers in Australia, Kuala Lumpur, Holland and West Africa.

For Gay Biddlecombe the market place for her 'St George's' English Wine is wider than the vineyard shop or local wine merchant – here she is selling her product at Covent Garden.

David Westphal of Penshurst sells English Wine to Holland too and to Denmark. Karl-Heinz Johner declares that oysters with English Wine is the height of fashion in Paris these days. *Le snobisme* for the exotic. 'Our customers buy Carr Taylor English Wine as a curiosity item at first', says Louis Jarousse, their Paris distributor. 'But when they taste it, they find it is a correct wine.' Stephen Spurrier sells Carr Taylor wine at both his Paris wine shops. Every year the French drink some 20,000 bottles of Carr Taylor wine.

VIP foreigners visiting Britain as guests of HM Government might well find themselves tasting their first English Wine at Lancaster House or 10 Downing Street. 'We won a contract to supply the Government Hospitality Fund with "Chiltern Valley" wine for the exclusive use of the Prime Minister and her ministers entertaining their foreign counterparts,' says David Ealand whose wine has also been supplied to Buckingham Palace, the British Council and the Victoria & Albert Museum. Hopefully they will return home and tell their fellow countrymen of their surprise at being told that what they had found so agreeable with the Scotch Salmon was English Wine.

Russell Collins's 'entirely new concept for the marketing of English Wine' – the 'Wines of England' range offered by his company, Wines England Limited.

The key to persuading foreign wine buyers to invest in English Wine, as Colin Gillespie asserts, is having a firm UK market which is what Russell Collins is helping to create with 'Wines England Limited'. A 30-year-old international commodity broker, he gave up his job in 1985 to introduce 'an entirely new concept for the marketing of English Wine', which was simple and ideally suited to the fragmented English Wine producers. With the help of his brother Paul Collins he set out to produce 'a generic label with unmistakable evocations of the English countryside and to develop a range of carefully selected vineyards under a number of county appellations'. He started with 'Lamberhurst Vineyards' medium dry wine from Kent, dryish 'Moorlynch' from Somerset, richly textured 'Lymington' from Hampshire, and dry 'Westbury' from Berkshire. He then added 'Chiltern Valley' from Oxfordshire and 'Pulham' from Norfolk. Selection was supervised by David Stevens, Master of Wine. The range is marketed as 'The Wines of England'. 'English Wine is no longer an overpriced, poor relation of Hock,' says Russell Collins, 'but a quality wine in its own right with a character and breed of its own. Because Wines England Limited, the purchasing and distributing company, are able to buy in quantity from the vineyards which we select for our label, prices are much more competitive.'

In October 1987 the Whitbread Delivered Trade division introduced the range to selected up-market tied outlets. Stocks are held at Whitbread depots, and trade prices are quoted on the Whitbread wholesaling list. Selfridges of London take the whole Wines of England range; Collins sells 'Moorlynch' and 'Chiltern Valley' to the Waitrose chain and 'Lamberhurst' to the Duty Free Shops at Gatwick and Heathrow airports and the Victoria Wine Company's new 'Gare du Vin' and 'South of the Bordeaux' shops. Collins believes that the evocative packaging of the Wines of England label coupled with the most stringent selection supervised by Master of Wine David Stevens will encourage consumers to look at English Wine in a new light. Certainly recent additions, Crest Hotels and the London wine bar chain Davy's of London, have done just that.

Proclaiming the virtues of English Wine to the North of England are two people from Northern Ireland, Susanne and Michael Breene, who in October 1986 started the wholesale 'Fine English Wine Company'. Operating from their 125-year-old house in Copmanthorpe outside York, they carry a stock of 210 cases of more than 25 different brands of English Wine. 'We intend gradually to expand the range we can offer,' says Susanne, 'to insure we are the English Wine Centre of the North.'

> We are looking for a range of quality English Wines that not only cover the different growing areas of southern Britain, but include the more interesting wine from the medium sized vineyards that will appeal to the genuine wine lover. We also decided to offer our own label, 'House of York' wine, using 'Three Choirs' Medium, associating the revival of English Wine in Yorkshire with the original introduction of wine by the Roman garrison in York. So far our sales have met our expectations, but from the outset we did realise it would be a slow and difficult educational job.

The estate-bottled white brands which she has chosen, and she sells by the case of 12 bottles, are 'Carr Taylor', 'Three Choirs', 'Breaky Bottom', 'Astley', 'Pilton Manor', 'Adgestone', 'Wootton', 'Biddenden', 'Bruisyard St Peter', 'Cuckmere', 'Downers', 'Elmham Park' and 'Ditchling'. Her own label, 'House of York', which celebrated the visit of the Duke and Duchess of York to the city in 1987 she sells at £37 a case, the rest range from £38.50 a case to £49.99, and £88 for a dozen of 'Carr Taylor Sparkling'.

Once a part-time teacher at Askham Richard Prison, Susanne Breene took a wine and spirits course at Thomas Danby College in Leeds. Selby Council gave her a grant for converting her garage into an insulated wine warehouse, and for a year she was on the Enterprise Allowance Scheme. Her Fine English Wine Company sells mostly to hotels and restaurants but also to any individual customer who will take a case.

In the South The English Wine Shop in London run since 1985 by Maureen and Robin Aikman who have the Heywood Vineyard at Diss in Norfolk, operates on similar lines, though their off-licence means they can sell single bottles. It is in Harcourt Street off Old Marylebone Road. 'It is the only shop in London which sells English Wine exclusively', says Maureen. She has between 20 and 30 wines on her List, including 'Fonthill', 'Frogmore', 'Hambledon', 'Hillgrove', 'Michaelmas House' (from Essex), 'Adgestone', 'New Hall', 'Pilton Manor', 'Stocks', 'Three Choirs', 'Wake Court', 'Westbury', 'Wraxall', 'Biddenden' and their own 'Heywood'. The main stock consists of vintages from 1984, but she also holds a number of older vintages such as Gamlingay 1979 and Cuckmere 1980. On her List too is 'Carr Taylor Sparkling', vintage and non-vintage.

Maureen Aikman takes delivery of another crate of English Wine for The English Wine Shop in Marylebone.

Every month she has a wine tasting for customers and potential customers, wine writers, local traders and overseas visitors. On such occasions the English Wine Shop becomes a talking shop in which the various makes are critically appraised. It is a convivial gathering for trying out what is new and telling those to whom English Wine is still a novelty something of its traditions. On the eve of St George's Day 1988 the Aikmans mounted a Special Tasting at which anyone tempted to buy a bottle or two was given a special discount.

One day maybe there will be more marketing operations like these specialising in English Wine, but in 1989 producers who look for sales beyond the vineyard gate have to rely on the wine trade, the wholesale vintners, to stock English Wine along with the foreign wine which has been their stock-in-trade for centuries and they buy in bulk from all over the world. They hope that more will follow the example of Hew Blair, Purchasing Director of Justerini & Brooks of St James's Street, London, established in 1749 when Charles Hamilton's Painshill Vineyard was in its heyday. In 1988 he had three sorts of white English Wine to offer his connoisseur customers, Kenneth McAlpine's 'Lamberhurst', David Ealand's 'Chiltern Valley' and Keith James's 'Bodenham' (two varieties) which he has had on his list for some years.

In August 1988 Grants of St James's were stocking 'Three Choirs' 1986, 'Carr-Taylor Kerner-Huxelrebe' 1986 and 'Astley Huxelrebe' 1986. These were selected at a blind tasting in May. They listed no English Wine in 1977. Corporate Affairs Director Jeremy Bennett says though the volume of English Wine sold through the firm is at the moment very small, demand will continue to grow. 'Even if the market were static, the English Wine trade will increase as awareness of its products spread.'

The Victoria Wine Company which is owned by Allied-Lyons (who also own Grants of St James's) had nine brands of white English Wine on their 1988 wine list from which the managers of their 860 retail shops can choose – or elect not to stock at all. They are 'Bruisyard St Peter', 'Biddenden', 'Adgestone', 'Cranmore', 'Wootton', 'Lamberhurst Priory', 'Three Choirs', 'Lexham Hall' and 'Gamlingay'. The prices range from £3.89 to £5.57 a bottle. In April 1988 a Victoria Wine shop near Holborn had four of these on their shelves, a 'Lamberhurst' Reichensteiner, a 'Gamlingay' Müller-Thurgau, a 'Bruisyard St Peter' and a 'Cranmore' Müller-Thurgau from the Isle of Wight.

Besides the Somerset 'Moorlynch' from Wines England limited, the wine department shelves of most Waitrose stores carry bottles of another Somerset wine, the Woosnam Mills's 'Castle Cary' blend, as seen, W. R. B. Foster's 'Lexham Hall' from Norfolk, Cliff Sentance's Hampshire 'Lymington' (at the Lymington branch at least), and 'Carr Taylor Reichensteiner' from Sussex. Tesco Stores have offered 'St Edmund' from Suffolk since 1984, and in 1987, says Buying Executive Claire Gordon-Brown, customers bought 2,500 cases of it. Patrick Fisher says that altogether Tesco have taken 14,000 cases of English wine. Recently, as seen, Tesco have also been stocking Moira Gammell's 'Swiftsden' wine of Sussex. Sainsbury's, Britain's largest food retailers, once sold 'Biddenden Ortega 1983', says Allan Cheeseman, Director of Off-Licence and Delicatessen Buying, although no longer. 'But we have recently spread the net again in an attempt to review the present position, and the English Wine now available; and we may be able to stock another English Wine later in 1988.' Antonia Hadfield, Senior Wine Buyer, Beers, Wines & Spirits, ASDA Stores, the Leeds-based food chain, was also looking for a suitable English Wine of quality to stock in 1988.

In the St Michael Wine Cellar at the Oxford Street, London branch of Marks & Spencer, Britain's second largest retailers, a litre bottle of 'French Medium White' was being sold for £2.99 in May 1988, and a 75-centilitre bottle of 'French Country Wine' from the Pyrenees at £1.99 reduced from £2.15. But there was no sign of a wine from the South Downs or the Meon Valley. Over the road at Selfridges department store, however, beside the wines from Chile and California were five brands of English Wine, 'Penshurst', 'Lamberhurst', 'Lymington', 'Moorlynch' and 'Hambledon'. Time was when Selfridges also stocked 'Tenterden' and 'Staple St James'.

A larger stock and a wider variety of English Wine is to be found out of town at Hewitts Farm Shop at Knockholt in Kent. Diners at Aunties in Cleveland Street off Great Portland Street in London W1, and at The Refectory in Richmond, Surrey, will also find a surprisingly large choice of English Wine on the wine list. David Allcorn makes sure his selection of English Wine catches the eye of customers to his Vats Wine Bar and Restaurant in Lambs Conduit Street, London, by putting it at the top of the first page of his wine list containing 60 white wines. They are 'Wootton', 'Cuckmere', 'Breaky Bottom' and 'Croffta'. The businessman who chooses to order a bottle of English Wine for his business lunch at Vats, and in the evening dines at the Savoy Hotel in the Strand, will find his English taste is equally satisfied there. Ken Barlow's Isle of Wight 'Adgestone' has been on The Savoy's wine list for 13 years, and at Claridge's and The Berkeley, and at their restaurant, Simpson's. Wine Buyer Giles Townsend says they sell about 50 dozen bottles of it every year. Guests at the Savoy Group's Lancaster Hotel in Paris have no opportunity as yet of sampling English Wine – but maybe soon?

Trusthouse Forte have six brands of English Wine on their wine list from Gloucestershire, Sussex, Suffolk, and Kent – 'Three Choirs', 'Carr Taylor Reichensteiner', 'St George's Reichensteiner', 'Finn Valley Müller-Thurgau', 'Lamberhurst Seyval-Blanc' and 'Saxon Valley'.

Gay Biddlecombe sent Lord Forte two bottles of her 'St George's' wine on 23 April, St George's Day, with a covering letter chiding him for running the largest catering operation in England (and the world), having 16 Italian wines on his huge wine list but not a single English one. 'I said it was about time that they had at least one English Wine on their wine list. He took the point.'

There followed a year of negotiation and discussion. 'Out of 200 or so commercial vineyards in England we short-listed 40 which we felt met our needs and could give us continuity of supply for a particular vintage,' explains G. B. Chiandetti, Deputy Chief Executive and Director of Catering, Trusthouse Forte. The wines themselves are carefully selected:

The wine from these 40 vineyards was chosen for its style, freshness, fruitiness and elegance. All of it had good bottle age. From these 40 we made a final selection of six. We felt it would be preferable to give our guests a wine which had mellowed with age rather than one which still had some of the sharpness of youth. For this reason we have to make changes. In 1988 we replaced 'Adgestone' with 'Saxon Valley', and the 'Lamberhurst Reichensteiner' with a 'Lamberhurst Seyval'. The Wine Policy Committee of which I am the chairman, meets periodically to review all the wine on our wine lists to determine not only the wine which will appear in the next reprint but also what we should purchase for laying down and featuring perhaps ten years hence.

They introduced the English Wine they selected for the first time at the St George's Day Festival in April 1987. In the two months following that event guests at Trusthouse Forte hotels and customers at their restaurants bought more than 12,000 bottles of English Wine, and by April 1988 they had bought 60,000 bottles of the six brands.

Lord Forte, whose Trusthouse Forte group of hotels have six types of English Wine on their wine list, with Gay Biddlecombe on a visit to St George's Vineyard.

BEYOND COMPARE

WILL THE WINE WAITER AT THE hotel and restaurant, the shop assistant at the wine merchant or on the wine counter at the department store and supermarket, respond with a blank look of incomprehension to any request for English Wine?

Ten years ago almost certainly – followed probably by a pained smile from which the customer was to infer that to have asked for English Wine demonstrated a regrettable unfamiliarity with what (in his establishment at any rate) was meant by 'wine' – *real* wine – a social indiscretion comparable with asking a Savile Row tailor for a suit off-the-peg.

Today such a reaction is rare. The catering and retailing fraternity, responding to increasing demand not only for English Wine but for as much information about it as is always over-abundantly available on continental wine, is making sure that there is no pained smile on the face of the customer, dismayed that his favourite restaurant or store should be so behind the times, so staidly traditional in its attitude to wine.

'It is all changing,' says David Carr Taylor, whose wine is available at Hilton hotels, the Midland Hotel Group, the London Waldorf Hotel, Saccone & Speed, Grants of St James's, Victoria Wine, Waitrose to name a few of his 380 live purchase ledge accounts.

New fashions have taken over in the wine-drinking world. The new wine-drinking public are more discerning, more willing to experiment with new varieties of wine than the traditional wine drinker whom, God forbid, I don't meet very often and don't want to meet. His palate has been trained to nice wine that is not very interesting however, wine that has been carried on its name not its reputation.

It is something of which Gino Chiandetti at Trusthouse Forte is fully aware, and of which he makes sure his wine waiters are aware. 'We require our wine waiters to be as knowledgeable about English Wine as they might be for others,' he says. 'To this end we have periodic training sessions which include tastings to ensure that this requirement is met.' Each wine waiter has the Trusthouse Forte Hotels' 'Personal Wine Training Booklet' which carries a section describing the six brands of English Wine stocked. Under 'Food and Wine', giving a list of 'reliable relationships' to help wine waiters guide customers in their choice of wine, the advice for Light Dry Whites reads:

Fresh water fish, mussels, whitebait, hors d'oeuvres, salads, fish or shellfish, pasta.

Muscadet, Verdicchio, English Wine, Soave, Pinot Grigio,
Greco di Tufo, Ferrari Spumante, Ayala NV, Bouquet d'Or.

English Wine has its place too in the Savoy Group's Training Centre courses. 'All our wine waiters possess a basic knowledge of English Wine,' says Giles Townsend.

Change in the patronising attitude to English Wine of the influential Wine and Spirit Education Trust came in 1986 with the appointment as Director of David Bowyer who had joined them the year before – or rather his 'conversion' a year later when one of a party of English Wine producers visiting Intervitis, the international wine-making and vine-growing fair which takes place every other year in Stuttgart.

TASTE THE WINE TODAY

The Trust was set up in 1969 to educate and train all those engaged in or connected with the Wine and Spirit Trade. It sets standards of professional knowledge, conducts examinations, runs courses of instruction and has duties in connection with exams for the Mastership of Wine. David Bowyer had looked after the training and personnel aspects of Whitbread's wine and spirit division, and been with wine merchants Threshers and Stowells of Chelsea where, he says, in the nineteen-sixties and-seventies English Wine was never talked about – 'we had "Adgestone" on our list but it was just a line we carried'. There was in any case, a fair amount of confusion between 'English' and 'British' wine.

His lack of acquaintance with English Wine was still worrying him when, at the suggestion of Cecil Paynter, one of his trustees, he accepted the invitation of the Weald and Downland Vineyards Association to join their Intervitis party headed by Stephen Skelton. Cecil Paynter and Arthur Bone, then the Trust's Director of Studies, went too. Each member of the party brought three bottles of his best wine. Sampling some of this on the coach *en route* was an eye-opener for David Bowyer.

> Someone would open a bottle and we drank English Wine out of plastic cups – not the ideal thing to drink wine out of. But even out of plastic cups I thought the wine was very good. I had the Master of Wine exam papers in my pocket – it had taken place the week before and everyone was anxious to take a look at them. That started it! No mention of English Wine!

At Stuttgart what was left of the wine was used for a Comparative Tasting in unmarked bottles with German Wine made by a local Co-operative.

> These Stuttgart wine makers clearly thought it was a joke, an opportunity to get rid of wine they could not dispose of in any other way. But English Wine came out better.

He was greatly impressed. In November 1987 a whole day Seminar on English Wine was held at Five King's House in London under the auspices of the Trust. It was attended by students of their Diploma courses, Masters of Wine, the Queen's Cellarer, and members of the Wine Trade. Robin Don, wine merchant, English Wine producer, and Master of Wine, organised a blind tasting of English and Continental Wine. The two which came out top were both English, costing £4.20 and £3.90 a bottle, and a Sancerre at £6 came third. Two German wines at £3.11 and £5 came tenth and 12th. 'The seminar,' wrote Gareth Lawrence, Courses Administrator of the Trust, to the English Vineyards Association who had organised it, 'will almost certainly encourage many people to take English Wine more seriously than they have done in the past.'

Stephen Skelton is now one of the Trust's consultants and regularly lectures to its students. Some 10,000 take the Certificate, Higher Certificate and Diploma courses each year. Six thousand of these take the Certificate, many of whom are hotel and catering students. Students are encouraged to spend a day visiting an English vineyard and winery.

'English Wine appeared in our curriculum before,' says David Bowyer, who was made Principal of the Trust from 1 August 1988, but he goes on to explain that the subject has only recently featured more seriously in the course structure:

English Wine got lip service on our courses until 1986 when it was introduced at Higher Certificate to complement the Northern European lecture. From 1989 it is being included as a full session at Diploma level, a two year course of study approximating to 'A' level. It will continue to be mentioned at Certificate level and given more importance at Higher. The review took place particularly bearing in mind the fact that, with the creation of the no-frontiers single European market in 1992 – larger than the United States – English Wine is likely to be available at a more competitive price.

IT IS LITTLE USE THE SOMMELIERS AND wine merchants knowing the answers however, if their customers do not know the questions.

In view of the many festivals, fairs and events which nowadays promote English Wine, no one so inclined should have any difficulty in learning all there is to know about it and in thoroughly enjoyable circumstances. They can ask questions galore, and have their first taste of it at the English Wine tents at county agricultural shows – the Suffolk County, the Royal Bath, the Devon County, the South of England, the Three Counties, the Royal Show, the Kent County, the New Forest and Hampshire, the Dorchester and the rest.

English Wine festivals are now a regular feature of the English summer – the Weald and Downlands Vineyards Association's marquees at the 1988 Leeds Castle festival.

People filled the English Vineyards Association's stand at the International Food and Drink Exhibition at Olympia, London, in February 1987, declaring they had no idea there were so many vineyards in England, no idea of the range of English Wine. All of them ended with 'But where can we buy some?' Seven producers in East Kent, calling themselves

Canterbury Winegrowers, mount an English Wine Sunday. Almost all the regional vineyards associations mount their own shows, like the Wessex Wine Fair at Wilton, and the Weald and Downlands association at Leeds Castle near Maidstone in June and at The English Wine Centre at Alfriston in September, which Christopher Ann has been running a few weeks before the grape harvest, since 1975. With its grape-treading competitions, prestidigitators and jazz bands, The English Wine Festival at Drusillas Corner is truly 'a day out for all the family.

Christopher Ann also thought up the Great English Wine Run for motoring enthusiasts which every year in September begins with a wine tasting at Drusillas and ends up in Paris. *The Motor* magazine, which for three years sponsored it with The English Wine Centre, gave a silver cup and a case of English Wine to The Most Thoroughly English Entry. The money raised goes to charity – in 1988 to Great Ormond Street Hospital – but it draws a lot of attention to English Wine from people who never knew it existed. After five years of driving to Paris, the 1988 Run was to Deauville on 1 October. Every so often Ann organises an English Wine Tasting on the Continent – in a chateau in Normandy, to Méréville in Essonne the *département* twinned with Sussex.

Christopher Ann of the English Wine Centre atop one of the trailers on the Great English Wine Run to France, a promotional idea of his which was launched in 1983 and has taken place each year since.

An English Wine festival has been held in Sussex every September since 1975, latterly at Drusillas Corner, Alfriston where, as the 1988 poster shows, there is a wide variety of attractions apart from the stalls of the wine producers.

David Carr Taylor does the occasional promotion in Brussels and Germany. In 1989 he will once again be taking a stand at VINEXPO the largest wine exhibition in the world with 12 miles of exhibition lanes, in Bordeaux. He is the only English vineyard exhibiting. It will be the third appearance of Carr Taylor Vineyards. In 1987 his stand was the meeting point for the many overseas agents appointed after the 1985 show.

> *Our stand acts as the British base for British buyers. They come on to it, leave their hats and coats, go round the exhibition and come back again. We are the only English Wine firm at VINEXPO. We export to 16 countries now. We meet our agents at Bordeaux on this occasion – from Singapore, Japan, Canada, Denmark and elsewhere – and negotiate contracts for the next two years.*

That is fine for the foreign wholesale buyer but the natives of Britain have no better way of discovering the pleasure to be had from drinking English Wine, and of developing English Wine one-upmanship, than visiting a vineyard – and then three or four more to compare notes. Anyone – and that goes for overseas visitors who in any case are more used to spending a day in a vineyard than the British – who is not sure how to start should procure a copy of the 1987 'Follow The Wine Route' leaflet (which however has not been reprinted). It is written in French and German as well as English, and lists 35 vineyards with the names of their owners and telephone numbers, and indicates in which part of England they are located on an outline map. It shows which vineyards have unguided, casual visitor facilities, catering, a shop where wine can be bought, and a winery, and which organise guided tours. It was compiled by the English Vineyards Association who also publish an annually updated list of the more than 70 vineyards belonging to their members which are open to the public – see pages 152 to 157 and 166 to 170. In November 1988 they published *Hugh Johnson's Map of the English Vineyards* – those belonging to EVA members, that is – indicating which of them welcome visitors.

Because of the nature of Britain's licensing laws, tasting English Wine at a vineyard, let alone drinking a glass or two of it or buying a bottle or two to take home, has not always been possible at whatever time of day a visitor happens to turn up. The retailing of alcohol and its consumption, as everyone in Britain knows, is confined to certain 'licensing hours'. The Sunday hours differ from the weekday hours. A vineyard is a licensed premise as much as a restaurant or public house, and the restrictions on a publican between three o'clock and six o'clock on weekday afternoons have applied equally to a licensed vineyard keeper. On Sunday, the day when he probably had more visitors than on any other day, he had to lock his bottles away before noon and after two. He had no wish or opportunity to offer his wine for tasting or for sale in the evenings in the way a publican did, but regretted not being able to do so between two and five on Sundays, and three and six on weekdays.

If the local licensing magistrates to whom he applied, with all its time-consuming formalities, considered the way he ran his vineyard and the physical arrangements he had made to separate tasting, drinking and buying, warranted it, he could obtain an 'on-licence', an 'off-licence' or both. With the former he could sell or give away wine for tasting at any time during licensing hours; with an off-licence he could only give free tastings. With the detail in fact making it a somewhat more complicated matter than that, many vineyard keepers were inhibited from even applying. Worried by this, the English Vineyards Association saw the solution in a tidier system which treated a vineyard, never envisaged as a licensed premise when the law was drafted, as a special case. What about creating a 'Vineyard Licence'? They lobbied the Home Office in the person of junior minister Douglas Hogg MP, and in February 1988 there was a House of Commons debate on the matter. The Government had a Licensing Bill going through Parliament, one effect of which would be to extend the weekday permitted hours for all on-licensed premises, including vineyards, to enable them to sell alcohol between 11 a.m. and 11 p.m. – it became effective from 22 August 1988. It also contained a provision to allow licensing justices, on application by the holder of an on-licence for any premises which formed part of a vineyard, to make an order varying the permitted hours for them on weekdays as well as Sundays. Such an order could vary the hours on weekdays up to a maximum of 12 licensing hours a day to enable vineyards to sell wine by the glass at a time earlier than 11 a.m. On Sundays the permitted hours as varied could not exceed five and a half hours, and could not start earlier than 12 noon. In making an order of this kind, licensing justices would have to satisfy themselves that the sale or offer of samples was ancillary to the main business of viticulture and wine production, and that the hours were necessary to accommodate visitors.

In April 1988, following representations made by the Food and Drink Industries Committee of the Conservative Party and during the adjournment debate instigated by Anthony Steen MP in February, there was the prospect of there being what Michael Shersby MP, chairman of the Committee, described as 'flexi-Wine Tasting' for a maximum of any 12 hours on Mondays to Saturdays. The precise hours were to be decided by the magistrates, he said.

> On Sundays, whereas pubs operate fixed hours giving a total of five and a half hours opening altogether, English vineyards will be able to sell wine for any five hours for a continuous period. Again, that period will be agreed by the local magistrates. The off-licences will merge with the opening hours to be operated by the vineyards. Such changes, we feel, represent a real improvement for those who enjoy visiting vineyards and tasting English Wine.

It certainly was – though the excellent Vineyard Licence idea is still something which many hope will be given serious consideration at some later date.

At the same time vineyard keepers were encouraged to develop their vineyards as 'tourist attractions' by the Ministry of Agriculture whose Farm Diversification Grant scheme came into operation on 1 January 1988. Under this they can apply for a grant towards the cost of setting up facilities for visitors inside the vineyard, as well as of any road, fencing and toilets for which the operation of the facilities are necessary. The grant is at the rate of 25 per cent of the capital invested, up to a maximum of £35,000. Any bona fide applicant under the age of 40 can apply for a further six and a half per cent, making a total to him of 31½ per cent. The production of wine, including the growing of grapes, is not eligible for a grant. Moreover it will only be given to someone who spends at least half his working time on the vineyard and derives at least half his income from it. He must show too that the business requires a minimum of 1,100 hours of labour a year, and he has already been in farming for five years – viticulture is an aspect of farming and agriculture.

It is an incentive which should spur many who have hitherto held back from getting involved in what, both in expenditure and time, is a heavy extra to the already burdensome business of running a vineyard and producing and selling wine. All keepers of English Vineyards will sell bottles of their wine to those who call at the gate, but not all will let them in to wander around. Only 108 of the 260 members of the English Vineyards Association feel able to open their vineyards to the public, though of course there are a number of those who are not in the EVA who do. And not all of the 108 open them unreservedly, but require notice or confine exposure to the public to a few open days. They differ in the arrangement they make for allowing visitors to sample their wine; some charge, some give free tastes.

Motorists searching for the vineyard they are hoping to visit will know where to turn off the road when they see this sign.

They will all sell visitors bottles or cases of it to take away, drink it maybe with their own picnic in the grounds or, where they have them, in the vineyard snack bar or restaurant. Some vineyard visitors are welcome to come in and wander around without charge, but will have to pay if they want a guided tour. Others will have to pay to enter, after which they can take themselves on the self-conducted tour of vines and (where there is one, which is by no means everywhere) winery, described in the generally free route diagram, pointing out the grape varieties they pass. There are all kinds of permutations and combinations of the ways proprietors think up to make the visit in the first place understandable (without too much jargon) and secondly enjoyable. They range from the simple walkabout to the elaborate escorted tour of vines and winery, beginning with an authoritative talk on English Wine which any layman can understand, and ending with a tasting and the opportunity to buy wine and books, T-shirts and other souvenirs, and a vine plant to put beside a warm southern wall at home.

Half of the 108 welcome visitors without notice; the other half will only take them by appointment, either in coach parties, in private cars or on foot. Spending a day in an English vineyard involves more than admiring the strange un-English sight of rows and rows of vines, some suspended high above ground on what, as the guide explains, is called the Geneva Double Curtain system, and others hanging lower down according to the Guyot ('Ghee-oh') system, and hearing the story of how it came to be planted and how the wine is made, the dramas and hilarities of the picking, the ploys for keeping the birds away, the disappointments of the bad years, the exhilaration of the good years. It can give the opportunity of seeing a fine old house, learning its history, walking in its garden, enjoying an open-air meal and maybe, as a bonus, seeing unfamiliar animals and birds.

Many vineyards have been designed to make a visit easy for disabled people in chairs, with special toilets and other facilities. There is always plenty of car parking space, and almost all provide for young children, some having special playgrounds. Along with Senior Citizens they are charged at lower rates, and often are allowed in free. The English vineyard visiting season for most is from May to September, though almost all have their wine shops open all the year round. Charges are in the region of £2.25 each for conducted tours in parties of at least 15 or 20, which have to be booked ahead, and £1.25 for walk-abouts which do not. Both generally include a wine tasting. The climax to the visit will be buying bottles of the wine made from the wine-grapes which unbelievably they have just seen growing, row on row, in a way they thought only happened 'on the Continent'. Some will only sell a case of a dozen bottles from their vineyard shop (at wholesale prices); but most will let their visitors buy a bottle or a pack of three (at retail prices).

For almost everyone these days a visit to an English vineyard and winery is a great new experience, something for unbelieving foreigners to write home about, for children to tell their unbelieving schoolmates and teachers about, for Mum and Dad to make a note of as the perfect day out when next they have to entertain Aunt Bertha, or the original summer setting for Arabella's 21st birthday party.

May | The vines begin to grow; they are protected against spring frost.
THE VINEYARD VISITING SEASON STARTS.

Three Counties Spring Show, Malvern
Vineyard & Winery Equipment
   Exhibition, Biddenden
London Wine Trade Fair, Olympia
Devon County Show, Exeter
English Wine Festival, Leeds Castle,
   Maidstone

June | The vines flower. Spraying against mildew stops until blossoming ends;
praying starts for fine weather to set the grapes.

Suffolk County Show, Ipswich
Royal Bath and West Show, Shepton Mallet
East Anglia Winegrowers Association Equipment Exhibition, Linton
South of England Show, Ardingly
Three Counties Show, Malvern

July | The vines grow vigorously, and are tied to wire trellises; summer
pruning.

Southampton Show
The Royal Show, Stoneleigh
International Wine Fair, Bristol
Kent County Show, Maidstone
English Vineyards Association presentation of 'English Wine of the Year
   Competition' in the House of Lords
New Forest and Hampshire County Show, Brockenhurst

August | Tying and tucking in continues; spraying.

RASE Town and Country Festival, Stoneleigh

September   Those who can afford it protect the fast maturing grapes from the birds with netting; others patrol energetically. The wise place jars of honey and vinegar at strategic points to lure the wasps from the grapes. They start cleaning their barrels in preparation for the vintage, and check the crusher and press are in good working order.
THE VINEYARD VISITING SEASON ENDS – for most.

Dorchester Show
English Wine Festival, Alfriston
Great English Wine Run, Drusilla's

October   Pickers are mobilised to harvest the now ripened grapes, and spend an

intensive two weeks or so removing them from the vines, putting them into baskets and carrying them to the winery on the estate or to the lorry which will take them to the not-too distant contract wine maker up the road. Fermentation starts.

November   Most is safely gathered in – some harvesting will still continue however. Fermentation stops; netting is removed; winter ploughing.

December   The wine is racked and filtered for the first time. Ninety per cent of the year's wood is pruned away; the ground is manured.

January   Pruning continues – until March.

February   The wine is racked for the second time.

March   Pruning, staking and wiring stops; fertilisers are applied to the ground.

April   Vines are planted to form new vineyards; replacement vines on old plot.

English Vineyards Association annual general meeting, London
Southern Wine and Foods Fair, Bournemouth

The Vineyards of England & Wales

as registered with the English Vineyards Association

Peter McClure 1989

SURREY

WEST SUSSEX

KENT

Ightham
Leeds Castle
Chiddingstone
Penshurst
Bardingley
Lamberhurst
Royal Tunbridge Wells
Biddenden
Conghurst & Harefield
Tenterden
Swiftsden House

Seymours
Bookers
Downers
St.Cuthmans
Nash & Steyning

Flexerne
Rock Lodge
St. George's
Breaky Bottom
Springbarn
Carr Taylor

EAST SUSSEX

Berwick Glebe
English Wine Centre
Hastings
Brighton
Eastbourne

Croft Castle
Astley
Studl Man
Broadfield

WORCESTERSHIRE & HEREFORD

Three Choirs
St.Anne's
Severn
Deerh

Tintern Parva
GWENT
GLOUCEST SHIRE

GLAMORGAN

Croffta
Cardiff

SOMERSET

AVON
Bristol

Shers
Earl
WIL SHIP
Elms Cross
Chisen Prior

Cheddar Valley
Wootton
Avalon
Wraxall
Oatley
Pilton Manor
Moorlynch
Staplecombe
HRH Vineyard
Castle Cary
Fonth
Chá

DEVON
Highfield
Whitmoore House
Yearlstone
Brympton D'Evercy
DORSET
The Partrid

Manstree
Exeter
Whitstone

CORNWALL
Plymouth
Sharpham
Beenleigh Manor
Loddiswell
Polmassick
Veryan

La Mare
JERSEY
St.Helier

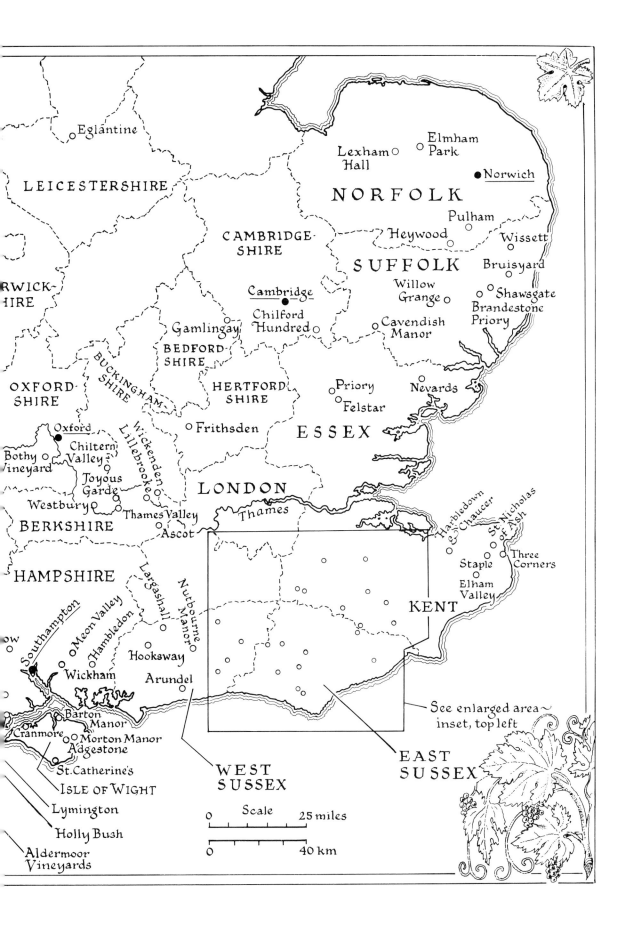

Eglantine

LEICESTERSHIRE

NORFOLK

Lexham Hall   Elmham Park

•Norwich

Pulham

Heywood   Wissett

SUFFOLK   Bruisyard

Willow Grange   Shawsgate

CAMBRIDGE-SHIRE

Cambridge

Chilford Hundred

Brandestone Priory

Gamlingay

BEDFORD-SHIRE

Cavendish Manor

RWICK-HIRE

OXFORD-SHIRE

BUCKINGHAM-SHIRE

HERTFORD-SHIRE

Priory   Nevards

Felstar

Oxford

Chiltern Valley

Lillebrooke

Wickenden

Frithsden

ESSEX

Bothy Vineyard

Joyous Garde

Westbury

Thames Valley

Ascot

LONDON

Thames

Harbledown & Chaucer

St. Nicholas of Ash

Three Corners

Staple

Elham Valley

KENT

BERKSHIRE

HAMPSHIRE

Largashall

Nutbourne Manor

Southampton

Meon Valley

Hambledon

Hooksway

Arundel

ow

Wickham

Barton Manor

Cranmore   Morton Manor
Adgestone

St. Catherine's

ISLE OF WIGHT

Lymington

Holly Bush

Aldermoor Vineyards

See enlarged area
inset, top left

EAST SUSSEX

WEST SUSSEX

Scale

0   25 miles

0   40 km

VISIT THE VINEYARDS FOR PLEASURE

HE INDIVIDUALISTS WHO PEOPLE the English Wine scene of today each have their own idea on how best to make their vineyards attractive to visitors. Here will be no describing the arrangements made by all of them, but giving an impression – a taste – of what lies in store for the English vineyard visitor and his wife (and family) by taking a look, from the West Country (but first the Channel Islands) to East Anglia, at what some vignerons are doing to hold their interest, to persuade them to return (with their friends), to make their day entertaining and informative, and encourage them to drink and develop a taste for English Wine.

Robert and Ann Blayney invite visitors to their La Mare Vineyards in the Channel Islands to 'follow the trail through the vines, sit in the orchard, and savour the peace of Jersey'. Their alternative crop of apples helps to ensure a balanced economy, should the vines fail. Robert tells visitors how the Blayneys have been involved in wine for 150 years, a tradition which has guided them in developing La Mare since they came there and planted the island's first vineyard in 1972. As in Bordeaux, he grows roses at the end of each row of vines. They suffer the same mildews as vines and show the effects sooner – his early warning system. He has recently built a smart new winery, cellars and visitor reception area which he has called The Vintry.

Laura and George Barclay have open days on Spring and August bank holidays, and every Tuesday during August, at Whitstone Vineyards, Bovey Tracey in South Devon. Richard and Ann Trussell like people telephone to for an appointment if they want a conducted tour of their Whitmoor House Vineyard at Cullompton, but welcome casual visitors on any day; and the same goes for the Symons's at Manstree Vineyard at Shillingford St George near Exeter. R. H. Sampson shows visitors video films of Loddiswell Vineyard at Kingsbridge and has guided tours and walkabouts.

Visitors to the 22-acre Pilton Manor Vineyard in Somerset which J. M. Dowling has taken over from Nigel Godden hear of Pilton's 800 years of history, how the monks of Glastonbury Abbey first planted vines there in the mid-twelfth century. They see the manor house which Abbot Michael of Amesbury built in 1252, and can enjoy a wine tasting, lunch or supper in the mediaeval walled garden. Parties can book a special tour for a Tuesday or

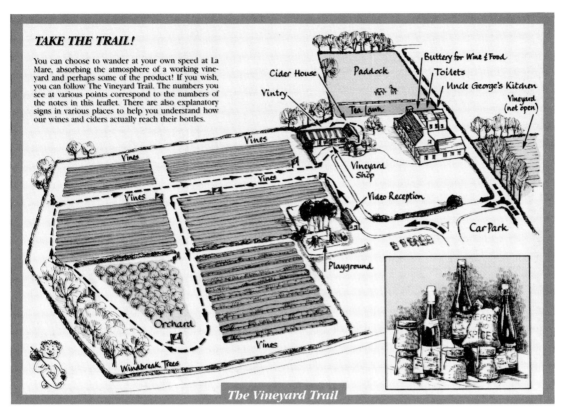

TAKE THE TRAIL!

You can choose to wander at your own speed at La Mare, absorbing the atmosphere of a working vineyard and perhaps some of the product! If you wish, you can follow The Vineyard Trail. The numbers you see at various points correspond to the numbers of the notes in this leaflet. There are also explanatory signs in various places to help you understand how our wines and ciders actually reach their bottles.

The Vineyard Trail

Most proprietors make it easier for visitors by providing a leaflet outlining a suggested route, such as this Vineyard Trail which Robert and Ann Blayney have devised for their La Mare Vineyard in Jersey in the Channel Islands.

Friday evening ending with a talk and a wine tasting. Tom and Judith Rees invite visitors to walk round their 15-acre Moorlynch Vineyard at Bridgwater with a printed guide to the grape varieties they see growing and the cultivation systems. At the farm they can see the small herd of horned Red Devon cattle which locals call Ruby Reds, and some unusual chickens which go by the name of Lavender Araucanas and Cuckoo Marans.

Colin Gillespie's Wootton Vineyard at Shepton Mallet is a popular rendezvous for Round Table, Womens Institute and Gardening Club evening wine tastings. 'For the vineyard we suggest sensible shoes!' warns Colin. After a conducted tour of the vines and into the winery, the party sits down to taste various kinds of English Wine and have a lively discussion on the problems of producing it, ending with hot soup and cheese. Visitors hear that the Wootton wine label of two grape stealers is from a thirteenth-century carving in Wells Cathedral.

The Producers Marketing Co-operative who call themselves A Taste of Somerset, based in Taunton, invite people to take The Somerset Wine Trail of eight vineyards – Pilton Manor, Moorlynch, Wootton, Castle Cary (open May to October) and four others. The Curshams at Staplecombe Wines at Staplegrove near Taunton like visitors to telephone first. At Brympton d'Evercy at Yeovil visitors will find 'a magnificent home steeped in history and heritage, with elegant rooms, beguiling atmosphere of unhurried pleasure'. Apart from the vineyard, there are peaceful gardens at Brympton, a country life museum, an exhibition of cider-making through the ages, and the I Zingari Cricket Club Collection. Charles Clive-Ponsonby-Fane currently has cream teas served in the afternoons but visitors will have to wait till the summer of 1990 to taste his Brympton Brandy, though

Eight vineyard owners got together in the West Country to work out this Somerset Wine Trail – a treat for the eye as well as the palate, they say, giving a flavour not just of Somerset wine but of Somerset itself.

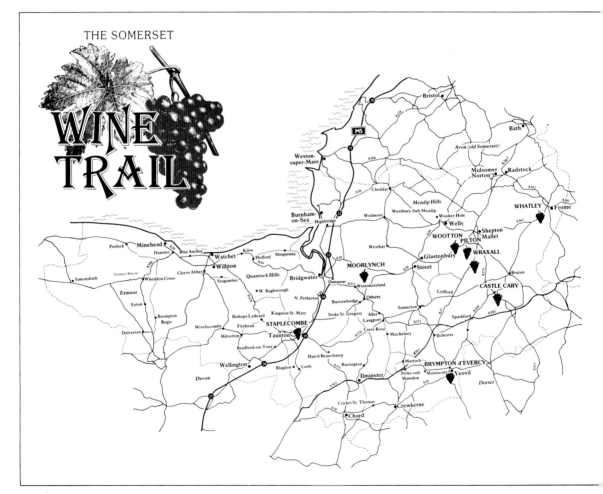

Brympton Distillery is already in production. The Witts of Whateley Vineyard near Frome, another on the Somerset Wine Trail, give evening English Wine tastings with a light meal in their cellar, apart from guided tours around their vineyard, winery and herb garden. David Holmes welcomes Somerset Trailers to Wraxall Vineyard near Shepton Mallet all the year round, though it is only from June to September that he serves light lunches in the wine bar.

Full details of what the eight vineyards on The Somerset Wine Trail have to offer visitors are given in A Taste of Somerset's illustrated leaflet which carries a good map showing their locations. All of them, it states, are family affairs.

> The owners of the vineyards are those who run them and in some cases do all the work from planting in the vineyard through to wine-making, with only a little extra help at picking and bottling time. Sometimes a vineyard is literally a one-man affair. Where this is so, growers may not, during the growing season, always be able to spare as much time to talk to visitors as they would like.

A visit to several of Somerset's vineyards, it says, will be a treat for the eye as well as the palate. 'It will give you the flavour not just of Somerset wine but of Somerset itself.' The vineyards were the newest element in the modern Somerset landscape. In 20 years their number had grown from nothing to twelve, and every year the acreage was increasing.

> Somerset wines have in extra measure the qualities which distinguish English Wine at its best: intensity of fruit and bouquet, lightness and freshness, an aromatic character which makes them particularly suitable for summer drinking . . . Somerset has long been famed for its apples and pears, and for the ciders and perries made from them. The same conditions that favour the production of these fruits also help the Somerset wine-grower to produce excellent wine-grapes.

The small size of Somerset vineyards helped to underwrite the quality of the wine. In plots of that size the growers could manage differences in varietal performance, could judge and control the picking to ensure that the grapes were at their peak when harvested. The county's vineyards are to be found in every setting, nestling in valleys at the foot of the hills, in the walled gardens of old monastic establishments, or country mansions, looking out across the wide Sedgemoor plains to the hills beyond or surrounded by rolling landscapes of orchards and farmland.

The settings of the Wiltshire vineyards are equally lush, but anyone proposing visiting either Fonthill Vineyard at Tisbury or Chalkhill Vineyard near Salisbury is advised to make an appointment.

Anthony Goddard has introduced a cut-price 'Welcome Return Ticket' scheme for anyone making further visits to his Barton Manor Vineyard at Whippingham on the Isle of Wight. Here the visitor sees not only the six acres of vines but the magnificent old house which was mentioned in Domesday Book and was bought by Queen Victoria in 1845 to form part of the Osborne House Estate to house Crown equerries and European royalty. Prince Albert laid out the gardens, and the water garden was once the royal skating rink.

King Edward VII made Barton Manor his Isle of Wight 'pad'. The Goddards bought it in 1976 and the vineyard dates from then. Ken Barlow allows visitors to stroll through the Adgestone Vineyard he planted in 1968 most of the year but depending on work in progress. It now covers 28 acres. He sells his wine at the vineyard only in cases at wholesale prices – the wine which guests drink at The Savoy Hotel and MPs at the Palace of Westminster. It is one of the oldest and most enduring vineyards of the English Wine Revival, following in the footsteps, in his choice of the Isle of Wight, of Sir Richard Worsley who, according to Richard French in his *Nineteen Centuries of Drink in England* (1884), 'planted the most hardy species of vine in a rocky soil at St Lawrence, Isle of Wight and engaged a French vine-dresser'. Unlike Barlow, he achieved only temporary success and finally abandoned the project.

The beautiful setting of the six-acre Isle of Wight Barton Manor Vineyard at Whippingham, owned by Anthony Goddard, chairman of the English Vineyards Association, to which a warm welcome is given to visitors.

Tom Day offers conducted tours of his Three Choirs Vineyards at Newent in Gloucestershire for groups of any kind between 20 and 55 in number, day or evening, any day of the week including weekends *throughout the year*. The tour starts in the vineyard where he runs briefly over the history of English Wine and his own beginnings in the business. He explains the various growing, pruning and cultivation techniques, and in the tasting room they all sample the end product. He shows them colour slides of the grape varieties he grows at various times of the year, gathering them in and pressing them. His visitors taste as he talks. If they wish it, they are served with a substantial Ploughman's Lunch of Diana Smart's Double and Single Gloucester Cheese, local bread from the Daffodil Bakery in Newent and Terry Harris's crisp salads. Michael and Wendy Baerselman too will arrange guided tours and tastings in the evenings and afternoons for up to 30 people at their Aldermoor Vineyards at Ringwood in Hampshire, and Chris Hartley does the same at The Meon Valley Vineyard at Swanmore. Keith James has tours and wine tastings at Broadfield Court Vineyard at Bodenham in Herefordshire every Thursday between 11.30 and three in the afternoon, and will take parties of 20 and upwards by arrangement to tour his vines, ending with wine and a meal in the winery. Plenty of club outings take place at Michael and Betty Bache's Astley Vineyards in the Severn Valley near Stourport. They are given an introductory talk on planting and care of vines, followed by a tour of the vineyard to see how this has been put into practice, and then Astley Wine and others are sampled.

Martin and Gay Rogers welcome visitors at any time to their four-acre Tintern Parva Vineyard at Tintern in Gwent, but John Bevan prefers them to make an appointment if they wish to come and see him at his Croffta Vineyard at Pontyclun in Glamorgan, perhaps after they have been to nearby Castell Coch, though the site of Lord Bute's nineteenth-century vineyard is now built over.

John Bevan, in his Croffta Vineyard at Pontyclun in Glamorgan, who is living proof that good English Wine can be made as well from grapes grown in Wales as in any other part of the United Kingdom.

World Wine Tours included, as an optional visit, Westbury Vineyard at Purley near Reading as part of their Fine Wine Weekends in November 1988 and March 1989. But throughout the summer Bernard Theobald offers three kinds of tours of his 15-acre vineyard for 25 people or more. He gives them a talk in the Tudor barn of the ancient Westbury Farm which had early British and Roman remains. If they pay a little more they will get The Vineyard Meal of home-made soup, eight English cheeses, village-made bread, English butter, pickles and coffee ad lib.

David and Fiona Ealand like to see people coming to Old Luxters Vineyard and Winery at Hambleden near Henley-on-Thames for a talk and wine-tasting; and the Skuriats who run Eglantine Vineyard part-time at Costock in Notts (though their postal address has to say Leicestershire) prefer evening or weekend visiting, and hope people will give them notice on the phone.

Vineyards owned by members of the English Vineyards Association which were open to the public in 1988 in the Channel Islands, Somerset, Cornwall, Devon, Dorset, Oxfordshire, Wiltshire, Isle of Wight, Gloucestershire, Avon, Hampshire, Herefordshire, Worcestershire, Glamorgan, Gwent, Berks, Bucks, Herts and Leicestershire are listed here.

Facilities Available:

V	– Visitors Welcome	WTF	– Wine Tasting Free
VA	– Visitors by Appointment	WTC	– Wine Tasting Charged
CP	– Coach Parties	VS	– Sales from Vineyard/Shop
CP/BA	– Coach Parties by Appointment	S	– Snacks available ⎫ usually by
OD	– Open Days	M	– Meals available ⎬ arrangement

Explanatory notes: 'Visitors Welcome' can be said to include casual visitors, particularly those who wish to buy wine; growers will, in many cases, provide information and if possible, conduct the public around the premises. It must be remembered that although few people are needed to run a vineyard, there are always jobs to be done and sometimes it might not be possible to stop the particular task in hand. It would be helpful if intending visitors telephone beforehand. The entry 'Coach Parties' needs a little explanation, but vineyards which accept them will obviously insist on prior booking (CP/BA). 'Open Days' means that growers will welcome visitors on certain days which are convenient to them. Where the letters M or S appear Meals or Snacks are, or can be made available, but at most vineyards only by arrangement – so please check first.

CHANNEL ISLANDS:

LA MARE (6 acres) [V. CP/BA. WTC. VS, M(light)]
R.H. & A.M. Blayney,
St. Mary, Jersey.
(0534) 81491

SOMERSET:

AVALON (2 acres – organic) [VA. WTF. VS]
Dr. H. Tripp, The Drove,
East Pennard, Shepton Mallet.
(074986) 393

BRYMPTON D'EVERCY (1 acre) [V. CP. VS. S.]
Charles E.B. Clive-Ponsonby-Fane,
Yeovil.
(093 586) 2528

CASTLE CARY (5 acres) [V. VA. CP/BA. WTF. VS.]
Mr. & Mrs. P.C. Woosnam Mills,
Honeywick House,
Castle Cary.
(0963) 50323

CHEDDAR VALLEY (2 acres) [V. CP/BA. WTF. VS. S.]
N.A. & P.K. McDonald, Stoneleys,
Hillside, Axbridge.
(0934) 732280

H.R.H. VINEYARD (8 acres) [V. VS.]
Nigel Hector, Alastair Reid, Derek Hector,
The Willows, Curload,
Stoke St. Gregory,
Taunton.
(0823 69) 418

MOORLYNCH (12 acres) [V. CP/BA. WTF. VS. M. S.]
T.B. & J.A.H. Rees,
Spring Farm,
Moorlynch, Nr Bridgwater.
(0458) 210393

OATLEY (6 acres) [VA.]
Ian & Jane Awty, Cannington,
Bridgwater.
(027 867) 340

PILTON MANOR (22 acres) [V. CP/BA. WTC. VS. M.]
Mr & Mrs J.M. Dowling,
Pilton Manor,
Shepton Mallet.
(074 989) 325

STAPLECOMBE (4 acres) [VA. CP/BA. VS.]
M.M. Cursham, Burlands Farm,
Staplegrove, Taunton.
(0823) 45217

WHATLEY (4 acres) [V. CP/BA. VS. WT/M/BA.]
M.J.E. Witt, Old Rectory, Whatley,
Nr. Frome.
(037 384) 467

WOOTTON (6 acres) [V. CP/BA. VS.]
C.L.B. Gillespie, North Wootton,
Shepton Mallet.
(074 989) 359

WRAXALL (6 acres) [V. VA. CP/BA. WTF. VS. M. S.]
A.S. & D.J. Holmes,
Wraxall, Shepton Mallet.
(074 986) 486 and 331

CORNWALL:

POLMASSICK (1½ acres) [VA. CP/BA
WTC. VS. S.]
G.R. & B.S. Musgrave,
St. Ewe, PL26 6HA.
(0726) 842239

VERYAN (1½ acres) [V. WTC. VS.]
Dr. G. L. Kington, Tregenna,
Portloe, Nr. Truro.
(0872) 501404

DEVON:

BEENLEIGH MANOR (1 acre) [VA.]
A.K. Wilson-Gough, Beenleigh Manor,
Harbertonford, Totnes.
(080423) 234

HIGHFIELD (1 acre) [V. VA. WTF. VS.]
Ian & Jennifer Fraser, Long Drag Hill,
Tiverton.
(0884) 256362

LODDISWELL (4 acres) [V. OD. CP. WTF.
VS. M. S.]
R.H. & B.E. Sampson, Lilwell, Loddiswell,
Kingsbridge.
(0548) 550221

MANSTREE (3 acres) [V. VA. WTF.]
Mr. G. Symons, New Barn Farm,
Shillingford St. George, Exeter.
(0392) 832218

SHARPHAM (4 acres) [VA. VS.]
Mr. M. A. Ash, Sharpham House,
Ashprington, Totnes.
(080 423) 216

WHITMOORE HOUSE (2 acres) [VA.
CP/BA WTF. VS. M.]
Richard and Ann Trussell, Ashill,
Cullompton.
(0884) 40145

WHITSTONE (1½ acres) [V. VA. WTF.
VS.]
George and Laura Barclay,
Bovey Tracey, Nr. Newton Abbot.
(0626) 832280

YEARLSTONE (2 acres) [VA. OD. WTF.
VS.]
Miss G. Pearkes, Chilverton, Coldridge,
Crediton.
(9925) 302

DORSET:

THE PARTRIDGE (5 acres) [V. CP/BA.
WTF. VS.]
Mr & Mrs. R. B. Partridge,
Keynston Mill, Tarrant Keynston,
Blandford.
(0258) 52596

OXFORDSHIRE:

BOTHY VINEYARD (3 acres) [VA. WTC.
VS. S/BA.]
R. & D.B. Fisher, The Bothy, Bothy Cottage,
Frilford Heath, Abingdon.
(0491) 681484

CHILTERN VALLEY (3 acres) [V. VA.
WTF.]
D.J. Ealand, Old Luxters Farm,
Hambleden, Nr. Henley.
(049163) 330

WILTSHIRE:

CHALKHILL (6 acres) [VA. WTC.]
Capt. D. Mann, Knowle Farm,
Bowerchalke, Salisbury.
(0722) 780041

CHISENBURY PRIORY (2 acres) [VA.
OD. CP/BA. WTF. Teas.]
A.H. & M.A. Robb,
Chisenbury Priory, Nr. Pewsey.
(0980) 70406

ELMS CROSS (7 acres) [VA. OD. CP/BA.
WTF. VS.]
R. & G.K. Dunkley,
Bradford-on-Avon.
(022 16) 6917

FONTHILL (13 acres) [VA. CP. WTF.]
C.P.M. Craig-McFeeley & J.F. Edginton,
The Old Rectory, Fonthill Gifford, Tisbury.
(0747) 870231/871230

SHERSTON EARL (3 acres) [V. VS. WTF.]
Norman Sellers,
Sherston, Malmesbury.
(0666) 840716

ISLE OF WIGHT:

ADGESTONE (8½ acres) [V. WTF. VS.]
K.C. Barlow (and Others), Upper Road,
Adgestone, Sandown.
(0983) 402503

BARTON MANOR (10 acres) [V. CP/BA.
WTC. VS. S. M.]
Mr. & Mrs. A.H. Goddard, Whippingham,
East Cowes.
(0983) 292835

CRANMORE (12 acres) [VA. WTC.]
N. Valentine, Solent Road,
Cranmore, Nr. Yarmouth.
(0983) 761414

MORTON MANOR (1¾ acres) [V. VA.
CP/BA. WTC. VS. M. S.]
J.A.J. Trzebski,
Morton Manor Vineyard, Brading.
(0983) 406168

ST. CATHERINE'S (3 acres) [VA.]
T. & M. Aldridge, St Catherines House,
St. Catherines Road, Niton.
(0983) 730465

GLOUCESTERSHIRE:

DEERHURST (4 acres) [V. CP. VS.]
P.J. Hall, Wells Farm,
Apperley.
(045 278) 435

ST. ANNE'S (2 acres) [V. CP/BA. WTF. VS.]
A.V. & B.R. Edwards, Wain House,
Oxenhall, Newent.
(098 982) 313

THREE CHOIRS (20 acres) [V. CP/BA. OD.
WTF. VS. S. M.]
T.W. Day, Rhyle House,
Welsh House Lane, Newent.
(053 185) 223 or 555

AVON:

AVONWOOD (1 acre) [VA. VS]
Dr. J.D. Minors, Seawalls Road,
Sneyd Park, Bristol, Avon.
(0272) 686635

HAMPSHIRE:

ALDERMOOR VINEYARDS (4 acres)
[VA. WTC.]
M.F. & W.A. Baerselman, Aldermoors,
Poulner Hill, Ringwood.
(04254) 2912

BEAULIEU (6 acres) [VA. CP. VS.]
The Hon. Ralph Montagu,
John Montagu Buildings,
Beaulieu, Nr. Brockenhurst.
(0590) 612345

HOLLY BUSH (4 acres) [V. CP.]
C. & E. Landells, Holly Bush Farm, (A337)
Brockenhurst.
(0590) 23054

LYMINGTON (6 acres) [V. CP/BA. WTC.
VS.]
C.W. & M.M.R. Sentance, Wainsford Road,
Pennington, Lymington.
(0590) 72112

MEON VALLEY (8 acres) [VA. CP. WTF.
VS.]
C.J. Hartley, Hillgrove,
Swanmore, Southampton.
(0489) 877435

WELLOW (80 acres) [V. CP. WTF. VS. S.]
Andrew Vining, Merryhill Farm,
Tanners Lane, Shootash,
East Wellow, Romsey.
(0794) 522431/522860

WICKHAM (7 acres) [VA. WTF. VS.]
John & Caroline Charnley,
Wickham Vineyard,
Botley Road, Shedfield.
(0329) 834042

HEREFORDSHIRE:

BROADFIELD (12 acres) [VA. CP/BA. OD.
WTC. VS. S. M.]
Mr. & Mrs. K.R.H. James,
Broadfield Court Estate,
Bodenham.
(056 884) 483 or 275

CROFT CASTLE (½ acre) [V. VS. CP.]
The Hon. Mrs. F. Uhlman,
Croft Castle (National Trust)
Nr. Leominster.
(056 885) 246

WORCESTERSHIRE:

ASTLEY (4½ acres) [VA. VS.]
R.M. & C.B. Bache, The Crundels, Astley,
Stourport-on-Severn.
(02993) 2907

WALES: –

GLAMORGAN:

CROFFTA (3 acres) [VA. WTC. VS.]
J.L.M. Bevan,
Groes-Faen, Pontyclun.
(0443) 223876

GWENT:

TINTERN PARVA (4 acres) [V. CP. WTF.
VS.]
Martin & Gay Rogers, Parva Farm,
Tintern, Nr. Chepstow.
(029 18) 636

BERKSHIRE:

ASCOT (3 acres) [V. CP. WTF. VS. M. WTF. VS.]
Col. A.R. Robertson, Ascot Farm, Winkfield Road, Ascot.
(0990) 23563

JOYOUS GARDE (2½ acres) [VA. OD. WTF. VS.]
D.T. Dulake, Crazies Hill, Wargrave.
(073 522) 2102

LILLEBROOKE (1 acre) [VA.]
Mr. & Mrs. Wheeler, Lillebrooke Farm, Cox Green, Maidenhead.
(0628) 32131

THAMES VALLEY (17 acres) [VA. CP/BA. WTF. VS. M. S.]
J.S.E. Leighton, Stanlake Park, Twyford.
(0734) 340176

WESTBURY (12½ acres) [V. VA. CP. WTC. VS. M.]
B.H. Theobald, Westbury Farm, Purley, Nr. Reading.
(073 57) 3123

BUCKINGHAMSHIRE:

WICKENDEN (4 acres) [VA. CP/BA. WTC. VS. S.]
R.H. Lock, Wickenden, Cliveden Road, Taplow.
(0628) 29455

HERTFORDSHIRE:

FRITHSDEN (3 acres) [VA. WTC. VS.]
Peter Latchford, Frithsden, 38 Crouchfield, Nr. Hemel Hempstead.
(0442) 57902

LEICESTERSHIRE:

EGLANTINE (3⅓ acres) [VA. OD. WTF. VS.]
A.M. & V. Skuriat, Ash Lane, Costock, Nr. Loughborough.
(050 982) 2386

SINGLETON RAILWAY STATION was built on the Sussex South Downs in 1880 to handle the crowds, including the future King Edward VII as Prince of Wales, who came to Goodwood Races. The last passenger used it in 1935 and the Midhurst to Chichester Line on which it was a stop was closed in 1953. Today its booking hall and waiting rooms are the 60,000 bottle winery of the 13-acre Chilsdown Vineyard which visitors reach by walking under the line by the subway and up on to Platform 4. A free eight-page leaflet tells them the story of how the Paget brothers acquired the site and planted the vineyard in 1971. While their parents are walking the vines and buying wine and container-grown vines in the 'Sip & Shop', children can admire the sheep, goats, ducks and bantams.

Further along the South Downs Ditchling Vineyards are open for anyone to walk around by themselves with the aid of another excellent guide leaflet, though Ann and David Mills the proprietors will come and accompany them if at all possible any time after 11 a.m. On certain days the vineyard is open for inspection between May and October, but it is as well to telephone and check. 'An opportunity to see an estate in miniature,' says Hector and Beryl McMullen to anyone who calls in by appointment at Seymours Vineyard near Horsham. Self-conducted and pre-booked tours are possible too at Downers Vineyard at Fulking near Henfield and at Berwick Glebe Vineyard near Alfriston. Groups of visitors to Rock Lodge Vineyard at Scaynes Hill near Haywards Heath, who give due notice, are sure of being escorted around the vines and into the winery by a member of the Cowderoy family – Norman, Jennifer or David – and at the informal wine tasting and talk that follows. A week's notice is required if they are going to round off the visit with a Quality Ploughman's Lunch or Supper (only £2). Norman Cowderoy has built a separate on-licence 'wine parlour' for drinking in, and another, as the law requires, for tasting and buying Rock Lodge wine.

An outing to a vineyard, which they thought was only to be found on the Continent, is now part of the summer programme of every self-respecting social club and wine appreciation society in England – here is a coach load of visitors hearing all about it, and tasting the product, on the terrace at Barnsgate Vineyard, Herons Ghyll, with its magnificent view across Sussex Weald.

Apart from sampling, drinking and buying wine, callers at Nutbourne Manor Vineyard near Pulborough can acquire a pack of five assorted vines to start a mini-vineyard at home, and in any event can be assured of a very warm welcome from Jeff Sanger.

Facilities at Barnsgate Manor Vineyard on the edge of Ashdown Forest at Heron's Ghyll near Uckfield embrace not only walking through the 20-acre vineyard with its magnificent view over the Sussex Weald, but looking around a wine museum of traditional and contemporary vine-growing and wine-making methods. A romantic wine cellar contains historic equipment used by vintners and cellar masters. For anyone giving General Manager Martin Hoare advance notice, the estate with its tasting rooms and shop, is open all the year round. A special walkway through the vineyard provides an enjoyable tour of one of England's largest vineyards. With its spacious internal accommodation, terraces and car parks, it caters for conferences, weddings, and social club outings of every kind – a short half-hour visit, a two-and-a-quarter-hour Ploughman's Lunch/Supper, or English Cream Tea visit or, for a minimum of 35, the Sussex Evening visit in the Wine Hall.

Historical wine-making paraphernalia are also to be seen in the Sussex Barn cellar of The English Wine Centre in the Cuckmere Valley at Alfriston seven miles from Lewes. It adjoins Drusillas Zoo Park with its ample car parking. It is geared to cater for wedding receptions, conferences and social functions throughout the year. Christopher Ann will arrange wine tastings and gourmet dinners with everyone sitting at a single refectory table in the candle-lit wine cellar. Parties of English Wine enthusiasts home in on The English Wine Centre's vine garden which shows nine grape varieties growing under three pruning systems, its historical curate's vinery and herb garden. Available to them too, of course, are all the attractions of Drusillas with its country pub, and high class shops.

David and Linda Carr Taylor offer Vintners Platters to the people – 20 per cent foreigners – who take the go-as-you-please walk around the 21-acre Carr Taylor vineyards at Westfield near Hastings in the summer. The vineyard is open from April to December however. Anyone can drive in, park their car, buy a ticket at the vineyard shop, follow the signposted vineyard trail by themselves, sit and eat their picnic in the Bluebell Wood, and end up having two wine tastings in the winery where plaques explain the processes. There is a short 15-minute walk of a third of a mile and a larger one around the perimeter of one and a quarter miles taking 35 minutes. Guided tours, talks and comparative tastings are given to groups of from 20 to 40. In their barn the Carr Taylors can seat up to 50 and serve them anything from a smoked salmon and Carr Taylor Sparkling breakfast to a six-course banquet, preceded maybe by a 'tutored tasting' of different sorts of English Wine. Local branches of professional societies and sporting clubs – architects, lawyers, doctors, cricketers, golfers – find it a congenial and 'different' rendezvous for the annual dinner.

St George's Day, 23 April is the start of the vineyard walkabout, audio-cassette and personally conducted tours season at St George's Vineyards near Heathfield, the home of Gay Biddlecombe's 'St George's' English Wine. She had 20,000 visitors in 1987, the year the local Buxted Players presented *A Midsummer Night's Dream* in the vineyard. Her summer programme has included art and antique exhibitions, Sussex food fairs, craft displays and mediaeval banquets in the eleventh-century tithe barn. But the gift shop is open every day, and so is the on-licence restaurant for lunch (stuffed vine leaves) and for cream teas. Visitors, who pay no entrance fee, can make up their own picnic and take it into the vineyard beside, perhaps, the vine they have adopted under Gay's 'Adopt-A-Vine' scheme. It has their name plate on it; they watch it grow and when it is mature they pick its grapes and receive a bottle of 'their' wine with their name on the label. Anyone who adopts 96 vines (the maximum) gets 96 bottles.

A typical vineyard shop in country-kitchen style. This one is at St George's Vineyards, Waldron.

IN THE KENT VALLEYS WHERE the mediaeval archbishops of Canterbury had their vineyards and wineries, the British on weekend and holiday sprees and visitors from foreign parts, can see row upon row of leafy vines with white and red grapes growing and ripening as they did then.

Near Faversham whose wine Henry III exempted from royal duty in 1302, Syndale Valley Vineyards at Newnham St Peter give an opportunity to walk back into history. Jonathan Abbs invites visitors to take his nine-acre vineyard trail any day of the week, and see his winery (parties, as usual, by arrangement). He tells them that though wine-making in the valley goes back at least to mediaeval times, there are traces of far earlier habitation. A pin that once fastened the toga of a Roman farmer was picked up on the farm; and when he was planting the vineyard in 1977 Abbs found a rare palaeolithic flint working site, dating from the time some 250,000 years back when a deep river ran through Syndale Valley and mammoths and woolly rhinos roamed the countryside. But there is no fear of meeting any in what today is designated the Kent Downs Area of Outstanding Natural Beauty, where just south of Canterbury, lie also Elham Valley Vineyards and Winery at Barham to which visitors are also welcome but not till 1 June and never on a Monday.

Evocative of the days when the Church was the experienced patron of viticulture and the best English Wine was considered 'Theologicum', Staple Vineyards, some seven miles east of Canterbury, face the ancient church of St James the Great, the lychgate of which, erected in 1664, is featured on the label of Bill Ash's 'Staple St James' wine. The scallop on the neck label is the symbol of St James the Apostle. Bill invites visitors to take the seven-acre vineyard trail clutching his excellent descriptive leaflet, to picnic where they will and test his wine in his attractive vineyard shop.

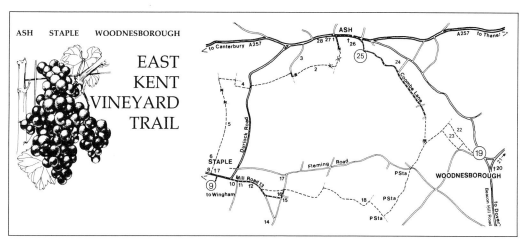

A circular walk of five miles, mainly on public footpaths, gives English Wine addicts and those anxious to have their first taste, the chance to visit three typical English vineyards in adjoining villages on the East Kent Vineyards Trail.

Staple Vineyards are one of three forming the East Kent Vineyard Trail devised by James and Pat Wilkinson of St Nicholas Vineyard, and open from Easter to October. It is a circular walk of some five to six miles mainly on public footpaths over gentle countryside – though for a stretch it takes to a disused railway track.

'It gives the wine enthusiast and walker a unique opportunity to visit three vineyards in adjoining villages in east Kent each producing fine English Wine,' says James, whose idea it was. The way round is clearly indicated with 'vineyard trail' signs. People can start where they like. Pat Wilkinson walked the trail several times with the Footpaths Officer of the Dover District Council to see if it was feasible and to put the signs up.

> *I then had a meeting with the Tourism Department of the District Council who agreed to have a leaflet printed with a map and description, and to help distribute it, if we supplied the artwork. Just shows what can be done with a little co-operation between local vineyards and the local Council.*

The three vineyards on the trail are St Nicholas Vineyard, Moat Farm, Ash; Staple Vineyards, Church Farm, Staple; and Three Corners Vineyard, Woodnesborough. At each, walkers doing the trail are welcome to look around individually or in groups, self-guided or conducted, and then rest their feet and picnic, washing down the food with a bottle of the product of the grapes they have seen growing. As usual, guided tours generally have to be arranged in advance and there is a charge between £1.25 and £1.50 a head, with accompanied children mostly free. Groups are normally limited to 30. Each vineyard has a shop or a cellar where, after a free tasting, not only the vineyard's wine but all sorts of other gifts can be purchased.

At St Nicholas Vineyard trail-takers will find a sixteenth-century farmhouse, a timber-framed winery, a thatched vineyard shop and a picturesque lily pond. *En route* they will pass the site of an Anglo-Saxon burial ground; the site of a large mediaeval lake; the dovecote and walled garden which are all that remain of Grove House, the sixteenth-century home of the Lynch family which was burnt down at the beginning of the last century; the ancient church of St James with its Saxon window and one-handed clock; and Reed Cottage which has had only three different families as owners since 1528. They will also see Gander Court, built around 1425 as a hostel run on commercial lines – not charity, though run by the See of Canterbury – to give lodging to pilgrims landing at Deal and making for Becket's shrine; the sixteenth-century 'Black Pig' inn; and Woodnesborough church and spire (replaced in 1740 by a curious cupola), once a landmark for sailors heading for Sandwich.

A reminder that the noblemen grew vines around their country mansions and castles as well as the clergy within the walls of their monasteries and bishops' palaces, the mediaeval vineyard at Leeds Castle in the Garden of England near Maidstone has been re-planted on the same two-and-a-half-acre site. It can be visited along with the many other attractions: the aviary, maze, grotto, gardens and parkland, as well as the castle itself originally a Saxon fortress, rebuilt by the Normans and converted into a royal palace by Henry VIII.

When King Henry went to Small Hythe ('smalide', a small landing place) to inspect warships being built there in 1537, there were no vines growing where today visitors can see the 18-acre Tenterden Vineyards at Spots Farm from as early as mid-March right up to Christmas. They are encouraged to take their baskets of sandwiches and hard-boiled eggs, legs of chicken and ham rolls, to the landscaped lake and picnic area, browse through the herb nursery and garden centre, walk around the vineyard at their leisure and learn about grape growing and wine production from their guide booklet. Afterwards they can relax on the terraced wine bar and non-picnickers can buy a Kentish cold lunch or tea and scones.

VISIT THE VINEYARDS FOR PLEASURE

Anyone who turns up at Richard Barnes's 18-acre Biddenden Vineyards at Little Whatmans outside the lovely old Wealden village of Biddenden just north of Tenterden can pick up a leaflet from the box in the car park and set off on either a short route or a long one. Both will land them up in the wine shop where they can have a free taste of any of the seven kinds of 'Biddenden' wine. David Westphal's experience at Penshurst Vineyards, where in 1987 he had 30,000 visitors, is that people come to be entertained, to learn something and to buy the English Wine they find it hard to get elsewhere. People who have come to visit the famous Penshurst Place in the picturesque village which is not far from Tonbridge, can come and (after giving advance notice) cook their sausages and chops on the barbecues at the vineyard or picnic in the grounds without charge, and then wander around the 12 acres of vines. They inspect the modern winery with the 4,000-litre wooden cask in the centre where David makes some 60,000 bottles of wine every year. Children are entertained by the mob of breeding Red Neck wallabies, the black swans, the Indian Runner ducks, the snow geese, the Black Welsh Mountain sheep, the Soay sheep from the Western Isles of Scotland, and other rare breed sheep and exotic wild fowl. David charges for pre-booked parties of wine buffs and catering students of at least 15 in number, or indeed of any able to appreciate

Many English vignerons who open their vineyards to the public have more to show their visitors than rows of vines and a modern winery – like David Westphal seen here at Penshurst Vineyards with some of his wallabies.

a detailed explanation of wine-making and the growing of outdoor grape vines. There is no charge for conducted tours of schoolchildren escorted by a teacher. At the end of it all visitors can sample 'Penshurst' wine in the log cabin tasting room which accommodates 70.

Set deep in the Garden of England, on the A21 at Lamberhurst – Kenneth McAlpine's vineyard, one of the country's largest and best known, covering 60 acres.

The signposts along the A21 past Scotney Castle reading 'Vineyard Trail' point to what in 1988 was England's largest vineyard. The facility is organised by the Kent County Council Amenities and Countryside Committee in collaboration with Kenneth McAlpine who planted it at Ridge Farm, Lamberhurst outside Tunbridge Wells in 1972 after consulting Professor Dr Wilhelm Kiefer of the Geisenheim Wine Research Institute in West Germany. The Lamberhurst Vineyard trail is open for anyone to take on their own with the aid of a guide leaflet any day throughout the year. Guided tours booked in advance are confined to the usual May to October summer season. During August guided tours of the 60-acre vineyard and winery, ending with a free tasting of 'Lamberhurst' wine, take place three times a day and without an appointment. Lamberhurst Priory, built in the sixteenth century, belonged to the Priory of Leeds, home of the Augustinian order of monks who cultivated the mediaeval vineyard now revived at Leeds Castle. The large farm has an attractive apple orchard too, through which plans are afoot to lay a miniature gauge railway track on which rides will be given to visitors on carriages drawn by steam locomotives. The Oast House is to be converted into a restaurant able to seat a hundred, and rooms for meetings, conferences and receptions. The Wine Shop and Tasting Bar of 1976 was rebuilt in 1988, and light lunches, snacks, tea and coffee are served in a room next door. The year saw the launch of a Lamberhurst Vineyards English Wine Club and a *Newsletter*.

North of the Thames near Maldon in Essex, Bill Greenwood and his family hold a two-day English Wine festival of their own at New Hall Vineyards each September. Apart from the 22 acres of vines and the winery, other attractions are performances of folk plays by the Thameside Mummers, country dancing, sheep shearing, a craft fair and endless supplies of Colchester oysters. Every day from May to September, however, Sheila Greenwood and her son Piers, who trained as a vine grower in France, give parties of 20 and more a two-hour guided tour of the vineyard at Purleigh, its press house, fermentation chamber, bottling room and fourteenth-century cellar under the farmhouse where they can store 48,000 bottles maturing or ready for sale. The tour ends with a wine tasting at which Sheila gives them tips on wine appreciation, and a film on the vineyard year.

Ten miles south of Cambridge lies the county's largest vineyard which Sam Alper planted in 1972 at Chilford Hall, Linton and which has grown to 22 acres. For their money groups visiting Chilford Hundred Vineyard get a tour of the vines with a knowledgeable guide, and of the cool winery decorated with carved stonework and huge vats standing on a marble floor. They are told at the tutored tasting of 'Chilford Hundred' wine which follows that they can take away the tasting glass as a souvenir of their visit. Sam and Simon Alper welcome individual callers, but in the usual opening hours between 10 a.m. and 5 p.m. and in the season. Ploughmans Lunches with a glass of Alper's wine, and tea and coffee with or without sandwiches and cakes can be served by arrangement in one of the three historic Chilford barns which are always in big demand for private functions.

Tours of the winery at Brandeston Priory Vineyards at Woodbridge near Ipswich across into Suffolk take place six times a day in the season. Apart from wandering through the six-and-a-half-acre vineyard, visitors can take pleasure from the fine garden with its pond and fountain, and take their luncheon packs into the wooded picnic area within which there is a children's playground. Not only 'Brandeston Priory' wine with its gallows label, but cider, honey and pottery can be bought in the vineyard shop. The Dows will open the vineyard and winery in the evening and at weekends for booked private parties.

'Suffolk Riesling may sound as unlikely as Bordeaux Bitter, but do come and see for yourself,' says Basil Ambrose in the hope of attracting people to Cavendish Manor Vineyards at Nether Hall Manor House, his home near Sudbury behind the fourteenth-century church on Cavendish village green beside the River Stour in the high Suffolk Constable country region. A glass of his 'Cavendish Manor' wine goes with a visit to Nether Hall (listed in *The Treasures of Britain*). The house and grounds, with their strange collection of byegones, are open daily all the year round. The charge includes a look around the adjacent ten-acre vineyard via the *route du vin*. Ambrose organises conducted group tours with a lecture, a tasting and, if wanted, light refreshments. He likes to have coach parties – as long as they give him due warning.

Visitors to Shawsgate Vineyard at Framlingham, where there are guided tours, vineyard trails, wine tastings and a well-stocked vineyard shop, are assured of a friendly welcome from Moira Harris.

Picnic area and childrens' playground once more feature in Ian and Eleanor Berwick's ten-acre Bruisyard Vineyard and Winery near Saxmundham which is open from Easter to the end of November. Visitors can taste the 'Bruisyard St Peter' wine in the winery courtyard while they browse through the well-written booklet *Wine Growing in Bruisyard.*

Further north Robin Don tells his callers that under the Cathedral Vineyard, one of three in his Elmham Park Vineyards complex at North Elmham in Norfolk, lies part of the graveyard of the ruined Anglo-Saxon cathedral. North Eltham was the seat of the Bishops of East Anglia from 631 to 1071. There is no other pre-Norman cathedral visible above ground in England. Carol Taylor arranges tours of the vineyard and the modern winery in the old outbuilding for parties of between 12 and 50. They will be invited to taste the 'Elmham Park' dry wine which its maker, a Master of Wine, says is at its best drunk as an accompaniment to the Cromer crabs of the Norfolk coast.

The Isle des Vignes is alive and well and gathering strength in East Anglia.

Vineyards owned by members of the English Vineyards Association which were open to the public in 1988 in Sussex, Kent, Essex, Cambridgeshire, Suffolk and Norfolk and are listed here.

Facilities Available:

V	– Visitors Welcome	WTF	– Wine Tasting Free
VA	– Visitors by Appointment	WTC	– Wine Tasting Charged
CP	– Coach Parties	VS	– Sales from Vineyard/Shop
CP/BA	– Coach Parties by Appointment	S	– Snacks available ⎱ usually by
OD	– Open Days	M	– Meals available ⎰ arrangement

Explanatory notes: 'Visitors Welcome' can be said to include casual visitors, particularly those who wish to buy wine; growers will, in many cases, provide information and if possible, conduct the public around the premises. It must be remembered that although few people are needed to run a vineyard, there are always jobs to be done and sometimes it might not be possible to stop the particular task in hand. It would be helpful if intending visitors telephone before-hand. The entry 'Coach Parties' needs a little explanation, but vineyards which accept them will obviously insist on prior booking (CP/BA). 'Open Days' means that growers will welcome visitors on certain days which are convenient to them. Where the letters M or S appear Meals or Snacks are, or can be made available, but at most vineyards only by arrangement – so please check first.

SUSSEX:

ARUNDEL (1½ acres) [V. VA. CP/BA. WTF. VS.]
J. & V. Rankin, Church Lane,
Lyminster, West Sussex.
(0903) 883393

BERWICK GLEBE (2 acres) [V. VA. WT. VS.]
Jane Broster & Doreen Birks,
Frensham Cottage, Berwick,
Nr. Polgate, East Sussex.
(0323) 870361

BOOKERS (5 acres) [VA. VS.]
J.M. & R.V. Pratt, Foxhole Lane,
Bolney, West Sussex.
(044482) 575

BREAKY BOTTOM (4 acres) [V. WTF. VA. CP. WTF. VS. M.]
Peter Hall, Northease, Lewes, East Sussex.
(0273) 476427

CARR TAYLOR (21 acres) [V. VA. CP/BA. WTC. VS. M. S.]
David and Linda Carr Taylor,
Westfield, Hastings, East Sussex.
(0424) 752501

DOWNERS (7 acres) [V. VA. WTF. S.]
Commander & Mrs. E.G. Downer,
Downers, Clappers Lane, Fulking,
Henfield, West Sussex.
(079 156) 484

ENGLISH WINE CENTRE (1 acre) [V. VA. CP. OD. WTF. VS. M. S.]
Christopher & Lucy Ann,
Drusillas Corner,
Alfriston, East Sussex.
(0323) 870532

FLEXERNE (5 acres) [VA. WTF.]
Peter & Brenda Smith,
Fletching Common, Newick,
East Sussex.
(082 572) 2548

HOOKSWAY (3 acres) [VA. WTF. VS.]
S.R. Moore, c/o Lares,
Bepton Road,
Midhurst, West Sussex.
(073 081) 3317

LEEFORD (34 acres) [VA. WTF.]
John & Pam Sax, Whatlington,
Battle, East Sussex.
(04246) 3183

LURGASHALL (Winery only) [V. VA. CP/BA. WTF. VS. S/BA.]
Virginia & Jerome Schooler,
Windfallwood, Lurgashall,
Nr. Petworth, West Sussex.
(0428 78) 292 or 654

NUTBOURNE MANOR (14 acres) [V. CP. WTF. VS. M/S/BA.]
J. J. Sanger,
Nutbourne Manor,
Nr. Pulborough, West Sussex.
(07983) 3554

ROCK LODGE (7 acres) [VA. CP. WTF. VS. M.]
Norman Cowderoy, Scaynes Hill,
West Sussex.
(044 486) 224

ST. CUTHMAN'S NASH (5¾ acres) [VA. WTC.]
J.F. Sherman, Ashurst Road,
Steyning, West Sussex.
(0903) 814054

ST. GEORGE'S (20 acres) [V. CP. OD. WTF. VS. M. S.]
Mrs. Gay Biddlecombe,
St. George's English Wine,
Waldron, Heathfield, East Sussex.
(043 53) 2156

SEYMOURS (2 acres) [VA. OD. CP/BA. WTF. VS. M/S/BA.]
Mr. & Mrs. H. McMullen,
Forest Road, Horsham, West Sussex.
(0403) 52397

SPRINGBARN (2 acres) [VA.]
Mr. & Mrs. C. Reed, Cleavers Bridge,
Laughton, East Sussex.
(032 183) 218

STEYNING (3 acres) [V. VA. CP/BA. WTF.]
Miss J. Elsden,
Nash, Horsham Road, Steyning,
West Sussex.
(0903) 814988

SWIFTSDEN HOUSE (3½ acres) [VA. VS. WTF.]
William & Moira Gammell,
Swiftsden House, Hurst Green,
East Sussex.
(058086) 287

KENT:

BARDINGLEY (2½ acres) [V. WTC. VS.]
H.B. Smith & I. Winter,
Babylon Lane, Hawkenbury,
Staplehurst.
(0580) 892264

BIDDENDEN (22 acres) [V. CP/BA. WTF. VS.]
R.A. Barnes, Little Whatmans,
Biddenden, Ashford.
(0580) 291726

CHIDDINGSTONE (14 acres) [VA. WTF.]
J.M. & D. Quirk, Vexour Farm,
Chiddingstone, Edenbridge.
(0892) 870277

CONGHURST (¾ acre) [VA. WTF.]
Miss J. Bridgwater,
Conghurst Oast,
Conghurst Lane, Hawkhurst.
(05805) 2634

ELHAM VALLEY (3 acres) [VA. WTC. VS. OD.]
Mrs. J.V. Allen & Mr. P.W. Warden,
Breach, Barham, Canterbury.
(0227) 831266

HARBLEDOWN & CHAUCER (2 acres) [V. WTC.]
A.G. Fisher & L.C.W. Rea,
Isabel Mead Farm,
Harbledown, Canterbury.
(0227) 463913

HAREFIELD (2 acres) [VA.]
Dr. Ivan Williams, Harefield,
Stream Lane, Hawkhurst.
(058 05) 2333

IGHTHAM (4 acres) [VA.]
J.M.B. & K.R. Corfe,
Ivy Hatch,
Nr. Sevenoaks.
(0732) 810348

LAMBERHURST (60 acres) [V. CP. WTF. VS. S.]
K. McAlpine, Ridge Farm, Lamberhurst, Nr. Tunbridge Wells.
(0892) 890844 & 890448

LEEDS CASTLE (2¾ acres) [VA. CP. OD. VS. S.]
Leeds Castle Foundation,
Leeds Castle, Maidstone.
(0622) 65400

PENSHURST (12 acres) [V. CP/BA. WTF. VS. M/S/BA.]
D.E. Westphal, Grove Road,
Penshurst.
(0892) 870255

ST. NICHOLAS OF ASH (2 acres) [V. CP. WTF. VS. S.]
J.G. Wilkinson, Moat Lane,
Ash, Canterbury.
(0304) 812670

STAPLE (7 acres) [V. CP. WTF. VS. M/S/BA.]
W.T. Ash, Church Farm, Staple,
Canterbury.
(0304) 812571

TENTERDEN (18 acres) [V. CP/BA. WTF. VS. M. S.]
W. Garner & D. Todd, Spots Farm,
Small Hythe,
Tenterden.
(05806) 3033

THREE CORNERS (1½ acres) [V. VA. CP/BA. VS.]
Lt. Col. C.S. Galbraith, Beacon Lane,
Woodnesborough.
(0304) 812025

ESSEX:

NEVARDS (1 acre) [VA.]
W. Hudson, Boxted, Colchester.
(0206 230) 306

PRIORY (6 acres) [VA. WTF. M. S.]
Col. D. W. Cooper,
Little Dunmow.
(0371) 820577

CAMBRIDGESHIRE:

CHILFORD HUNDRED (18 acres) [VA. CP/BA. WTC. VS. M/BA. FD.]
S. Alper, Chilford Hall,
Balsham Road,
Linton, Nr. Cambridge.
(0223) 892641

THE ISLE OF ELY (2½ acres) [V. VA. VS.]
Mrs. H. Graham, Twentypence Road,
Wilburton, Ely.
(0353) 4960

SUFFOLK:

BRANDESTON PRIORY (6½ acres) [V. VA. CP/BA. WTF. VS.]
H.P.B. Dow, The Priory, Brandeston,
Woodbridge.
(072 882) 462

BRUISYARD (10 acres) [V. CP/BA. WTF. VS. M. S.]
Mr. & Mrs. I.H. Berwick,
Church Road,
Bruisyard, Saxmundham.
(072 875) 281

SHAWSGATE (14½ acres) [V. CP/BA
WTF. VS.]
I.S. Hutcheson, Badingham Road,
Framlingham.
(0728) 724060

WILLOW GRANGE (1 acre) [VA. OD.
CP/BA. WTC. VS.]
W.A. Sibley, Street Farm, Crowfield,
Nr. Ipswich.
(044 979) 234

WISSETT (3 acres) [VA.]
J.R. & J.A. Craft, Valley Farm,
Wissett, Halesworth.
(098 685) 216

NORFOLK:

ELMHAM PARK (3 acres) [VA. CP. WTF.
VS.]
R.S. Don, Elmham House, Dereham.
(036 281) 571 or 363

HEYWOOD (1½ acres) [VA. OD.]
R.C. Aikman, Heywood, Holly Farm,
The Heywood, Diss.
(0379) 2461 and 01-340 9635

LEXHAM HALL (8 acres) [VA. CP. WTF.
VS. M/S/BA.]
W.R.B. Foster and Partners, Lexham Hall,
Nr. Litcham, Kings Lynn.
(0328) 701288

PULHAM (6 acres) [VA. CP/BA. WTC. VS.]
P.W. Cook, Mill Lane, Pulham Market,
Diss.
(037 976) 672

SWAFIELD HOUSE (⅔ acre) [VA. WTF.]
P.F. Bowles, Swafield House,
Swafield, North Walsham.
(0692) 402348

EACH YEAR THE ENGLISH vineyard is being discovered by more and more as a place to visit on holiday and at weekends, for entertaining relations and friends who come to stay, for 'different' parties and conferences, for contemplative meandering, for romantic escape, for relaxed family picnics, in a way that has been part of the lifestyle of people on the Continent for centuries.

At last we in Britain are catching on; at least we are catching up.

≈§ 6 §≈

WHAT THE FUTURE HOLDS

OW THAT THE RISKY ACTIVITY resumed by Sir Guy Salisbury-Jones and Mrs Margaret Gore-Brown has re-established itself in England and become an industry, albeit a small one compared with the Continent's, is it here to stay? Will it never again be abandoned in the way it was for the 25 years following the scrubbing of the Castell Coch vineyard in 1920? Is everyone confident that it can be made to work sufficiently consistently to make money out of it? And have people come to like the end product enough to buy enough of it to earn its makers a living?

Much has been learnt about open-air viticulture in England since 1952, about the vine varieties which will grow and ripen here, and the circumstances which growers need to create to stimulate them. With the advice available from Joanna Wood, and since January 1987 from Sheila Baxter, the Ministry of Agriculture's ADAS national vine consultants (Cromwell House, Andover Road, Winchester, SO23 7EN; telephone 0962 63500), few vine growers have failed to keep up-to-date with technical developments enabling them to maintain and improve their grape crops. The wise ones still consult them, and anyone contemplating putting spare ground under vines or looking for somewhere to start a new vineyard, can (for a fee) benefit from the experience of ADAS on such matters as site assessment, financial planning, field drainage, land preparation, vineyard planning, the sort of buildings to erect and farm machinery to buy, and every aspect of crop production. Some take advantage of the ADAS subscription schemes which give them ready access to information and services together with an option on advisory time at advantageous rates.

Apart from obtaining professional solutions to *ad hoc* problems in this way, England's wine producers add to the general store of their viticultural know-how by attending courses. Sheila Baxter was one of the tutors in the series of one-day training courses (£42 a time) for commercial vineyard owners given at The English Wine Centre, Alfriston, by the Agricultural Training Board in 1988, for which Christopher Lindlar was the main instructor. When a decision was being made to enter a new industry such as viticulture, said the ATB, one was immediately faced with many questions that needed urgent answers. Mistakes could be very expensive both in time and money, crops might be lost through disease or delayed because of mismanagement.

≈§ 171 §≈

As with any new venture there is a great deal of skill and knowledge required. This may be acquired over the years by experience, but time may not be on your side and few people have unlimited resources. Most people want a return on their capital investment as quickly as possible.

Their training courses should be regarded as an investment. They were designed to enable those who took them to make the right decisions and acquire essential skills.

For people in the West Country (and elsewhere) Gillian Pearkes ran Viticultural Courses for Vine Growers at her Yearlstone Vineyard at Tiverton in Devon. Each of the one-day seminars took place on a Sunday and cost £20 – or £80 for anyone taking all five of them spread from April to October. Gillian, who is a Nuffield Scholar on Viticulture and Oenology, is alarmed at the proportion of vineyards in England which have been planted without any advice on the site, its preparation or any discussion on the choice of vine for that particular plot.

As a result many very expensive mistakes have been made, several proving to be total failures. Others have been unable to produce a return on the outlay, let alone a profit. Typical examples of plant in haste, repent at leisure. Certain of these vineyards have yet to produce a grape, which is disastrous.

At Yearlstone she had shown that in the five past difficult growing seasons, one or two of which had been really cold and wet, given the advantage of knowledge on site improvement and by planting only culturally sound, early ripening vine varieties, a vineyard could be a viable enterprise regardless of the weather. Her course was designed to prevent failure.

I emphasise that growing vines and making wine is a simple, natural process, so long as the grower keeps mildew and other ills away. I demonstrate that the Wine Production Year is an enjoyable commitment, with the end result proving an attractive, even exotic, reward for one's labours. The sight of that first crop ripening on the vines is a tremendous experience.

In May 1986 Gay Biddlecombe of St George's Vineyards conceived an ambitious, comprehensive scheme – a Northern Europe Geisenheim? She felt that vine growers and wine makers in England had struggled very much on their own without, on the whole, any formal training similar to that available on the Continent. As the industry was expanding and more were concentrating on achieving quality and had to start to compete with other markets, she felt the need for a more comprehensive course in viticulture and wine-making.

As a result I approached two major colleges here in the south with a view to setting up a formal training course. I am obviously aware of the course already organised by the Agricultural Training Board, but I think we would all accept that this serves as a basic introduction to establishing a vineyard, whereas I feel that the industry, and those interested in working in the industry or establishing new vineyards or wineries, could benefit from a more detailed course, more in line with those held in other wine producing countries. I also feel that this would help establish England as a serious wine producing country, and put our industry on a completely different footing.

The two colleges she approached were Brighton College of Technology and Plumpton Agricultural College. In taking up the matter with Dr Roger Young of the Brighton College of Technology that June, the chairman of the EVA agreed that in recent history English vineyards had been managed by owners who were mostly untrained in the conventional skills of vines and wines but surprisingly capable none the less. The more wealthy ones imported wine makers from the Continent, and some had sent their sons and daughters to the Continent for training at viticultural universities. Those whose families were not in the business trained their staff on site with perhaps some light-weight days with the ATB.

A winegrower on the Continent can call on help from the Ministry of Agriculture, from a local specialist university or even from a neighbour. Here we survive remarkably well despite the lack of back-up. But there is no doubt that it would be beneficial if we had skilled advice on tap, and indeed if we could attend courses to improve our skills and knowledge.

Following this exchange of views, heads of agreement were signed to carry out a feasibility study in establishing a training scheme on the lines Gay Biddlecombe had suggested, and the Department of Education and Science offered a grant of £15,000. A press notice issued on this occasion announced 'plans to give England's growing wine industry the same academic and technical resources as French and German wine-makers' which were being backed by the Government. That amounted to official recognition that the English Wine business was expanding, said Toby Moore in the *Sunday Times*: 'Wine is now a lucrative crop, after being seen for years in the words of one producer, "as a hobby for retired majors".'

To involve the other agencies already working in this field, an English Wine Education Consortium was brought into being, with Lord Forte as Patron, consisting of the two colleges, Gay Biddlecombe's St George's Vineyards and other vineyards, the Wine Development Board and the Wine and Spirit Education Trust.

At the launch of the Local Collaborative Project, as the feasibility study became known, Peter Hodges, Head of Brighton College of Technology's Applied Science Department, said the English Wine industry had come of age:

It is no longer a hobby. It is now a genuine industry. It provides more and more employment. And of course it pays substantial taxes to Government. We believe the time has come to give it the necessary academic and technical resources it deserves if it is going to continue to develop and expand.

Excellent, said Colin Gillespie, chairman of the EVA. But it would be a mistake to perpetuate the errors of training too many students for non-existent jobs. It would, however, be good policy to provide a trickle of students with the skills required, and at the same time to have the facility to provide courses for those already in the trade in detailed aspects of the work in a vineyard and winery.

Others expressed doubts too as to the wisdom of setting up a training scheme on the scale envisaged which, year after year, turned out men and women as well qualified vine growers and wine makers for whom there might be posts in England the first year and for some of them the second year, but not for much longer. Though of course if it became the Geisenheim of Northern Europe with commensurate reputation it might soon be training people of all nationalities whose services were keenly sought by vineyard proprietors and wine makers all over the world.

In the course of his research for the feasibility study, Dr Roger Young, who is a senior lecturer on micro-biology at Brighton, visited 46 vineyards. The strongest impression he received was of individualism – 'not surprising if you consider what it takes to fly in the face of accepted wisdom and plant vines in the open in this damp island'. The owners of 23 of the 46 were 'doing their own thing' and making their own wine in their own wineries. In about 13 cases the vineyard provided a sole source of income; in eight it was related to an agricultural or allied enterprise; in 18 cases the major source of income was from other business or occupation; six vineyards were run by people who had retired.

The Consortium found the scheme feasible and Plumpton Agricultural College, which is near Lewes in Sussex, embarked on its first 'Growing and Making Wine in England' course in January 1989. It is part-time insofar as students gather for one week (Monday lunchtime to Friday lunchtime) each month for ten months – Viticulture from January to June; a break from July to August; and Oenology from September to December (some modules of which are at Brighton College of Technology). It can take up to 15 full-course students who will pay £480, and will award those who pass with an English Wine Education Consortium Certificate and hopefully* National Examination Board (City & Guilds) and Business & Technical Education Council certificates. There will be written papers, projects and practical tasks. In addition to those taking the complete 10-month course, anyone can attend for a single day for instruction on, say, fermentation (£16), or a half day reviewing, say, wine-making equipment (£9). Or they can sit in on the Viticulture part only (£300) or the Oenology part only (£200).

Course lecturer is 33-year-old Christopher Foss, B.Sc. (Hons) in microbiology, Leeds University, Brevet Technicien Superieur (Merit), Bordeaux Agricultural College. He has a French mother and was born in Paris. For some time he was Assistant Oenologist at Chateau d'Yqem, and during six years in France managed a highly mechanised 60-hectare vineyard, organised the fermentation of 250,000 litres of wine for a Co-operative and was *Maitre de Chai* at two Bordeaux wineries. Also an experienced lecturer and teacher, for the last three years Christopher Foss has been teaching Rural Science at Sutton Centre Community School. Dr Roger Young will cover sensory evaluation analysis and oenological microbiology.

*At the time of writing NEB and BTEC certification was being sought.

A two-acre plot was planted at Plumpton in 1987 with 15 varieties of vine – five of each – and a further area in 1988.

HAVING LEARNT THE BASIC TECHNIQUE, students will be able to go away and apply it to making wine of whatever kind they, or their employer, chooses. Though the small band of existing wine makers now have a much clearer idea of what a definitive 'English Wine' is, there is as yet no sign of it settling down into a pattern. Pending the emergence of a school of English wine makers, moulded maybe to some extent by what is taught at the Plumpton-Brighton 'Wine College', people like Kit Lindlar will continue in the work of finding that pattern and will share the knowledge they accumulate on the way with the English Wine movement as a whole. Says Lindlar:

> *The industry is still in a dynamic state of growth. The experimental element is less than it used to be, but the thing is moving, advancing. The spirit of adventure is still alive, though sometimes I think there is too much adventure and not enough reality. We are lucky we don't have years of tradition behind us. At the viticultural school in Germany where I was a student, we had a day meeting local wine makers who were all following the practices of their grandfathers. This does not apply to England. We have a completely fresh piece of paper to draw on.*

It was lucky timing. If it had been possible to lift a monk out of the Middle Ages and put him down in a winery of the nineteen-fifties, he would be perfectly at home, he would recognise all the equipment and take over without the slightest uncertainty. The dramatic changes in the science and technique of wine-making have only taken place in the last 25 years, the period when the English Wine Revival was getting into gear. With their *carte blanche* situation, the English Wine makers could start off on the right foot – to mix metaphors – instead of having to face the problems inherent in change.

> *We can choose from the latest equipment. Over the last ten years the old huge machines have been reduced in size. The technology has been reduced so that one does not need to bottle 100,000 a day in order to have the advantages. One can bottle 5,000 bottles a day and have the benefits of modern technology, modern filtration methods and less aggressive systems which achieve very much more consistent results. The wine maker can be more confident about leaving the wine as it is without manipulating it, because the modern methods enable him to intervene less frequently, more effectively, more subtly.*

Mediaeval monks who recognised the winery of 1970 would be lost with the new equipment of 1989. The winery of today is capable of producing a very much more drinkable, harmonious, intrinsically satisfying, aesthetically satisfying wine than any made in 1170 or 1970. For Kit Lindlar there was no question of compromising on principles or quality. What he and his fellow wine makers of the nineteen-eighties were doing was using modern tools to maintain an approach built up over the centuries.

What today's French and German wine producers have by way of beneficial tradition are the sites which they have inherited from their forebears. It was regrettably noticeable to Karl-Heinz Johner when he came to England. For so long he had assumed a tradition which gave his family an advantage they took for granted and could never be wiped out. At Lamberhurst he had to contend with ground which had been planted with vines for the only reason that Kenneth McAlpine already owned it. It was what had happened at Hambledon in 1952, and then elsewhere, in most of the years that followed. English viticulture had struggled to its feet handicapped by having to survive on sites which their owners rather than Nature had made suitable – or as suitable as circumstances and financial resources allowed.

The consequences of 'making do' are being mitigated by the new technology which has come to the rescue just in time, or rather can do so if it is applied by someone who knows what he is doing. Most, but not all, of the new generation know it is not as easy as it seems when dreaming of the romance of becoming the owner of a vineyard, and take advice before plunging in – if only because, with the larger initial plantings they are making, the wrong site or planting at the wrong time of year on the right site, can be prohibitively expensive.

Colin Gillespie is afraid a lot of people are still planting on the wrong sites. They only get one good crop every ten years.

> *They say it is going to be all right in the future, but you must produce ten crops, let alone ten good crops, in ten years. And you must average three tons of grapes to the acre. To do that you*

must plant the vine variety that does that every year, *which in my experience is Seyval-Blanc and perhaps Madeleine Angevine.*

Many people were pulling out because they were in the wrong place, and setting off to find the right place, with the text-book southern slope, suitable soil, ideal protection and the rest. Some found it and then the owner would not sell.

Stephen Skelton agrees. It is no longer enough, he says, to look out of the window and say 'Lucy's pony has gone now, let's plant some vines!' People who had done that were no longer in business. Sometimes it had worked, but mostly not. Site was more important than soil. It was something to be learnt from continental vignerons.

You can find two vineyards side by side. One is better angled to the sun, nearer the river, better protected by trees, and the wine from it is more highly valued than that from the plot next door. Each feature added together make one site better than another. I know vineyards in the locality which for no apparent reason had much higher sugars than we had at Tenterden Vineyards at Spots Farm. Bill Ash always has at Staple, but just looking at his site cursorily you might dismiss it out of hand.

His advice to anyone seeking land for a vineyard is to get at least the basic requirements: south sloping; 100ft up better than 300ft; light soil better than heavy soil; some protection better than no protection. At Tenterden he has never had grapes which were not ripe, grapes from the vineyard which they have had to de-acidify. In his opinion it should not be necessary to de-acidify.

Quality is not so much a worry, however, as quantity. The concern of many who have made the grade on the site they started with, and have no wish or reason to move, is to increase their grape crop. Those who have no surplus land or find their acreage under vines is just about as much as they can handle, are more than ever buying in grapes from other sites. Gay Biddlecombe is hoping to double the 130,000 bottles of 'St George's' she makes from the 20 acres she has at Waldron by doing just that. Her new winery has a capacity of at least 260,000 bottles. She seeks to emulate the Champagne houses in France, most of whom do not own a vineyard but have grapes grown for them.

It would certainly be the saving of the smaller vineyards, many of which David Westphal of Penshurst sees as surviving only as hobbies because of the reluctance to give the English Wine industry adequate funding, particularly for promotion. The English Vineyards Association had no funds for that. To the Government he thought English Wine was just an irritant:

It has been much more successful than anyone anticipated. This annoys them. To the EEC and the British government English Wine is like a boil on the skin. They would like it to burst and go away. But it won't. There will be more and more English Wine but fewer and fewer vineyards.

He would like to see co-operatives in England, each with a wine maker to whom vine growers send their grapes for making into wine which he has to sell, the growers dividing the profits. Kit Lindlar disagrees. A more collective approach to growing, clustered round wineries, yes; but not in the form of co-operatives in the legal sense. However that depended on the attitude, characters and ambitions of the newcomers. David Allcorn would like to see a semi-co-operative scheme introduced into every serious wine-producing county. By this the owner of Bashem Vineyard with an average grape crop of 20,000 bottles, say, sets aside perhaps a quarter of it for 'Co-operative Wine'. The other 15,000 bottles he sells at a higher price as 'Bashem Wine'. There is a sliding scale for how much he sets aside, adjusted to each year's circumstances. All the other vineyard keepers in the county do the same.

Lack of a regular income, warns Stephen Skelton however, will never make it a viable proposition for the person growing grapes as part of a co-operative and never making wine. If the average cropping level of the wine producer is three tons an acre a year – six in one year, two the next, one the next – he can even that out in his sales pattern, since he can *store* wine. So to a certain extent an irregular cropping pattern does not matter to him. But with the price and yield of grapes, which he cannot store, rising and falling each year, the person who only grows and sells grapes cannot rely on regularity of income.

In France, Germany, Spain and Italy co-operatives work because, if you are a peasant to start with, you have nothing to lose. But if you are a gentleman farmer or someone with capital to put into English vineyards, you do not want to join a co-operative where you are going in at the lowest level, getting a basic price for your grapes. If you are proud of what you do, you want to have your own wine and own label. That's why I do not believe co-operatives in the true sense will work here.

Contract growing was different; but even for that there was not yet enough regularity of cropping for anyone to say he was going to sink £10,000 in an acre of grapes and then get back so many thousand each year as a return.

If you are selling your grapes on a contract you have to have some guarantee of return. No one, as far as I can see, is prepared to give that guarantee. When there is a glut of grapes the price the buyer will pay for them drops dramatically. And the buyer only buys them on condition they reach a specification he lays down.

It is the specification which, Stephen Skelton hopes, will produce the kind of wine he wants them to make, the kind of English Wine which he believes the English people who are his main customers will buy and drink.

And what is that?

When Dr Roger Young first started drinking English Wine he was over-critical, and the same goes, he thinks, for most people. It seems to him they do not apply the same standards to, say, French Wine which they accept without question. Dry wine, he points out, is an acquired taste, and in the course of doing his feasibility study for the proposed training scheme, he came to like his wine much drier than he used to.

I am sure I am fairly typical in this respect, and as wine drinking is continually increasing in this country, I think we will see the development of a public following for the drier white wines. If I have correctly detected a trend towards more English vineyards producing a genuine dry wine, I am sure this trend is a good one. Since appreciation of drier white wines demands a moderately educated palate, I do feel that English Wine would benefit from a collective marketing campaign to establish a cogent identity. A well managed exercise of this type would not stifle individuality but would produce a clearly identified place for 'English' in the world of wine.

That can only be done by everyone conforming to the same grape growing specification – varieties, style. But, as Stephen Skelton points out, the trouble about having a distinctive flavour and taste for an area – England, say – is that vine-growing and wine-making have to be so tightly controlled that people get fed up. The distinctive taste of Chianti comes from their having to use a certain number of specified grape varieties in it, and having to make the wine in a style precisely ordained. If someone started growing, say, Cabernet Sauvignon in the Chianti area and made a better quality wine which they could sell at a higher price, they could only call it *Vino da Tavola*, since they were not growing grape varieties which were 'classic' for that area. The Muscadet growers could grow Chardonnay but are not allowed to, and when they see the price fetched by Muscadet remaining low and that for Chardonnay wine going up, they feel very aggrieved.

At our level I think it is best to keep things as they are. If we were restricted to growing Müller Thurgau, Seyval-Blanc, Reichensteiner and Schönburger, say, and that was 'English Wine', and it had to be medium dry to medium; and it had to be bottled with a certain degree of acidity and with a certain amount of sweetness and in a certain style, I don't think that would work. But that is the only way you could get a distinctive taste for 'English Wine'.

In his view, central marketing would not work either. There was not enough English Wine being made to put a bottom in the market. There had to be wine to fill out the basic price, so that everyone else could be above it. If there was not a good supply of cheaper wine for sale as generic English Wine, which others could be above, Roger Young's idea of central marketing would not work.

Should English Wine be a blend or a single grape variety wine? Skelton thinks the association in this country of a blend with lower quality is unfortunate and misleading. 'Adgestone' he points out, is a blend and a fairly highly priced one. But he sees little future in the County Wine blend idea. 'Why sell your wine as a County Wine when it is in direct competition with your own brand?'

Kit Lindlar deplores the fact that the English wine industry has so far not involved itself in the art of blending in the way of whisky blending. Some of the smaller vineyard owners have an insufficient amount of one variety and pick their two varieties at the same time. Both go into the basket together. They have to have a blend of the two, or else they would not have a viable crop. Because of the English climate the proportion of one variety to the other is never the same from one year to another. The vigneron has no control over it. There is always a degree of variability. The vintage of one year will rarely taste the same as the next year's. It may be basically the same, Lindlar points out, with similar dryness or sweetness, but the nuances are different from one year to another.

What is thus seen as in any case a far-from-straightforward matter is bedevilled by the fact that the EEC will only grant the 'Quality Wine' status which most English vignerons seek to a specific wine region. A region in this context is very large – 'Rheingau' or 'Côte d'Or' produces a volume of wine each year which is a hundred times that of the whole of England. But the whole of England could be a wine growing region in so far as it is an area within the Member State 'United Kingdom'. But the Quality Wine made in 'England' could only be made from certain approved grape varieties. (See pages 69 to 74.)

THE ENGLISH WINE INDUSTRY, on course for greater quantity and improved quality, finds a trip across both paths. Heading confidently for the kind of volume that would encourage big wine buyers like supermarket chains and hoteliers to place orders for Table Wine, the industry finds its output in peril of being compulsorily curtailed. Heading confidently for official recognition of the kind of quality most English Wine has already attained, the industry finds its specification and style in danger of being compulsorily circumscribed.

Praiseworthy high production becomes disgraceful 'over-production'. The achievement of producing 25,000 hectolitres of English Table Wine a year which would put English Wine on a firm market base, is likely to be regarded as thoroughly reprehensible by a body whose creation, so far as the development of English Wine is concerned, is a coincidence.

Britain's Ministry of Agriculture is well aware that the English Wine industry has become the victim of the EEC who set up the rules for the main wine producers on the Continent with no regard for those in England. The Ministry is striving to save them from being trapped by circumstances which they could never have foreseen*, and but for the existence of the EVA might already have overwhelmed them.

The danger is by no means past. For that reason the Ministry has its eyes firmly fixed on the point at which the industry might still find itself hamstrung by the EEC's wine production rules – the 25,000-hectolitre horizon which they might get erased altogether or lifted to 50,000 hectolitres to give the 'special case' English a breathing space. But since they may well fail to persuade the EEC to do either of these things, they are giving very little grant aid to English Wine producers. A vigneron can qualify for aid under the Agricultural Improvements Scheme for posts and wiring, and under the Farm Diversification Grants Scheme for aid towards visitor facilities, as seen, – their policy is that the English Wine industry is as good for 'tourism' as it is for agriculture – but that is all. They do not want the industry to expand so rapidly and in so disorganised a fashion that they breach the 25,000-hectolitre barrier *without being ready for it* – and it becomes a trip wire.

Their apprehension stems from the fiercely independent attitude they have found among English vignerons who do not want to know about rules which they regard as designed for the lot across the Channel and not them. They may not now regard them as their business, say the Ministry, but it will be their business as soon as they start producing more than that 25,000 hectolitres. It is going to affect not only the newcomers; all existing producers will become subject to the obligatory distillation rules and the ban on new planting overnight. The Ministry do not consider it is in the interests of English vignerons to rush madly at this figure without any thought of the consequences.

What they, and the English Vineyards Association, should be doing, in their view, is to develop the scheme for Quality Wine status. And in regard to this they are very anxious to disabuse the industry of the belief that wine production in England is an 'experimental' area. It is not – and never was. Many have the impression that there was something called 'experimental status', but that is a myth. Because the United Kingdom is exempt from obligatory distillation, the requirement of limitation of planting and having to keep a Vineyard Register, does not give it any special status beyond this. There is no question for instance of English Wine producers, because they operate in an 'experimental' area, being allowed to make Quality Wine from non-approved grape varieties.

*Treaty of Rome creating EEC, 1957; UK's entry 1973; full member 1978.

TASTE THE WINE TODAY

The Ministry's policy is one of 'gentle encouragement' of the English Wine Industry and protecting it from the savage future that lies ahead for it. It will do anything to help. Luxembourg has been exempted from obligatory distillation by claiming that demand for its wine exceeds supply. The Ministry may well point to that precedent in making out a case for English Wine to be similarly treated. But it sees the priority as educating wine producers in the legal aspects that govern their continued existence; getting across the message that they do not enjoy a wide-ranging 'experimental' status, but are subject to the same rules on oenological practices and vine-growing as everyone else in the EEC. The Wine Standards Board which enforces the regulations on behalf of the Ministry issued a booklet explaining the legal requirements at the beginning of 1989.

Anthony Goddard, chairman of the English Vineyards Association, saw 1987 as a turning point in the general acceptability and stature of English Wine. There had been no one specific event to bring that about 'but it is an impression many of us have got'. He was under no illusions however of the difficult road that lay ahead in regard to what the Ministry of Agriculture was warning. 'We are increasingly having to keep an eye on what comes out of Brussels and the EEC', he stated in his 1987 Chairman's Report.

It is difficult not to be jaundiced about it all. Some of the draft regulations made you wonder if the proposers lived in the real world at all. Perhaps I shouldn't say this, but I also fear that MAFF who are 'responsible' for us in EEC terms, will play the game with a straight British bat (as I think they should), whilst the rest of the member states continue to duck and weave round the regulations that get enacted to suit themselves. We will then finish up like the sacrificial goat, especially as we have relatively little 'clout'.

Luxembourg managed to get exemption from obligatory distillation only by an annual haggling match, and in that small state wine and milk between them represent a sizeable chunk of their gross national product. The Ministry of Agriculture point out that no other Member State is in the same position as the UK – *increasing* its wine production – except the Republic of Ireland which in 1987 increased its output from one vineyard to three. They have little doubt that *eventually* the UK will become subject to the two general provisions of obligatory distillation of 'surplus' Table Wine (not relating to Quality Wine), and the ban on new planting. Two recent regulations by which English Wine producers must already abide are that from 1 May 1988 all labels have to show alcoholic content with a figure giving the percentage of alcohol in the whole volume of liquid; and from 1 January 1989 the 70-centilitre bottle became illegal and wine had to be sold only in 75cl bottles, but past vintages in 70cl bottles could still be sold.

TO WHAT EXTENT THE NEW generation of English Wine producers are aware of the Ministry's exhortations is not clear, but in recent years there has been an upsurge of new planting on an unprecedented scale. And to Kit Lindlar the people who are plunging in are quite different from those he knew when he started at Merrydown in the nineteen-seventies.

The days were only just past then when the only real qualifications were a major's pension and a double-barrelled surname. They had earned a little money in the services or the professions, or were businessmen anxious to get out of the rat race, and they planted a small vineyard of two or three acres on small country house estates. All that is now changed. What we see in the nineteen-eighties is a rather different individual, younger (between 35 and 50, say), self-made, reasonably wealthy, active, with a longish spell of business life ahead of him to whom the commercial aspects of wine production appeal. He is interested in business in the countryside, not in farming, *not in breeding or training horses or gentleman farming. He has entrepreneurial experience and knows how the wheels of commerce go round. He looks upon a crop such as grapes as an end product capable of being actively marketed.*

Many of the new wine producers *are* taking it cautiously, starting on small sites and planting many grape varieties to see which take to the position, the soil and the rest. Michael and Pamela Judd look forward to seeing their first 'Crickley' wine in 1990, made in their own winery from the three acres of vines they planted on the lower slopes of Crickley Hill at the foot of the Cotswolds at Little Witcombe in Gloucestershire. Crickley Windward Vineyard is five miles from Cheltenham and overlooked by the site of the pre-historic fort on Crickley Hill. The Judds planted six white varieties and one red in 1986 and 1987 from which they propose making both red and white wine. They were Kerner, Huxelrebe, Seyval, Schönburger, Bacchus, Reichensteiner and Zweigeltrebe. Cider was the product at Peak View Farm until the middle of the nineteen-sixties, and they still have the horse-powered crusher and the press with which it was made. They intend welcoming any visitors who phone and say they are coming, and are preparing a shop in which to sell them 'Crickley' wine at the end of their tour of the vineyard and winery.

John and Caroline Charnley also chose Kerner, Bacchus, Schönburger and Reichensteiner for Wickham Vineyard near Botley in Hampshire which they finished planting in 1985, but made up their six varieties with Faber and Wurzer – seven acres which should be maturing around 1989. Alan Haickney has kept to two varieties Ortega and Reichensteiner, however, for the seven acres of his Landford Vineyards near Salisbury in Wiltshire. He has planning permission for the winery where he hopes to make 20,000 bottles a year of 'Earldoms' wine. This will be dry white, and a sparkling white wine produced by the bottle fermentation method. He will open the vineyard to the public and sell 'Earldoms' not only at the gate but through other outlets he has already established. On the civil engineering side of the aircraft industry, Alan Haickney's interest in English Wine led him to plant vines on his estate in 1984. He has room to enlarge the vineyard, and hopes to find other growers in the vicinity to supply him with grapes on a contract basis.

Enlargement of their present area is also the plan of James and Pat Wilkinson at their St Nicholas vineyard at Moat Farm House, Ash in Kent. 'East Kent is increasingly becoming recognised as a premier wine-growing area with its longer growing season and milder climate,' says Pat.

We planted our vines in north-south rows to take full advantage of the sun's heat and light throughout the day. The land is about ten to 20 metres above sea level, allowing for a full growing season. The vineyard is four miles inland from Sandwich Bay and the English Channel which gives the vines the benefits of a milder sea climate but protects them from the salt spray and the worst of the wind. At St Nicholas Vineyard we are very fortunate in having two of the best sites in the country as well as in the area. When the second site is planted we shall have approximately 20 acres under vines.

Inspired by Robert Blayney's La Mare Vineyards on Jersey in the Channel Islands, Steve Dugnemin has put down vines at his Le Pergnage estate in St Peters Valley, and in 1988 stayed with a wine maker in Australia. Blayney says the Department of Agriculture are investigating the possibility of a vineyard on Guernsey. He had three separate would-be Channel Island vignerons coming to benefit from his experience recently, and one of them an ex-Malayan banana grower. On Alderney it seems there are no vineyards, unless the plot of vines which John Arlott has in his garden rates as a vineyard!

Three of the four young men who in 1986 formed The Isle of Wight Wine Company and in 1989 have 55 acres under vines near Ryde – Conrad Gauntlett, his brother Neal Gauntlett, and Peter Godber.

Conrad Gauntlett, his brother Neal and two friends Peter Godber and Richard Sopar have gone for a no-nonsense co-operative of the kind advocated by David Westphal. Each owns and controls adjacent vineyards near Ryde on the Isle of Wight: Rosemary Vineyard, Whitefield Vineyard, Ashey Vineyard and Smallbrook Vineyard. They started by planting 16 acres of south-facing grazing land some 60 feet above sea level in 1986 when they formed the Isle of Wight Wine Company Limited. They bought another 20 acres in 1987, and overall planted 15 varieties – eight acres each of Reichensteiner, Schönburger and Seyval-Blanc, seven of Madeleine Angevine, four of Müller-Thurgau, three of Kerner, two each of Triomphe d'Alsace, Bacchus and Pinot Gris, and one of Chardonnay. In 1988 they acquired and planted another nine acres making the whole area under vines 45 acres, with 600 vines to the acre, mostly white and a few red. They are building their own winery and look forward to having a first vintage from the original 16 acres in 1989 which they intend to sell on the island and at the vineyards which will be open to the public.

Conrad Gauntlett explains more about the way they operate:

> Though we own our respective vineyards, we share all the plant and machinery we need such as tractors, grass cutters and sprayers, and also the winery buildings and wine-making equipment, which are owned and controlled by the co-op – The Isle of Wight Wine Company. In forming the co-operative we had the help and advice of the 'Food from Britain' people. We hope it is based on all the good points of the continental co-operatives. As well as buying in all our consumables – corks, bottles, labels, packs and the rest – the co-operative will handle the marketing of the wine made from the grapes grown at all four vineyards.
>
> All four of us work full-time out of agriculture. I am a computer engineer; and the others are a marine engineer on a British Telecom cable ship; a British Gas fitter; and an engineering technology buyer for Vickers. So we are all part-time in the vineyards, with much help from wives and friends. We seem to cope – just.

When insurance loss adjuster Robert Cole of Rotherfield, used to travelling the world on his business, bought the small 60-acre Harden Vale Farm near Penshurst in Kent in 1980, it was with a view to breeding horses there and planting a small vineyard as a retirement hobby. He planned to retire when he was between 60 and 65 when he reckoned he would need a bit of peace and quiet in the country with moderate physical and mental exercise. He was drawn to doing something he knew nothing about as the best way of keeping his mind active. He consulted David Carr Taylor who put him in touch with Alan Furneaux who pronounced his soil and situation suitable for vines. So in 1980 he planted a half-acre plot with vines, and two years later, encouraged by their growth, made a first commercial planting of five acres. He took out a hedge and a ditch and extended them to ten acres.

> Having started planting, I was bitten by the bug, and I thought I would go for something larger. If you have five acres you can manage with one helper. If you go bigger you have to go carefully. It means going into another gear. You have to buy expensive equipment, and if you do that you have to make maximum use of it. From ten I went to 15; and then to 18 acres which is what we have in 1988.

He knew it would take time to find the grape variety most suited to his site, but started with Huxelrebe, Schönburger, Reichensteiner, Regner, Bacchus and Faber. He had the whole vineyard drained for £20,000. Vines, posts and wire cost him another £20,000.

Robert Cole plans to experiment, under advice, by first having very small quantities of wine made from his grapes, just for his own consumption. For the first few years he will only sell grapes while he discovers the character of the wine which they make, and how best to market it. He is in no hurry. In this way he will build up a demand ahead of supply. He will not rush into having a large quantity of commercial wine available, but looks to producing a really high quality 'Harden Vale' wine in 1991 or maybe 1992. His full 18 acres will not have matured until 1992. The wine will be white and red (not rosé) but no sparkling. Eventually he will set up his own winery and make the wine himself. His daughter is helping him. It will be a family business. He has no wish to open it to visitors.

Robert Cole realises it is all a bit of a gamble, but not, he thinks, as big as it used to be. As a rough guide (after two very cold winters) he intends to add £1,000 an acre to the cost of running the vineyard each year for eight years. In year eight he expects to be on a fairly balanced production. He will then start writing off that £8,000 an acre for the next 20 years.

The gently gently approach is favoured too by Denys Randolph who planted six acres of vines at Wallingford in Oxfordshire in 1987, another six in 1988 and a final three in 1989. Clapcot Vineyard is now its full 14-acre complement. 'We shall not be building our own winery,' says Denys, 'the grapes will be shipped to a processor who will sell under his own name. The vineyard will not be open to the public, and for the time being we will not be selling wine at the gate.'

Will he be able to stick at 14 acres, or like one-time Cavalry officer Mark Lambert, who spent 18 months looking for a suitable site with a view to planting five acres, increase to ten 'and quietly vegetate', then get carried away and end up with 35?

After two years at Sandhurst, Lambert served five years with the 14/20th King's Hussars in Berlin and the Luneburger Heide south of Hamburg. He left the army in 1962 but not Germany where he remained for three years as a civilian racehorse owner/rider, at the same time running an army stable of 25 horses. On his return to England he found himself, in his own words, 'totally unsaleable'. 'After five years in the army,' he says, 'you are pushed for qualifications, and no British employer is interested if you have none. You can say "man management", but when you have said that, they still ask what your qualifications are.' But an American firm who were starting up in Britain took him on to help with their Energy Audit service, and he stayed with them for five years, running their Düsseldorf office for two years. Another five years with an English company in the same game followed, and then in 1978 Lambert set up his own consultancy providing similar advice on how to reduce electricity, gas and water bills.

Mark Lambert bought Barkham Manor estate near Piltdown in East Sussex in 1985 on the strength of ADAS assuring him that it qualified as the centre of wine production he had set his heart on establishing. Alan Furneaux approved the soil and Hartley Vince told him what would be needed by way of drainage. ADAS warned him off buying two places to which he had taken a fancy. By doing his own homework, by copious reading, and by talking to people who had gone through it all themselves in Kent, Sussex, Hereford and Wiltshire, he became reasonably adept at judging a potential vineyard site for himself. It was sorting out the varied advice they gave him which presented the difficulty:

Everyone I spoke to had a problem, but it was never the same as the last man's. Adrian's handicap was being too high up; Arnold's that the day was too short; Alistair's that it was all too labour intensive; Justin's that he was landed with 100,000 bottles of wine and hadn't a clue how to get rid of them – he knew damn all about marketing.

Everyone poured their problems out to him, but he could find no common theme. No one major drawback emerged which they all agreed had to be surmounted – and would deter *him* because he knew it would be beyond him.

When the owners of Barkham Manor put the estate on the market split in two, Mark Lambert made an offer for one half of it, but ended up buying the whole house and its 52 acres – 'in for a penny, in for a pound'. Which of the 52 would be the best for the first planting? He had a horticultural dowser go over the ground to find out. Though the man had never dowsed for vine-suitability before, he took samples from the various fields and made a report. Baron Rothschild had employed one in France, and what was good enough for him was good enough for Lambert. Eventually he had a vineyard with five acres each of Kerner, Bacchus and Müller-Thurgau, four of Huxelrebe and 13 of Schönburger. In 1987 he planted an acre of Pinot Noir from which he hopes to make a sparkling wine. So now Barkham Manor's Piltdown Vineyards consists of 33 acres.

One time cavalry officer Mark Lambert whose 1989 'Piltdown' vintage was the first from his 35-acre vineyard at Barkham Manor in East Sussex.

He has persuaded his apple grower brother, Peter Lambert, to join him and apply his horticultural knowledge to grapes. He already has him wrestling with the mysteries of wasp and weed destruction, how best to scare the birds, to counter the perils of wind-blown pesticides and polluting weed-killers, whether to prune by hand or machine and which fertiliser to use. He is against going organic on the lines of Bewl Valley Vineyard at Wadhurst and Sedlescombe Vineyard at Robertsbridge where Roy Cook has been growing grapes without chemical fertiliser since 1983. The products of both these were exhibited at the first National Organic Wine fair at Ryton-on-Dunsmore near Coventry in July 1988. Lambert may be able to dispense with fertiliser, but he learnt early on that he would never produce the sort of wine he wanted without intensive labour; and the most up-to-date growing methods and sprays:

> *If you want good grapes – and they are the* sine qua non *of good wine – you have to look after them. This is where a lot are led astray. The fact is it is damn hard work, and there is a hell of a lot of it. It is not the week-end job so many are led to believe.*

Even more alarming was the cost. For the vines, having them planted and having the land drained, he paid out £35,000; for posts and rails another £40,000. He reckons the vineyard cost him £3,000 an acre to get going. And of course he would have no return on this outlay for five years, which was why during the week he was earning as much money as he could with his Energy Audit business in London.

He decided he would have his own winemaker make 'Piltdown English Table Wine' on the estate from year one. He converted a large building in the centre of the vineyard, which had been used for milking cows, into a winery for £50,000, and spent another £70,000 equipping it.

Mark Lambert started trying to recover all this in 1989 when he had his first 'Piltdown' wine to sell, made from the first harvest of 1988. For two years he will try and sell it all to visitors. The assembly point, tasting room and shop is the ancient barn which was shifted a good five feet sideways by the hurricane of October 1987 and sucessfully re-positioned in April 1988. He has devised a tourism packet which includes a walk around the vineyard, a conducted tour of the winery, admiring the beautiful garden, watching a video film of the vineyard being created, and – what no other vineyard visitor will have – an opportunity of seeing the spot in the grounds where the spoof fossilised skull of the so-called Piltdown Man was found by Charles Dawson in 1911. It was then hailed as the earliest European human remains ever discovered, but in 1953 was sensationally exposed as a hoax – the jaw was that of an orang-utang. It is believed to have been put in the garden of Barkham Manor by one Samuel Woodhead, a lawyer friend of Charles Dawson who was an amateur palaeontologist and died in 1916.

Lambert tells visitors of his French connection, the de Gruchy family who built La Mare on Jersey, now owned, as seen, by the Blayney Family who have planted the vineyard there. The Lamberts are related to Maréchal Grouchy on whom the Emperor Napoleon relied, with little success, to relieve his Army of the North from the crushing onslaught of the Allied regiments at the Battle of Waterloo in 1815. Lambert's family name is de Gruchy Lambert. He shows visitors the French marshal's coffee cup out of which Napoleon Bonaparte often drank during his campaigns, which Lambert treasures among the de Gruchy family heirlooms. He also tells of his Italian ancestors, the Lambertini family, and of cousins of that name still in Italy whose family crest he shares, whose fine Tuscan wine he imports. To assist him in this exciting venture he has secured the help of French-born Elizabeth Brooks as General Manager, who with five years experience in the marketing of English Wine should give 'Piltdown' a flying start.

The huge barn is available for banquets and conferences, christening, wedding and twenty-first birthday parties, concerts and fashion shows, for which catering is provided, accompanied by the Lambert of Barkham Manor estate-bottled 'Piltdown' house wine.

Andrew Vining also lays score on European ancestry – French and German wine maker forebears – but has shown himself to be a man of the twenty-first century by monitoring the

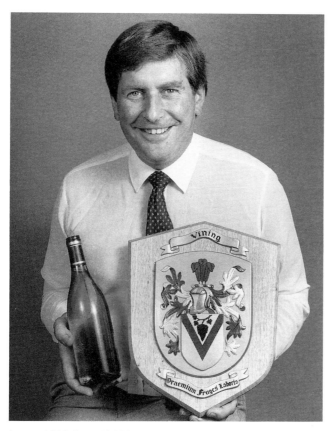

Andrew Vining, who in 1989 has 65,000 vines growing on his 80-acre Wellow Vineyards in Hampshire, which will not be in full production however until 1992.

growth and output of his Hampshire vines – all 65,000 of them – on a computer screen. Each one has been assigned a code number, and in the computer's memory are stored details of its variety, position, date of planting and the rest. Six weather stations record temperature and humidity on the 80-acre Wellow Vineyards estate he owns in the Test Valley near Romsey. Conscious too of creating history, when his first 1985 planting of 5,500 vines on five acres produced one and a half tons of ripe grapes from which he could not resist making 27 bottles of wine the following year, Andrew Vining was reported to be keeping 23 of them 'for posterity'. It had a light, fresh taste, he said. 'I suppose you could say it's the taste of things to come. It augurs well for the future.' Because of early flowering the grapes had been ready to pick before the hurricane hit the vineyard on 16 October 1987. It justified the advice he had been given that the Romsey area had a micro-climate favourable to vine growing.

Forty-five-year-old Andrew Vining spent his childhood on his parents' farm at Chandler's Ford near Winchester, and as a young man worked on it. To cleanse the cowhouse after an outbreak of salmonella poisoning, he bought a high pressure cleaning machine and did the work himself. He made so good a job of it that others who saw the results asked him to come and do the same for them. He formed Power Cleaning Ltd to provide a farming hygiene service which within a year was employing 22 people and was under contract to the Ministry of Agriculture. Power Cleaning later became Merryhill Contracting Ltd and today provides a wide range of specialist services from stone cleaning to asbestos removal. In 1977 he was asked to set up a company in Qatar on the Persian Gulf to service the oil industry, mainly cleaning and painting offshore oil production platforms and tankers. He called it HBK Power Cleaning Ltd.

Pondering the idea of starting a vineyard at the Hampshire farm which was his home base, he was given a copy of *A Tradition of English Wine*; and the story of past viticultural exercises in England, of which there might have been more but for native inertia, which he found in it, determined him to press on. Inertia had never been one of Andrew Vining's failings. And when he found the author of the book had the same initials as his Middle East cleaning company, he took it as an omen that could not be ignored. It was not the only coincidence, he says:

> *The name Vining is thought to be derived from vine, vine growing or wine and, according to genealogical research that I and others have conducted, the Vinings probably came from France originally. They may have been descendants of Vikings or Norsemen who settled in the vineyards of that country. One Malcolm Vining of Belfast has a coat-of-arms depicting seven grapes on top of a helmet; and near Avignon there is the Tavel vineyard which produces France's leading rosé wine made from the juice of seven grapes. Furthermore, it was purely by chance that I met wine consultant Mark Thompson who advises me on wine-making. I'm not sure whether I believe in fate or destiny, but the coincidences make you stop and think.*

The 5,500 vines he planted in four small areas round his house in Tanners Lane in 1985 were mostly Müller-Thurgau and Bacchus; there were some Auxerrois and a few

Reichensteiner. In the spring of 1987 he was so encouraged by their performance and the fact that he had been told his East Wellow was ideal for vine growing, that he increased the size of his vineyard ten-fold from five to 50 acres. The 45 acres on which he made his new planting was on rolling, loamy soil farmland between 145 and 260 feet above sea level, mainly south facing with an excellent, all-important micro-climate and less-than-severe frosts. Once again he planted mainly Müller-Thurgau and Bacchus (around 10,000 of them); nearly 4,000 Reichensteiner; 3,200 Ortega; 2,700 Chardonnay; more than 2,000 each of Kerner, Faber and Auxerrois; a thousand each of Triomphe D'Alsace and Huxelrebe, and a handful of pinot Noir, Riesling and Kernling. By 1987 he had 40,000 vines in 13 varieties, with the second plot changing from the Guyot to the Liar system of training.

But it was not large enough. In 1988 he planted another 30 acres.

When I do something I put everything I have into it, both energy and money. From the advice I have been given by consultants and others, it would seem the only way to create a really profitable vineyard is to grow vines on a very large scale. Small vineyards appear to have great difficulty in attaining commercial viability. But once you exceed the 15 to 20-acre size threshold, the cost per vine, in direct proportion to the labour and equipment used, is much lower. What you need for a 15-acre vineyard could easily manage a 50 to 100-acre estate.

A corner of Wellow Vineyards in 1988.

After ten years in the Middle East he intends to devote himself to producing top quality wine profitably on a large scale, and while making 'Wellow' a household name in wine-drinking and wine-making circles, stimulating greater interest in and appreciation of English Wine both at home and abroad.

Excellent wine is being produced in this country, but many people are reluctant to try it. There is a good deal of prejudice and apathy to be overcome and Wellow will be doing everything possible to promote good English Wine. I am not only confident that my vineyard will be successful, but that when people in Britain become aware of the quality of wine being made from home-grown grapes they will buy far more of it, and perhaps come to prefer it to some continental wine.

Twenty thousand of the 25,400 vines he planted in 1988 were Seyval-Blanc. 'This', he said, 'is becoming one of the most widely grown vines in England, and is one of the best croppers around, producing anything up to eight tons of grapes an acre in England.' But he also put in another 4,000 Chardonnay, plus a few more Bacchus, Müller Thurgau, Faber, Reichensteiner and Ortega. Andrew Vining now has 65,000 vines growing on his own 80 acres and on two other Hampshire vineyards totalling 15 acres for which he has complete management responsibility.

In the spring of 1989 a Wellow Wine Centre was opened to the public. An attractive barn-like rustic building it incorporates a visitors' reception area, shop, wine and snack bar, off-licence, restaurant, wine display area, a History of English Wine Museum and a Florence Nightingale Museum – the Lady of the Lamp spent part of her life at nearby Embley Park and is buried locally. There is no charge for visiting the Centre which is open all the year round. Vining plans a conservation area, woodland walks and play areas.

In June 1988 Vining announced that 40 of the 88 cases (1,000 bottles) of 'Wellow' medium dry white wine which he had had made from the one and a half tons of grapes harvested in October 1987 from the five acres of vines planted in 1985 had been sold at £72 a time. 'It's very nice,' he declared after taking his first taste of it. 'But then I'm biased. Seriously though, I'm very pleased with the result, and I've been told by an English wine expert that it is a very good wine. The main thing, however, is what buyers and the rest of the trade think of it. In 1988 we could well have a bumper crop. Growth on the vines is three weeks ahead of schedule. But of course we will not be in full production until 1992, and then we expect to produce around half a million bottles of dry, medium dry, sweet and single grape wine annually.'

The blends, says Mark Thompson who will make the wine, will be for general public consumption, and the varietal wine for connoisseurs, hotels and the like. He hopes the grapes from the 4,000 Chardonnay vines imported from France will ripen early enough to enhance the quality of 'Wellow' wine. 'We are confident that the mixture of German and French grapes will produce a very good, high quality medium dry wine.' From August 1988 the Wellow management team – Andrew Vining, Dee Thompson, Tom Ayers and Karl-Heinz Johner – were also offering a consultancy and management service.

Even more ambitious are the plans which Adrian White has for his 200-acre vineyard at Denbies Estate near Dorking in Surrey, which is being managed by his brother Jeremy. They planted it over four years – 35 acres in 1986, 30 in 1987, 70 in 1988 and another 65 in 1989 – with around 145,000 vines in about 20 varieties. They hope to have some 50,000 bottles of 'Denbies Estate' 1989 table wine on sale in 1990, both blends and single varieties and perhaps some sparkling. All of it will be made in their own winery from the vineyard's grapes. They intend to open the vineyard to visitors, build a shop, hold wine tastings and the rest. They reckon that their investment up to the end of 1988 has been in the region of £750,000.

The biggest vineyard in England? Easily. In the meantime plans are afoot to clear and re-plant the vineyard which was England's biggest in the eighteenth century, Charles Hamilton's at Painshill.

The 250-acre landscaped garden was divided up in 1948. Elmbridge Borough Council was persuaded by local enthusiasts and The Garden History Society to buy back what remained of the land, and in 1981 formed The Painshill Park Trust pledged to restore the 158 acres left, of which they took a lease, to its eighteenth-century layout.

By 1988 they had repaired the Gothic temple, mausoleum, abbey cottage, Chinese bridge and the water wheel which raised water for the lake from the River Mole. What they had done was inspected and praised by the Duchess of York and their royal patron the Prince of Wales. The rehabilitation of Painshill Vineyard is a later priority and will require sponsorship. It is however an important part of the restoration programme and one day, for sure, vines will grow again where David Geneste toiled to such effect – and to the admiration of so many incredulous visitors. Perhaps in their re-examination of the estate Mrs Mavis Collier, the Trust's archivist, and archaeologists will discover the site of the wine barn (probably close to the house) where Hamilton and Geneste made the still champagne which Hamilton had told Lord Ilchester that Lady Ilchester had liked so much in 1754 – 'and I'll answer for 'twill make Miss Cheek laugh and quicken her low spirits'.

ADRIAN WHITE, ANDREW VINING, MARK LAMBERT, Robert Cole, Michael Judd, John Charnley, Alan Haickney, Conrad Gauntlett and others, are the third tier waiting in the wings to enter the English Wine scene with a confidence that few would have deemed possible ten years ago. Stalwarts like Kenneth McAlpine, David Carr Taylor, Norman Cowderoy, Bernard Theobald, Christopher Ann, Sam Alper, Richard Barnes, Ken Barlow, Robin Don and Colin Gillespie, who have stayed the course from the earliest days of the English Wine Revival and inspired the second tier who entered in the nineteen-seventies, have been performing nothing inherently uncertain or untried. They have merely been re-enacting, in the English setting which the centuries have shown to be sympathetic, the processes of viticulture and vinification which are common to the whole world.

Sir Edward Barry's prophesy of 1775, that it was not improbable that in some time several vineyards might be propagated on account of the profit they brought, has come true. That time is now. The trot has become a canter. Several has become 250.

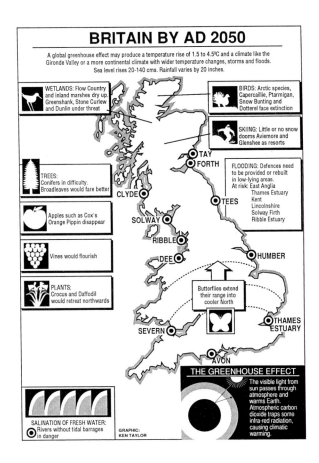

It is a fact that will not deter the woeful from continuing to assert that its weather will never make England a land where wine-grapes will consistently ripen sufficiently in the open air to make fine wine. And if our climate changes, as it seems it may, what then? Scientists sponsored by the British Government have predicted that the consequences of the irreversible 'greenhouse effect', producing a temperature rise of 1.5 to 4.5 degrees Centigrade, will be that by the year 2050 central England could have acquired a climate like that of the Gironde Valley and vines would flourish as never before.

But then English Wine will lose the character that distinguishes it from Mediterranean wine and makes it uniquely English.

APPENDICES

WINE-GRAPE VINE VARIETIES

WHITE

German

Riesling	makes Hock and Mosel; ripens very late; wine fruity acidity.
Sylvaner	also ripens late; less acidity than Riesling; wine earthy and neutral.
Müller Thurgau	cross between Riesling and Sylvaner; early ripening, heavy crop; shortish bottle life; wine curranty-grapey; widely grown in England.
Reichensteiner	cross between Müller-Thurgau, Madeleine Angevine, and Calabrese Frohlich; wine very neutral and delicate in flavour.
Bacchus	cross between Müller-Thurgau and Riesling-Sylvaner; high yield – 1335 gallons an acre; wine with Muscat-tinged flavour.
Huxelrebe	needs careful husbandry; dislikes chalk; good quality wine, peachy.
Siegerrebe	cross between Riesling and Traminer; early ripening; wasps and bees like it; wine powerful flavour and bouquet.
Scheurebe	cross between Sylvaner and Riesling; needs a good site; like Siegerrebe but more acidity; strong Muscat-like bouquet; much used in blending.
Schönburger	late ripener; pink grapes of Muscat parentage; wine Traminer-type with a grapey-curranty flavour.
Ortega	ripens very early; wasps like it; produces peachy-spicey wine with good bouquet; long bottle life; good for blending.
Faber	a heavy cropper from Alzey; Riesling-like characteristics; liable to stem rot.
Ehrenfelser	cross between Riesling and Sylvaner; ripens late; low acidity.
Gutenborner	likes a sheltered site; vulnerable to disease; wine elegant but neutral.
Kerner	ripens a bit late for England; a cross producing outstanding wine in the style of Riesling.
Regner	ripens as early as Huxelrebe; improvement on Müller-Thurgau.

APPENDICES

Wurzer	yields well, with a high sugar content; wine has fine bouquet.
Chasselas	prolific variety yielding medium quality, mellow soft wine, drunk young.

French

Seyval-Blanc	produces crisp dry wine; good for blending; England's second most popular.
Madeleine Angevine	a Muscat-type grape; very grapey wine.
Auxerrois	from Alsace; poor yield – 450 gallons to acre; naturally acidic; good for blending; wine similar to Pinot Gris; EEC recommend it for England.
Pinot Gris (Rülander)	ripens earlier than Pinot Blanc; yields well; fussy about soil and site.
Pinot Blanc (Chardonnay)	makes Chablis, White Burgundy and Blanc de Blancs; part of Champagne blend; wine full-flavoured with crisp acidity; few suitable sites in England.

RED

French

Pinot Noir (Spätburgunder)	classic red grape of Burgundy; ripens late; poor yield; must have right site.
Pinot Meunier (Wrotham Pinot; Müllerrebe)	ripens earlier than Pinot Noir; low yield – 350/450 gallons to acre.
Triomphe D'Alsace	heavy cropper if weather is good; strong flavoured wine, rich colour.
Blue Portuguese	prolific yield – 1160/1425 gallon an acre; ripens reasonably early.

(*Note:* figures for yields are approximate.)

European Community wine regulations divide vine varieties intended for wine production into five categories:
    Recommended
    Authorised
    Temporarily Authorised
    Experimental
    Provisionally Authorised

'Unauthorised Varieties' do not fall into any of the permitted categories, and wine produced from them must not be sold commercially. It can be consumed by the producer's family or exported to a non-European Community country. Otherwise it can only be distilled or converted into vinegar.

Varieties classified as 'Recommended' in the UK at July 1988 were Auxerrois, Müller Thurgau and Wrotham Pinot, and are those which 'normally produce wine recognised to be of good quality'. 'Authorised' varieties for the UK seen as producing wine of an acceptable standard but lower than that from 'Recommended' varieties are Bacchus, Chardonnay, Ehrenfelser, Faber, Huxelrebe, Kanzler, Kerner, Madeleine Angevine, Madeleine Royale, Madeleine Sylvaner, Mariensteiner,

APPENDICES

Ortega, Perle, Pinot Noir, Rülander, Seyval, Siegerrebe. Reichensteiner and Schönburger are classified as 'Provisionally Authorised', and may not be submitted to the Wine Management Committee of the EEC for final approval before 1990.

Appendix 2 THE WINE DEVELOPMENT BOARD'S
DRY TO SWEET WINE GUIDE

In the Wine Development Board's *Dry to Sweet Wine Guide* 'the leading white wines of the world have been graded from 1 to 9 in terms of dry to sweet' from Muscadet (1) to Marsala (9).

In it one of the leading white wines of the world 'Medium Dry English' is graded, along with six others, in Grade 3.

GRADE 1	GRADE 2	GRADE 3
Muscadet	*Soave*	*Brut Sparkling wine*
Champagne	*White Burgundy*	*Gewürztraminer*
Chablis	*Fino Sherry*	*d'Alsace*
Dry White Bordeaux	*Sercial Madeira*	*Dry Amontillado Sherry*
Manzanilla Sherry	*Rioja*	*Medium Dry Montilla*
Tavel Rosé	*Penedes*	*Dry White Vermouth*
		Anjou Rosé
		Medium Dry English

Appendix 3 THE ENGLISH VINEYARDS
ASSOCIATION 1989

President — Lord Montagu of Beaulieu
Chairman — Anthony Goddard
Secretary/Treasurer — Kenneth McAlpine
Chief Executive — Geoffrey Bond
38 West Park, London SE9 4RH
Tel: 01-981 0452
Registered Office: 71 Lincoln's Inn Fields, London WC2A 3JF

Appendix 4 REGIONAL ASSOCIATIONS AFFILIATED TO THE ENGLISH
VINEYARDS ASSOCIATION AND USEFUL ADDRESSES

EAST ANGLIAN WINE GROWERS ASSOCIATION
Contact: Mrs Eleanor Berwick, Bruisyard Wines Limited, Church Road, Bruisyard, Saxmundham, Suffolk. Tel: 072 875 281

WEALD AND DOWNLAND VINEYARDS ASSOCIATION
Contact: Dr Ivan Williams, Harefield, Stream Lane, Hawkhurst, Kent. Tel: 05805 2333

APPENDICES

WESSEX VINEYARDS ASSOCIATION
Contact: Mr Chris Hartley, Meon Valley Vineyard, Swanmore, Southampton SO3 2PZ.
Tel: 0489 877435

SOUTH WEST VINEYARDS ASSOCIATION
Contact: Miss Gillian Pearkes, Yearlstone Vineyard, Chilverton, Coldridge, Crediton, Devon.
Tel. 03635 302

THAMES & CHILTERN VINEYARDS ASSOCIATION
Contact: Mr Roger Fisher, Amphora, Crays Pond, Reading, Berkshire. Tel: 0491 681484

OTHER USEFUL ADDRESSES

Wine & Spirit Education Trust Limited, Five Kings House, Kennet Wharf Lane, Upper Thames
Street, London EC4V 3AJ. Tel: 01-236 3551

The English Wine Centre, Drusilla's Corner, Alfriston, East Sussex. Tel: 0323 870532

ADAS: Sheila Baxter, National Vine Consultant, Cromwell House, Andover Road, Winchester,
Hants SO23 7EN. Tel: 0962 635000

'Growing and Making Wine in England' Training Course: Principal, Plumpton Agricultural
College, Lewes, East Sussex BN7 3AE. Tel: 0273 890454

FURTHER READING

General

H. M. Tod. *Vine-Growing in England*, London: Chatto & Windus, 1911

A. L. Simon, *English Wines and Cordials*, London: Gramol Publications, 1946

Edward Hyams, *The Grape Vine in England*, London: Bodley Head, 1949

—— (ed.) *Vineyards in England*, London: Faber & Faber, 1953

R. Barrington Brock, *Outdoor Grapes in Cold Climates*, Report no. 1, Viticultural Research Station, Oxted, Tonbridge, 1949

—— *More Outdoor Grapes*, Report no. 2, 1950

—— *Progress With Vines and Wines*, Report no. 3, 1961

—— *Starting A Vineyard*, Report no. 4, 1964

S. M. Tritton, *Grape-Growing and Wine-Making from Grapes and other fruits*, Almondsbury: The Grey Owl Research Laboratories, 1951.

George Ordish, *Wine Growing in England*, London: Rupert Hart-Davies, 1953

Margaret Gore-Brown, *Let's Plant A Vineyard*, London: Mills & Boon, 1967

Gillian Pearkes, *Growing Grapes in Britain*, London: Amateur Winemaker, 1969

Alan Rook, *The Diary of an English Vineyard*, London: Wine & Spirit Publications, 1969

A. Massel, *Basic Viticulture*, London: Heidelberg Publishers, 1971

—— *Viticulture in Britain*, lecture to Nuffield Scholars Association, December 6, 1971

W. B. N. Poulter, *Growing Vines*, London: Amateur Winemaker, 1972

Sir G. Salisbury-Jones, 'Wine growing in Great Britain', *Journal of Royal Society of Arts*, pp. 455–65, 1973

J. Cochrane, 'Meteorological Observations in Hambledon Vineyard in 1972', *Weather*, vol. 29, no. 4, April 1974

F. W. Beech, E. Catlow, E. G. Gilbert, *Growing Vines in the Open in Great Britain*, Long Ashton Research Station, Bristol, 1974

William Younger, *God's Men and Wine* (for the Wine & Food Society)

Norman Sneesby, *A Vineyard in England*, London: Robert Hale, 1977

Anthony Hogg, *Guide to Visiting Vineyards*, London: Michael Joseph, 1977

Joanna Smith, *The New English Vineyard*, London: Sidgwick & Jackson, 1980

Oz Clarke, *Websters Wine Guide*, 1987

—— *Sainsbury's Book of Wine*, 1987

Wine-Making

A. Massel, *Applied Wine Chemistry and Technology*, Pt 1 Viticulture, Pt 2 Vinification, London: Heidelberg Publishers, 1969

W. B. N. Poulter, *Wines From Your Vines*, London: Amateur Winemaker, 1972
F. W. Beech & A. Pollard, *Wines and Juices*, London: Hutchinson
—— *Wine Making and Brewing*, London: Amateur Winemaker
Bravery & Turner, *Home wine-making and vine growing*, London: Macdonald, 1973
L. Frumkin, *The Science and Technique of Wine*, London: H. C. Lea, 1974
F. W. Beech, 'Harvesting and Wine Making Techniques' *Journal*, no. 9, June 1975, p. 57, English Vineyards Association, Horam
Ben Turner, *Growing Your Own Wine*, London: Pelham, 1977

Index

INDEX

INDEX

INDEX